THE SPIRIT OF DR. BINDELOF
THE ENIGMA OF SÉANCE PHENOMENA

ROSEMARIE PILKINGTON

Anomalist Books
San Antonio • New York

An Original Publication of ANOMALIST BOOKS

The Spirit Of Dr. Bindelof
© 2006 by Rosemarie Pilkington

ISBN: 1933665130

Book design by Ansen Seale

All rights reserved, including the right to reproduce this book or portions thereof in any form whatsoever. For information, go to anomalistbooks.com or write to:

Anomalist Books
5150 Broadway #108
San Antonio, TX 78209

Anomalist Books
PO Box 577
Jefferson Valley, NY 10535

For the two Gilberts:
I kept my promise.

CONTENTS

Introduction 1

Part One: The Bindelof Case

Prologue:	Gil's Story 5
Chapter 1	Family And Friends 6
Chapter 2	The Saturday Night Sitters 15
Chapter 3	A Shot In The Dark 20
Chapter 4	Bindelof's Boys 29
Chapter 5	Larry's Story 32
Chapter 6	The Doctor Gets Annoyed 39
Chapter 7	Trumpet For A Dead Man 42
Chapter 8	See Me, Feel Me, Touch Me, Heal Me 44
Chapter 9	The Portrait 50
Chapter 10	Speak To Me 53
Chapter 11	Bindelof Missing 60
Chapter 12	The New Bindelof Society 64

Part Two: A Brief History Of Physical Phenomena

Chapter 13	It Didn't Begin With The Fox Sisters 72
Chapter 14	The Extraordinary Powers Of D. D. Home 77
Chapter 15	Sir William Crookes 88
Chapter 16	The Phantom Of Katie King 102
Chapter 17	The Neapolitan Wonder 113
Chapter 18	The Case For Ectoplasm 124
Chapter 19	The Unique Pole 136
Chapter 20	Indridi Indridason Of Iceland 142

Part Three: Twentieth Century Mediumship

| Chapter 21 | Last Of The Old Time Mediums? .... 148 |
| Chapter 22 | The Russians Are Coming .... 160 |

Chapter 23	A Mini-Kulagina	164
Chapter 24	The Man Who Could Put His Thoughts On Film	168
Chapter 25	Breaking Mental Barriers	189
Chapter 26	The Impact Of Kenneth Batcheldor	202
Chapter 27	There's Something To Be Said For Spirits	218

Epilogue 227

Appendix: So You Want To Do It Too? 232

Sources: For Exploring On Your Own 236

Acknowledgments 239

Index 240

INTRODUCTION

If you ask most people what they think about what happens in séance rooms—knocks or raps, levitating tables, ectoplasmic forms, disembodied limbs and so on—they'll tell you it's all bunk and superstition. Any skeptic will inform you that it's all done by trickery carried out by skilled magicians to bilk the credulous. Ectoplasm? Nothing more than regurgitated cheesecloth. Houdini even demonstrated how tables could be surreptitiously levitated by sly swamis, especially if the sitters were uncritical bereaved families.

On the other extreme are the spiritualists who believe that these phenomena, which defy the laws of physics, are caused by the spirits of deceased persons who are trying to communicate with the living and are not bound by earthly physical restraints.

My view in this book lies somewhere between these two extremes. Yes, there have been, and are, frauds and magicians who produce miraculous-seeming effects, but there are also many cases in which the fraud theory collapses when they are scrutinized more closely and the evidence is examined.

I already subscribed to this middle view when I first met Gilbert Roller in 1973. I enrolled in Gil's course in "Paramechanics," or physical psychic phenomena, at the New School for Social Research in New York, and although I thought that I knew a great deal about psychic phenomena I was ignorant of some of the more spectacular and mind-bending phenomena of which he spoke. We eventually became close friends and over time I learned that Gil was a multi-talented artist who had had some unusual experiences as a child and even more extraordinary experiences in his teens.

At the time I knew of the psychiatrist named Montague Ullman but had no idea that it was because of his participation in Gil's teenage séance explorations that Ullman had become a parapsychologist. Though he had spoken to other psychic researchers of these early experiences, he had never gone public with them, fearing, I believe, that he would be ridiculed and ostracized by the medical and scientific community, a fate suffered by many scientists who dare report on anomalous findings that challenge the established world-view.

Some of the researchers who knew of Gil's séances, which became known as the "Bindelof Case," felt that it was incomparable because of the kinds of phenomena produced and because of its careful documentation. They felt that it should be published for more than just the parapsychological community. I agreed. Gil and Larry, another member of the original Bindelof group whom you'll meet later, urged me to write their story for the general public.

I felt it would be more interesting if Gil wrote his own story, but with his usual modesty, he was reluctant to do so. Consequently I wrote it and then had Gil and Larry, both of them known for their wit and humor, add details and go over it for accuracy. I think you'll find the result entertaining as well as fascinating.

In the second part of the book, I will delve into the history of physical phenomena, that is, phenomena such as psychokinesis (PK), or the moving or otherwise affecting of objects by psychic power, as opposed to "mental" phenomena or ESP. I have provided this historical background not only to educate the reader but also to place the Bindelof case within a wider framework and to help clarify what it means in the context of séance research. I hope as well to shed more light on these intriguing manifestations and the special people who produced them.

You will read here about true instances of levitating tables-- *and people*-- real organic ectoplasm (not cheesecloth) exuding from the bodies of entranced mediums and forming hands, limbs, and even phantoms who speak and walk among observers, all under the controlled conditions and the critical eyes of competent investigators.

Who or what the source of these mind-boggling occurrences is, however, remains a mystery. Are these forces the manifestations of discarnate spirits, as believers insist, or are they "merely" manifestations of certain gifted or extraordinary living people? What indeed *are* these forces and what implications do these phenomena have for science?

In the final section of this book I'll concentrate on 20th Century mediums, some of them "secular mediums," such as Ted Serios, who could imprint his mental images on film; Nina Kulagina, the former Soviet soldier and housewife whose feats were observed and filmed by Russian scientists; and the Canadian "Philip" group, who invented their own ghostly communicator.

I'll also provide suggestions for developing your own sitter-group, should you be encouraged to do so, and give additional sources of information on other mediums and paranormal phenomena so that you may continue to explore this mysterious and fascinating subject.

PART ONE:
THE BINDELOF CASE

PROLOGUE: GIL'S STORY

It was a Saturday night in the first week of October 1933. In Mayor Jimmy Walker's Manhattan people who had labored hard all week splurged on movie tickets to *Flying Down to Rio* featuring the new dance team of Fred Astaire and Ginger Rogers, while young men put protective arms around the shoulders of their dates in the dark theaters where Edward G. Robinson menaced the populace. Six floors above the street at 38 Fort Washington Avenue, behind drawn shades in a small bedroom, a group of teenage boys also sat in the dark.

I was with them, crowded around a small two-tiered nightstand, our hands resting lightly on top of the table, fingers touching those of the boy on either side. On the floor our feet touched also so that any movement by one would be felt by his neighbor.

We listened intently to the sounds of the pencil we had placed on the lower shelf as it raced across a piece of yellow paper, guided by an unseen hand. The writing stopped abruptly. The pencil was slapped down sharply. We heard the sound of crumpled paper. Then silence.

One boy sprang up to turn on the lights. Another reached under and retrieved the tightly crumpled ball, opening it carefully as the others impatiently crowded around to read. Near the end of a long printed message, written faster in the dark than any of us could have managed in the best of circumstances, we read the words "My name was Dr. Bindelof . . . Will you be the disciples of a dead man?"

This is not a scene from a Stephen King novel. This is a true story of mind-boggling but actual occurrences. How did this scene come about? Who was Dr. Bindelof? Who were these intense young men?

My name is Gil Roller. The first part of this book is my story, a story that may change the way you look at reality. But I'm getting ahead of myself. Let's start at the beginning.

CHAPTER 1

FAMILY AND FRIENDS

OLGA, LIZ, AND ME

My mother, Olga, was an unusually beautiful and gifted woman. Her lovely lyric soprano voice, her dramatic temperament, and her grace contributed to her success as a singing actress. She appeared in operettas, especially those of Victor Herbert, which were very popular in the first two decades of the century. She met and married the young scion of a prominent Argentinean family, who was in the United States to buy battleships for his government, and after I was born, in 1915, Olga moved to Argentina with her new family.

My mother's idea of marriage clashed with the Argentinean concept of what a wife and mother should be and it wasn't long before she returned to the U.S., obtained a divorce, and little Gilberto became me, Gilbert Roller.

To support us Olga went back to the theater, traveling all over the United States and Europe. I was cared for by governesses and later attended private schools here and abroad. My only playmate was my aunt Ellie, my maternal grandmother's change-of-life baby, who was only a few months younger than I was and lived with us for a time. We required *two* governesses because together we were a formidable team and too much for one poor woman to handle.

My first decade of life is shrouded in a dream-like mystery. I never really had a father, so to speak; I grew up like Topsy. My mother never spoke of my father and I didn't learn of him until I was seventeen or eighteen. We didn't live a normal family life. Mother was on the road all the time. I would be sent for, to join her, so my schooling was pretty well messed up. We went to Europe for a year. I was taken out of school again. Then when we came back from Europe, we took this apartment on Riverside Drive and I wondered why, because it was a fairly large apartment. It was all furnished. It was then that I was informed that the man whom I called Uncle Eddie was to be my father.

My mother was "a mystic." Two of her fellow performers, the Dolly Sisters, international vaudeville stars in the 1920s, were psychic and held séances in which Olga participated. She had many books on psychic phenomena, which I read avidly as I grew older. Psychic phenomena just became part of my life, like any other "normal" experience, resulting in a certain mystical personal philosophy.

My stepfather, Eddie Fink, was a basically warm, charming and lovable guy. He was a brilliant pianist who would sit at the piano in his pajama bottoms, with his hairy chest exposed and a cigar in his mouth, singing while he played. He was surrounded by women in his work and Olga was away performing much of the time: Trouble was bound to develop.

And, of course, Olga was a temperamental artist. My friends thought our home was wonderful, filled with music and art, and good times, but I remember the earlier times as monstrous and terrible. There was considerable tension between my parents and violent fights: Mother had a temper that was absolutely without equal. She'd scream, "Oh, no you don't!" and she would destroy a whole kitchen of china. The place would look like a battlefield, and Eddie would actually clean it up. I would of course become panicky. I would scream and yell. It was absolute madness.

These scenes were frequent occurrences. Often, after one of these marital wars, Olga would take me and move out. It became a ritual. I retreated into my many interests. I had inherited my mother's musical ability and played the piano. I loved to draw, and developed skill as a photographer. But I had troubling dreams.

One day, in the midst of this tumultuous life, when I was about 12 or 13, odd things began to occur at home. We would hear a soft "whizzing" sound followed by a "clink." Upon investigating we'd find one of the hairpins Olga used to do up her long, luxurious tresses. These hairpins would be "thrown" from her bedroom, when no one was in there. At times the pins would be flung from the dresser at the door as someone left the otherwise unoccupied bedroom. We would hear them striking the back of the door and upon reopening it we'd find the pins on the floor behind the door. Wooden knobs from shoe trees would be "pulled off" and flung across a room. We would enter the living room to find oatmeal scattered evenly over the rug. I was generally in the apartment during these occurrences but not always in the room where they took place. When I was not at home the phenomena were less intense.

Olga tried to make light of it. We named whatever this force was "Liz."

We'd speak to it commanding, "Liz, throw something!" And, sure enough, "ping," something would go flying across the room. It was exciting fun at times, but the manifestations became more violent.

Dishes would come crashing off counters or shelves. We'd return home to find the words "GO, GO" crayoned in huge--four or five feet tall--printed letters on the walls.

Some of the violence actually seemed directed against me. Once as I was walking in the street a milk bottle came plummeting down, crashing a few feet in front of me. Another time I heard a commotion coming from a wooden cabinet in which I kept my most treasured possessions including a shiny blue Lionel electric engine. The racket stopped abruptly as I opened the cabinet door. To my dismay I discovered the wreckage of my engine. It had been torn into pieces. Its body had been ripped away from the wheels; wires were dangling from it as from a disemboweled animal. It looked as if it had been senselessly attacked with a sledgehammer.

This time Eddie called in the well-known psychical researcher, Hereward Carrington, to investigate the occurrences. The tall, imposing Carrington regarding me with suspicion, went through my pockets, found some hairpins and a rubber band among the contents, and concluded that I was responsible for the outbreaks. What is more, nothing out of the ordinary took place while he was there, strengthening his opinion that "this highly emotional child" was most likely the cause. I was heartbroken. Not only was my favorite possession destroyed, but I was being blamed for these things that I hadn't done (as far as I was aware at the time) as well.

My case, however, might have contributed to Carrington's theories associating poltergeist outbreaks with puberty. In 1930 he was to write: "An energy seems to be radiated from the body . . . when the sexual energies are blossoming into maturity. . . .It would almost seem as if these energies instead of taking the normal course . . . find this curious means of externalization."

Whatever the researcher's conclusions, relations grew even more strained between my parents. Although Eddie loved me, he felt that these were mischievous pranks: He couldn't accept the "poltergeist" explanation. Olga felt, rightly or wrongly, that he had brought Carrington in to discredit *her* son. Their violent arguments escalated until Mother took "Liz's" advice to "GO," and went, taking me with her.

We rented rooms from some of my mother's old friends with whom she had had successful séances in the past with some minor physical occurrences. Once settled, Olga persuaded these people to sit for a séance. For the first time I was allowed to participate. Following Victorian tradition, we sat in a darkened room around a table. The room was hushed except for occasional muffled street noises. We waited in the dark room lighted only by the street lamps that filtered in through the heavy old-fashioned wide slats of the Venetian blinds. Suddenly the curtains at the closed window began to billow out as though blown by strong gusts of wind, and furniture began to slide away from the walls. A heavy, overstuffed easy chair came sliding toward us from a corner of the room. The landlords screamed and fled. That ended my first séance.

In time my parents reconciled their differences and decided to start again in another location, taking an apartment on the then upper middle-class Fort Washington Avenue. There we lived somewhat more peacefully with only sporadic outbreaks of "poltergeistery."

LEONARD AND ME . . . AND LARRY

It was late summer, 1929. New Yorkers went busily about their business, blissfully unaware of the great financial catastrophe about to shake the world. I was new to Washington Heights. I was kind of a loner, without friends or even acquaintances in this new neighborhood. My only acquisition as a friend was Leonard Lauer, another teenager nearly a year younger than I was, but advanced beyond me in school. Leonard was one of the generations of intellectually gifted New York City children who, like human express trains skipping certain stops, were sped through the school system, starting high school at the age of 12. At about 15 they were deposited, insecure and often out of emotional sync with their more mature classmates, at the doorsteps of colleges and universities. Leonard, at 13, was about to begin his second semester at Townsend-Harris High School, a school for gifted boys.

Lenny was handsome, self-assured to the point of arrogance, and convinced of his scholastic superiority. He wouldn't associate with anyone who he thought didn't have a sufficiently large brain. For me, I suppose it was more a matter of desperation than companionship at the beginning. But our chemistry was similar. It came as rather an emotional shock. Leonard was as much of an extrovert as I was an introvert.

He was attracted to my entire family. I suppose we were quite different from any of the other people he knew. He was charmed by Eddie, the personable pianist, and enchanted by the beautiful, talented Olga. As for me, not only was I someone who could match him intellectually, but in his eyes I had talents he lacked. I was a gifted musician and artist, and, as he told me later, he was in awe of my sensitivity and creativity.

Our intellectual conflict or rivalry, especially his attitude about his intellectual superiority, would result in a chain of events that changed our lives. As Lenny later commented about himself, "I was trying to be smart." And I wasn't about to let him lord it over me.

He had been reading H. L. Mencken and was showing off his information in oratorical fashion one day, trying to one-up me, so I retaliated by putting down my cerebral friend's knowledge as unimportant, especially as compared with the profound truths of which *I* was aware.

"Mencken!" That's surface knowledge. If you want to learn something really important I'll give you a few books that'll educate you to things you haven't even dreamed of."

"Like, what, Oh learned one?"

We went up to my apartment and I grabbed T. J. Hudson's *Psychic Phenomena and the Scientific Demonstration of the Future Life*. "Read this, oh smart ass, although I doubt that you've got the brains to comprehend it."

I started to talk about what seemed to him at first completely "crazy, irrational stuff"—the "occult" is what he called it. He knew nothing about psychic phenomena. He believed that things like this didn't happen. Up to that time Len had considered these phenomena and psychical research as fraud, pseudoscience, and charlatanism. He considered himself a budding young scientist and had a hard-nosed view of science as "the only source of truth." But he accepted the challenge. The book was so scholarly that he was willing to give it a go. It smacked of mystery—a sort of adventure that intrigued him.

I didn't reveal what had happened in my own home at first, but started by telling him about things I had witnessed with my mother at that séance at the boarding house. He trusted my intelligence and I was pretty sure he believed me.

I supplied him with other books from my own and my mother's library: F. W. H. Myers's *Human Personality and Its Survival of Bodily Death*, and books by some of the most respected scientists of their day. These included the great French physiologist, Charles Richet; the distinguished Italian physician, psychiatrist, and anthropologist, Cesare Lambroso; and the German physician, psychical researcher, and hypnotist, A. von Schrenck-Notzing.

Leonard was impressed, as I knew he would be, by the stature of these eminent scientists who had devoted a considerable portion of their lives to investigating and attempting to understand these phenomena. They wrote factual accounts of table tiltings and levitations, and of séances in which messages were seemingly communicated through mediums to the living from "discarnate entities" or dead people.

Leonard was fascinated and, as I became more at ease with him, I told him about my poltergeist experiences and of my mother's sittings with the Dolly Sisters and others. Now he was really intrigued. Well, the two of us decided, if the Dolly Sisters could do it, so could we!

One evening when the Lauers had gone out and Len's younger brother was asleep we took the opportunity to try our first sitting. We imitated the format traditionally followed in the Victorian séances we had read about in the books and in copies of the *Journal of the Society for Psychical Research* that we had found in the New York Public Library: You darkened the room, everybody was quiet, some person acted as spokesman, and you talked to thin air as though there were somebody there. And in these things we had been reading about, something responded.

We started with a light bridge table. We pulled down the shades and turned off the light. Of course this was New York City where, except in a blackout, the skies are never dark and light filters in and around drawn shades or blinds. Once the eyes dark-adapt other persons and objects in the room can be seen relatively well.

We held hands across the table sitting for periods of about 20 minutes with no results. Our arms got tired and we leaned on the table. We'd break for a glass of water or milk then resume, changing tactics, experimenting with sitting next to each other so we could just put our finger tips on the table and touch one another's hands without adding any weight. We rolled back the carpet so the table would be able to slide over the polished wooden floor—we never doubted that it would—but . . . no results.

A day or two later we tried again. This time we began to get "threatened movements," that is, creakings or slight motions. Every strain, every shift that your arms made produced a sound, and there was much more of that the second night: That was all the encouragement we needed.

In order to determine whether or not there was actual movement we chalked circles on the floor around the table legs and on the third or fourth evening we got what we thought was a sliding motion.

"You feel it move?"

"*You* feel it move?"

"It *did* move, didn't it?"

We jumped up to turn on the lights and, sure enough, *there* was the ring and *here* was the leg. Over on the other side *there* was the ring and *here* was the leg!

From then on things began to happen quickly. Instead of waiting forever, we'd sit there and wait for a little while and all of a sudden you could feel life in the table. We'd say, "Move to the right!" Zhoom, it would slide. "Move to the left!" Zhoom, the other way. We barely touched the table to insure that neither of us was exerting the force necessary to move it.

"OK," we said, "Now we're gonna communicate." We informed the table that we were going to call out letters of the alphabet and that it should move at the letter it wanted. At first the table would "get eager" and slide at every letter. Then we would recite, "A, B, C, D..." and it would be quiet, as though it were chastised, and wouldn't move at all.

We decided to try tilting instead of sliding. In a short time we got it to do that too. Two legs would come up off the floor and the bridge table would take a little bow. We asked it questions using the code of two tilts for no, one for yes, and tried to get it to spell out messages. Nothing very significant was communicated. Once in a while we would get a reflection of something that was on our minds, for example, if it was getting late it might spell out, "your mother," a reminder that Len's mother would be returning soon and Len was afraid of getting caught doing something "weird."

With each sitting, however, the table gained in strength and dexterity. At the beginning it tilted rather feebly or indefinitely. Later it became a smart, military kind of response and we were much encouraged.

One evening I said, "Let's try for levitation."

Now up until this point there was a great deal of distrust.

"Ya *sure* ya didn't lean on it?"

"You put your hands on top of mine!"

I was just as suspicious of Len as Len was of me.

Suspicions finally evaporated, however, during the levitation trials. We were working with the table on the bare wooden floor, the rug having been removed. We asked the table to levitate and sat and waited. Gradually it started to rotate under our hands. We tried to follow it around but this became impossible as the table slid out from under our fingers. It began to gyrate more rapidly, revolving around the room and rotating as it revolved, much the same as the earth's simultaneous turning on its axis and around the sun.

There was no sitting down, of course, or keeping in contact with each other's hands. The table was leading *us*.

On the second night of this wild movement, the table suddenly came up off the floor. It seemed to rise about six inches into the air before settling down again. Rather stunned, we switched on the lights and looked at one another. Had we really done it? We went back and tried again. Before the night was over we were getting the table up to about shoulder height. There was no mistaking it: Wonder of wonders, we had got it to levitate!

We were bursting with excitement. In our exhilaration we needed to share our experience, to show others what we had accomplished. But most people would think we were nuts! Len was afraid to tell his mother: He still felt as if we were doing something she would consider weird or wrong. And my family was still reeling from the poltergeist-like episodes: I thought my mother would be upset to know that we were consciously invoking these same phenomena that had created such dissention in our family.

But there was no sitting on this thing. We had to tell somebody. At the beginning of the new semester, in January or February of 1930, Len decided to confide in another unusually precocious and talented schoolmate of his at Townsend-Harris named Larry Levin.

Larry had an extremely unhappy home life, which he was to describe in black humor, many years later: "I was brought up in a lower middle class family. My father was a professional gambler, unsuccessful, and as a result, we were prematurely poverty-stricken. We had the distinction of having been dispossessed from an apartment in 1926 at the height of prosperity. But we had foresight. We knew the crash was coming and we didn't want to get into the bad habit of living well, so we started early."

This talented thirteen year old, who would leave high school in another few months to become an apprentice actor in the workshop of the famous actress Eva Le Gallienne, was a kindred spirit with whom Lenny had had many profound discussions during their first year at Harris. Larry also hung around the neighborhood because his home life was so depressing. He was part of a group of boys who were interested in hypnosis. One of them was a good subject and someone would put him in a deep sleep and put a penny on his arm suggesting it was hot. To their amazement, it left a burn mark on the boy's arm. It was Larry, therefore, to whom Lenny first entrusted our precious secret.

Larry reacted predictably with skepticism but went along for the ride. He became an instant believer. In his very first sitting, after a short wait, we got movement of the bridge table at which we sat, and some rapping sounds. Larry was hooked. By the third sitting we got an extremely powerful levitation. The table actually rose far above our heads so that we found ourselves in the peculiar position of feeling that we were holding it down. Larry, who was three or four inches shorter than we were, complained that he could no longer reach the table top. Leonard said, "Hold on to the legs." Larry grabbed the legs—and pulled! The table, which usually gentled itself down, came crashing to the floor, fracturing one of its legs in the process.

The three of us met on and off for the next year or so obtaining movements, tiltings, levitations, and "raps," or knocking sounds that seemed to emanate from the table.

But we saw little or nothing of each other in the summer of 1932. Larry came with my family and me to Sheepshead Bay where we rented a place for a couple of weeks. Then Larry got a job selling magazines that took him on a long trip west. He ended up with a friend of his family in Dallas. The friend gave him the $7.00 to pay a man who spent his time driving paying passengers around the country, and he arrived back in New York in December. We corresponded regularly during that time, writing nonsense letters decorated with funny drawings and addressing them with weird titles. Unfortunately, neither of us saved them for posterity.

CHAPTER 2

THE SATURDAY NIGHT SITTERS

Over time we invited more friends to join us. At the end of the summer, with Larry away, Leonard began rounding up some of his cohorts to expand the experiments. The fourth guy to be let into the inner circle was Leonard's cousin, Leo Kaiser, a quiet, personable, nondescript "follower," who had always been more than just a relative. He had been a playmate and friend to Len, which some of us found incongruous because Leo was a bit dim.

In the fall our group acquired a fifth member, Montague Ullman, another of Lenny's classmates, who by now was attending City College (CCNY). Monte, who at 16 was beginning his sophomore year, was a serious, spectacled student, somewhat cautious, retiring, and insecure. He was competing with older classmates in an effort to get admitted to a pre-med program. His father was a traveling salesman who was absent much of the time.

Leonard told him of the results we had obtained in our sporadic sittings in the past two years and introduced Monte to Hudson's *The Law of Psychic Phenomena*. Monte's first reaction was a mixture of amazement, curiosity, and skepticism. He too, as he was to write much later, "had read no serious work on the subject and, imbued with the scientific zeal of a pre-medical student, had relegated the entire field to the mystics and `spiritualists.'" He was, however, impressed by the Hudson book and thought Len's suggestion worth a try, even though he felt that nothing more than a social evening would come of it. As it turned out, the next few months would change the entire course of his life.

Nothing terribly exciting occurred for the first few sittings with Monte, but he persisted at our urging and very soon his patience paid off.

With the introduction of a new group member, and especially after a long break, it took a few weeks to get things going again. At about the sixth sitting with Monte we experienced a slight tilting of the table and in the next few sessions the tiltings became more frequent and more pronounced. The table also slid horizontally along the floor, at first unpredictably, but in time the table became more "obedient" to our wishes.

That is not to say that success was certain. There were evenings when nothing happened or in which we got very disappointing or weak results. These "blank" sittings became less frequent, however, as our meetings continued.

In our first attempts to obtain "raps" or knocks, it was the same story: After initial failure there were at first feeble noises, which could easily have been involuntary muscle movements causing creakings of the table. But, we thought, maybe not. And gradually these grew stronger, ultimately becoming unmistakably sharp "knocks" occurring on command and seeming to emanate from the center of the table.

In April 1933, at age 16½, Monte, even then the sober scientist, wrote an account of these sessions as part of his thesis for a course in logic he was taking at CCNY: "In these experiments, we . . . used an ordinary bridge table, keeping contact with the table and with each other by means of our hands. The room is usually light enough to permit us to see what takes place. After one or two moments the table would start to move and distinct knockings are heard, seemingly coming from beneath the table. One of the sitters utters commands (it is immaterial who does the talking as long as all the others are thinking along with him), and response is almost instantaneous. The table moves to the one whose name is mentioned."

He went on to describe how we first got the table to respond by tilting in any direction we asked it, and finally to elevate "to a height of two or more feet." We experimented with one or two of us taking our hands away and eventually we were all able to remove our hands, one at a time, from the table and it remained suspended in mid-air for about two seconds before falling to the floor. Thus encouraged, we kept trying until we were able to get the table to rise up to our hands, which we held about two feet above it. He concluded: "Success without contact of the hands we had always found difficult."

That was an understatement. That observation illustrates just how accustomed we had become to these "impossible" feats, and with what casualness we began to accept the minor miracles we performed regularly, taking them in stride as we pushed forward to see "what else" we could do.

Lenny corralled some more of his academic associates to further expand the experiments. He seemed to me to be the Robin Hood of the neighborhood with young intellectuals who came out of the woodwork at his beckoning. His goals were lofty. He felt himself the leader of a new and provocative parascientific inquiry. Certainly I could never by myself have brought together this motley adolescent crew he had at his disposal. Except for Leo, who perhaps served as Lenny's mascot, the boys were all remarkably intelligent. They were bright, unique personalities. I couldn't figure out how he lured these guys into sitting around a table in a darkened room, to entice these relatively rational young men from their Saturday night rounds in the search of more immediately satisfying pursuits.

We began to meet regularly in the late summer of 1933 and other teenagers were invited. These "regulars" included Howard Frisch, another serious-minded classmate of Len's at CCNY who considered himself a "materialist... interested in social forces, not psychic forces." Howard was tall, thin, highly-strung, and looked like Jimmy Stewart, giving the impression that he was a bit nervous and having trouble sitting still. He was cerebral and somewhat remote or secretive, perhaps defensive, protecting his sensitive, inner self. He never ate and never went to the bathroom, which was really none of my concern but for some reason it is part of my early remembrances of him.

Lenny had known Howard since Townsend-Harris High School and had become friendly with him at City College. As they were walking home from class one day Len abruptly asked, "What do you think about psychic phenomena?" Howard, taken off guard, blurted nervously, "What should I think about it?"

"How'd you like to sit in on a séance?"

Howard's curiosity and respect for Len's intellect were the selling points. He was in.

Leo's cousin, George Kaiser, was another loner who had no close friends before he met me. He was much brighter than Leo, had a more dynamic personality than did his cousin, and became intensely involved in the proceedings.

Then there was the eccentric, rebellious, resonant-voiced, would-be poet, Tom Loeb, later known as Tom Newman, or, "Timothy Bastard," who was also invited and became a regular. A few other "fringe" members were also present at various times.

Tom Loeb was even for that time a generation ahead of all of us. He was brilliant but completely off the wall. He preferred the name of Timothy Bastard, claiming he was a love child. His parents, he explained, were terrified of him, if they *were* his parents. Apparently they left him very much to his own devices. He was a pathological liar, which we all knew. His life was a complete invention, entirely apart from reality. He had no concern for the grandiosity and absolute impossibility of his fabrications. (He once showed us a picture he said he had painted. It was Gainsboro's "Blue Boy.") His voice was lush and affected in the Shakespearean manner. He regaled us with recitations of poetry that were really quite compelling and enjoyable, but he was mad as a hatter. We kept him under close scrutiny, convinced that he would willingly produce any phenomenon we wanted.

In contrast to the overly discrete Howard who was never observed to use the toilet, Tom had a great and aggressive preoccupation with his genitalia. (I suppose we all had the same fixations at that age, but not as overtly as "Timothy," and certainly no compulsion to exhibit them gratuitously to our fellow sitters.) After one séance when the bathroom was in use, Timothy casually mentioned that he had two urethral openings in his penis and urine flowed from each. This of course evoked a measure of curiosity and we challenged him on the matter. He invited us into the bathroom and withdrew his penis, which we scrutinized carefully. It was a perfectly normal organ. With this one exception, exhibitionism was not his thing. What prompted the episode will never be known except that we now had all seen Timothy Bastard's quite unremarkable penis. Evidently this satisfied some emotional need for him. We returned to the séance without further comment.

Horace Joseph was exactly the opposite. Horace today would be called a dweeb. Horace lived in my building. He had dark curly hair and eyeglasses that were as thick as bottle bottoms. He was a little older than the others, but severely retiring, timid, shy, and insecure. His intellectual brilliance didn't seem to help when it came to social savvy. We were merciless with him. And still he stayed, probably because he was fascinated by the results of our sittings and the challenges they presented to his scientifically oriented mind.

The locale of the sittings had been moved to my small bedroom. We had confided our secret to Olga and when she saw the seriousness of our investigations she agreed to allow us to use our apartment. We would congregate in our living room to shoot the breeze or listen to classical music, on our state-of-the-art RCA electric phonograph, then retire to my small bedroom where we would crowd around my nightstand.

Because of the crowded quarters we gave up the rickety card table and switched to this sturdy little nightstand, which was about three feet high and had an open lower shelf about 8 inches from the table top. We kept our knees and feet touching and our fingers glued to each other's atop the table. Although the small back bedroom was darker than Len's large living room, it was still not possible to get the room completely dark and after our eyes adapted to the existing light it was easy to make out the outlines of the other sitters.

The sessions generally began about 8:30 p.m. We would sit for about half an hour at a time with rest periods of ten to fifteen minutes in between, during which we would sometimes return to the living room for more chatting, bantering, or immersion in music.

After some sessions we would be in a state of sheer exhaustion. We'd troop inside and there would be no talking at first; we would just plop down on the sofa, or on a chair, or on the floor. I would put on Ravel or a Debussy recording, and we'd listen to it. Larry always sat with his head in the speaker.

We'd engage in light-hearted banter for a while, then go back in and try some more until we were beat or restless because of the late hour and we'd terminate the session, generally at about 11:00 p.m.

Since our meetings were usually on Saturday night, we would generally descend en masse to Stewart's cafeteria on Broadway and 157th Street where we would continue our teasing and verbal jousting while devouring quantities of food as only teenage boys can.

We established regular, once a week sittings. These regular meetings and our constant striving to see "what else" we could do had a dramatic effect on the development of the phenomena. We became dissatisfied with "mere" levitations and raps as our inquiring minds sought answers to all sorts of questions through "communication" with whatever "guiding spirits" or energies we might be reaching.

CHAPTER 3

A SHOT IN THE DARK

Eventually raps or knocks became our means of getting "information." These sounds varied from barely audible "scratches" and taps, to a frightening *fortissimo* intensity. They seemed to be the most erratic of the physical phenomena and the most difficult to evoke. One member, usually Lenny who liked to be in control, would act as spokesman addressing the "force" as if it were an intelligent entity. At a time when the knocks were occurring with considerable regularity, we attempted to elicit "yes" and "no" answers by using a code: Two knocks stood for "no" and one knock "yes." This limited the information we could obtain so we also employed the method of calling out letters of the alphabet and asking the "force" to indicate desired letters by knocking at, or right after, we had uttered them. In this way messages could be spelled out and our questions could be answered more speedily.

What was uppermost in our minds was to determine, if we could, whether or not we were dealing with "spirits" or discarnate entities, and to learn more about the nature of the force operating through us. We didn't keep any written records of these early probings but from our later logs and recollections it is obvious that we did establish, at least to our own satisfaction, that we were in contact with an intelligent but as yet unnamed force.

One of the most significant and interesting developments in regard to the rappings as a form of communication was the emergence of a unique pattern of rapid, "staccato" sounds, beginning softly, then swelling in a crescendo to a final resounding RAP. It was like a drum roll that serves to call attention to or punctuate some spectacular occurrence or act in a show. This "staccato," as we came to call it, became associated with a forthcoming message from the "intelligence" with whom we were communicating; a sort of "signature tune" announcing this unique personality.

Some of us tried to reproduce this "drum roll" with its final loud "Boom!" manually, but even I who was an accomplished pianist couldn't do it. The force it would take to produce such a fortissimo climax was beyond our physical abilities. Not to mention that anyone trying it would necessarily produce movements obvious to all the others.

Our restlessness and curiosity led us to adopt a pattern of attempting to develop each type of phenomenon to its highest pitch and then to turn to another phase of investigation.

My interests included photography and someone suggested that we attempt some experiments with film.

Lenny, ever the scientist, and convinced of the importance of establishing controlled experiments, went with me to buy the photographic plates. These emulsion-covered glass plates, about 4" by 5" in size, were factory-sealed with paper tape in wax-coated cardboard boxes. A "dark room" was set up in my bathroom where at least three or four of us crowded in the eerie infrared lamp's glow to witness the opening of the seal, the removal of the plates, and their insertion into metal light-proof holders.

We took the plates into the bedroom and placed one, chosen at random, on the table. For the first trial we decided to have someone place his hand on the plate in the darkened room. As usual we kept the vigilant contact of hands and feet. We sat expectantly in the dark waiting for a rap to signal us when the required time had passed. And we waited. After several minutes, we got discouraged and put the plate aside thinking it wouldn't be worth developing since it was impossible for the plate to have been affected.

We went on with the sitting asking the "force" to give us a message, if it had any, by knocking after the appropriate letter in the alphabet as it was called off by one of the sitters. The rappings immediately spelled out "p-l-a-t-e."

"Plate! Holy cow, that must mean develop it!"

We grabbed the metal holder, jumped up and made a bee-line for the bathroom. As I dunked the glass in and out of the chemicals, the others watched in awe. Sure enough, the distinct image of the hand appeared.

We repeated the experiment with the other plates; not only with hands, but also with any object we happened to think of. Someone put his keys on the plate holder. This time we received the "rap" signal after just a few moments. Again we ran to into the bathroom. Now we received a clear, distinct image of the keys. We tried a spoon and got a clear outline of it.

Besides the obvious fact that it was "not possible" to get such exposure through the metal container, especially in a nearly dark room, these pictures were unusual in that they were "shadowgraphs." That is, "positives" rather than "negatives." (The images on the negatives were light when they should have been dark and conversely the printed pictures show dark objects instead of light.) It was as though some radiation had penetrated from above the metal holders casting a "shadow" of the object onto the plate.

One spontaneous test proved conclusively to the ever-suspicious Monte that no one could have been "preparing" these plates in any way beforehand or by slight of hand during some point in the procedure. It involved one of the "hand" pictures. The hand on the plate was that of the guy next to Monte. At the last moment, as the hand was placed on the plate, Monte moved his own hand, already clasping the one to be photographed, and placed his thumb over the plate, on top of the other boy's hand. The developed plate showed the hand with Monte's thumb clearly superimposed over it.

Not content with these small miracles, we then attempted "thought photographs." Instead of placing an object on a plate, we had one sitter, usually Larry, hold the plate up to his forehead while we concentrated on some image we spontaneously decided upon.

We first lit upon a common object found in most homes in the 1930s, a milk bottle. We extinguished the lights and concentrated on the familiar image of a bottle. What emerged from the developing pan this time was a picture of, not a *milk* bottle, but an *iodine* bottle. Upon close examination a label could be seen bearing part of the skull and crossbones (used to warn users of poisonous substances) and part of the name of the local drug store, Rio Pharmacy. Both Lenny and I had such bottles in our medicine cabinets, but so did most other families in that neighborhood. It could also be observed that the bottle's image was somewhat distorted, as though the plate had somehow been slightly "bent" or curved. (This was not flexible film but rigid glass plates encased in almost equally rigid metal containers.)

In another trial we attempted to project the image of a page of a book none of us had seen. We asked my mother to take some book from her shelf, choose a page without showing it to us, and then to close the book again. We followed the same procedure. The image that appeared this time was definitely of printing but it resembled newspaper columns. Only a few words were distinguishable: It looked as though two pages of printing were superimposed so that most of the words were illegible.

Next we decided to attempt an image of a person known to only one of us. Larry had a new girl friend named Olympia whom none of us had met, so we decided to try to get a picture of her. Again Larry held the plate to his forehead while we all tried to obtain Olympia's image telepathically and project it onto the plate. My mind, however, for some reason kept turning to thoughts of American Indians. When we developed the plate, what emerged was the silhouette of a Native American amulet that I recognized as one that my aunt Ellie had bought on a trip out west and that I had seen years before. No one knew what had become of it but it was found sometime later, in cleaning, behind a dresser in the apartment.

Iodine Bottle *Amulet*

Howard claims he was the first to ask for a written message, having been engaged in college journalism and having a high respect for the written word. The truth is that we were all impatient with the labored knocking out of messages and would have welcomed a speedier means of communication.

Most of us had read Hudson's *The Law of Psychic Phenomena* in which the author reports on his experience with a "medium" in Washington, D.C., who caused writing to appear on small slates. Sometimes the writing was done silently but often the bit of slate-pencil placed between two slates (which were tied together and closely observed at all times by the wary sitter) would be heard moving with gentle but rapid scratching sounds. The slate writing was done, in broad daylight, without physical contact with the pencil either by the medium or anyone else, and the messages were pertinent answers to questions written in secret by the sitters.

Perhaps remembering, consciously or unconsciously, this account, one of us inquired of the table, "Can you write your message?" We received one loud knock— "Yes."

We placed a pencil and a piece of yellow foolscap paper on the open lower shelf of the nightstand. Again the room was tense as we waited in the dark for something to happen, scarcely breathing. In the stillness we could hear the pencil stir and fall down, stir and fall again, its lead point finally scratching marks on the paper. Gradually, just as with the other manifestations, over the next sessions the writing grew from short, sometimes indistinct markings, to a printed word or two and then, suddenly, the pencil began to fly across the paper. It was a frenzied scratching.

We could hear the pencil racing across the paper at a furious rate. Even at that whirlwind pace, the sound of the pencil was distinct. You could hear even such things as the dotting of an i and the stop at the end of a sentence.

The speed at which the pencil wrote was comparable to today's—or maybe the 1980s—computer printouts. Generally the writing was preceded by the "staccato" pattern of raps, then later, the computer-like speed of the writing would be followed by the sound of the pencil being "slapped" down and, sometimes, especially after long messages, the paper being crumpled into a tight ball.

Occasionally the paper was folded as well. The folding and crumpling was not consistent: a few short messages were crumpled and many long ones were not.

The messages gradually developed in clarity and substance. The first were all done in block printing and were characterized by a rather imperious tone and lapses in spelling.

On September 2, 1933, in response to a question that we had asked about the nature of the "force" at work in producing the photographs, the pencil flew across the foolscap. On and on it went until—thwack, the pencil was slapped down and we heard the sound of the paper crumpling. Then silence—not unlike a Teletype machine when the message is over. We switched on the light and there on the lower shelf was the paper in a tightly crumpled ball. Excitedly we pried it open and were awed to see a block-printed message occupying the entire sheet:

"THE FORCE IS GENERATED BY THE COMBINED EFFORTS OF THE SITTERS

OPERATING IN UNISON. THE PRODUCTION OF THIS FORCE BY THE SITTERS SETS INTO ACTION THE OTHERWISE DORMANT ENERGY PRESENT IN THE SURROUNDING ATMOSPHERE. THE FORCE HAS THE ABILITY TO PENETRATE ONLY ONE SOLID OBJECT OF A SERIES. AS IN THE PLATE IT PENETRATED ONLY THE PART OF THE PLATE UNCOVERED. HOWEVER IF THE OBJECT SUCH AS THE KEYS HAD BEEN WELDED INTO ONE SOLID PIECE (COMBINED WITH THE PLATE COVER) THE FORCE WOULD HAVE PENETRATED THE ENTIRE PLATE, RENDERING IT ENTIRELY EXPOSED. AFTER PENETRATING ONE OBJECT AND ENCOUNTERING ANOTHER SURFACE OF AIR IT IS INCAPABLE OF PENETRATING THE FOLLOWING OBJECT. THE FORCE CAN BE PROJECTED FROM ONE OF THE SITTERS IN THE SHADOW FORM OF AN OBJECT (THE CLARITY DEPENDING UPON THE ABILITY OF THE SITTER). IT IS NOT A CONSTANT PENETRATION DURING THE PLATE BUT AN ACCUMULATION OF FORCE WITH INSTANT PENETRATION AT A MAXIMUM POINT. MATERIALIZATION AND CONTACT YOU ARE INCAPABLE OF UNDERSTANDING."

This was more irrational than anything we had yet witnessed. My mind, too, started racing, somewhat in this vein: Fraud! It had to be. Which one was the sonofabitch who would try something like that? The message had to have been written beforehand, the blank paper removed and the crumpled paper substituted. All the skunk had to do was somehow first get his hand free, make scratching sounds with the pencil, remove the blank paper, get rid of it without making any noise, substitute the crumpled paper and get his hand back into the group. It would be safer with two skunks working together to pull it off. Three working together would make it a cinch. There were six sitting in the group. That meant that at least two had lost their minds.

We sat quietly during the break. Who was the Judas? I put on the Philadelphia Orchestra playing Ravel's "La Valse." I guess we were all thinking pretty much the same thing. Monte wore glasses. He didn't look clever enough. Larry? Maybe he sank into a fit of automatic writing. But it would take a long time to print out that message, and where did he hide the other paper? It had to match the kind we placed on the shelf. Timothy Bastard? He'd try anything. He was an exhibitionist and this was another variation. I don't know why we put up with him. He was insidious. He would have made a perfect warlock for a black mass. It was his voice and his whole lilting manner. He moved like a big Jewish cat. Leonard was clean, and I was asleep half the time. Leo? Too stupid.

Leonard suggested we knock off with the Ravel. He wanted to try something. We would put another paper on the shelf and ask questions hoping for pertinent answers. We all agreed that was a great idea—even the warlock. We made very sure all the hands were accounted for—even feet, although anyone who could pull that off with his toes was pretty good.

Lenny asked us to switch seats. I guess he too wanted to break up any conspirators. Then he asked a question concerning materialization. The answer came almost immediately after we had switched off the light and settled ourselves around the table:

"AS I SAID BEFORE, MATERIALIZATION YOU ARE INCAPABLE OF UNDERSTANDING. (IT INVOLVES THE MANIPULATION OF DIMENSIONS YOU CANNOT CONCEIVE). PLEASE BELIEVE ME WHEN I SAY THIS.
I SHALL BY DEMONSTRATION MAKE IT PERHAPS A BIT COMPREHENSIVE.
PLEASE TURN."

This last phrase meant that we were to turn the paper over to read the other side. That side contained instructions for eliciting materialization:
"1. SITTERS CONCENTRATE MILDLY ON CONTACT. (LEONARD WILL VERBALLY ORDER INTENSITY OF CONCENTRATION)
2. ONE OF THE SITTERS UPON FEELING CONTACT WILL ANNOUNCE IT.
3. SPOKESMAN WILL TELL SITTER WHAT TO CONCENTRATE ON (SUCH AS INCREASED PRESSURE, MOVEMENT, PULLING OF HAIR) NOTICE HOW DEGREE OF CONCENTRATION AFFECTS CONTACT. THIS IS THE ONLY SIMILARITY YOUR MINDS CAN CONCEIVE.
THE REST YOU WILL UNDERSTAND WHEN YOU ARE PART OF US."

Now we were really confused. As we did almost always after the séances, we would go to the neighborhood cafeteria, get some coffee and cake, and discuss the evening. Knocks, full table levitation, and responses to our questions by knocks as we called out the alphabet were acceptable phenomena to us. But this was a quantum leap and we were not ready to accept it. Was this some clever trick or were these sittings genuine? Why would anyone put themselves and us through two years of these séances and then spring this kind of "manifestation" and risk interception in doing it? It required clever substitution and concealment of the original paper, and a free hand that had to do a good deal of manipulating. It meant moving the pencil, crumpling the paper, getting rid of the original sheet, or substituting an already printed message, pre-crumpled, to replace the original paper, which still had to be carefully concealed on his person. It was a large sheet. It would have to be folded, placed in a pocket . . . and so on, and so on. Even a professional magician couldn't get away with all that. The clincher, though, was that the answers couldn't have been made up before since they were responses to spontaneous questions. No, this had to be the real McCoy.

As the messages indicate, we had asked about, and hoped to experience, some form of materialization, that is, some manifestation of physical phenomena. We had read of séances in which ectoplasm, a white smoky or gauze-like substance, emanated from the entranced medium. In some cases sitters had felt hands touching them or, as in the "Katie King" apparitions, which you will read about in a later chapter, witnesses claimed to have felt the warm life-like hands of the apparition and took samples of ectoplasm for analysis.

I, always reluctant to accept the onus of "mediumship," gladly allowed Lenny to lead the group. As the message indicates, we felt unseen hands tugging on our clothes and lightly pulling our hair, in sequence and simultaneously. We were scared and excited at the same time. And, as always when new phenomena occurred, we were even more suspicious of the others and made sure all our hands and feet were firmly connected. This feat however would have been impossible to accomplish by any one of us, even if his hands and feet were freed from the human chain, and if my bedroom were larger and pitch dark.

At the following session, on September 23, we asked for further materializations. One of us suggested using luminous paint on some object so that they might see any solid form against it. We received a written message praising the suggestion as "A SPLENDID METHOD FOR ME TO MANIFEST MY SHAPE. BY BLOCKING OUT RADIANCE YOU MAY OBSERVE MY FORM IN SHADOW." The sender then informed us that we were wrong in assuming that he had no identity in particular and even providing us with a chart to explain a hierarchy of manifestations:

"... IN THE LOWER FORMS OF PHENOMENA SUCH AS TABLE MOVEMENTS, NO ONE IDENTITY EXISTS, BUT MERELY AN EXERTION OF FORCE BROUGHT INTO PLAY BY THE SITTERS. IN THE HIGHER MANIFESTATIONS SUCH AS YOU ARE OBTAINING THE FORCE MOULDS ITSELF INTO AN IDENTITY WITH DEFINITE INTELLIGENCE."

DEFINITE IDENTITY IN FORM, INTELLIGENCE.

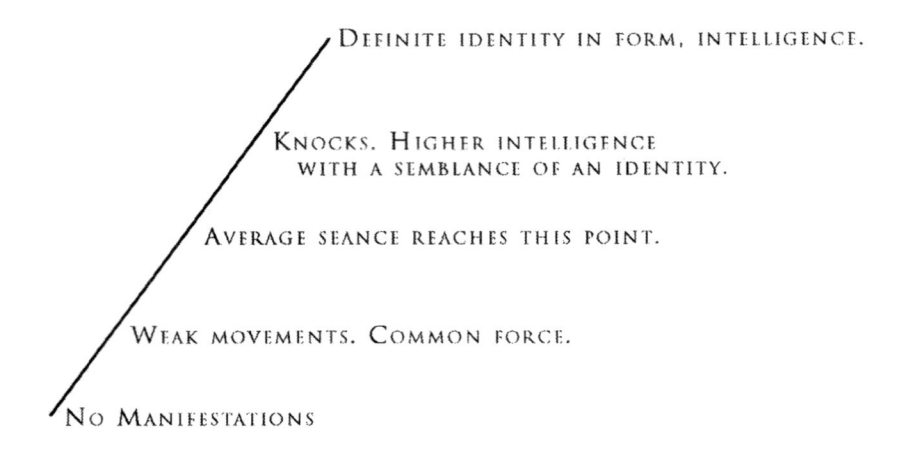

KNOCKS. HIGHER INTELLIGENCE
WITH A SEMBLANCE OF AN IDENTITY.

AVERAGE SEANCE REACHES THIS POINT.

WEAK MOVEMENTS. COMMON FORCE.

NO MANIFESTATIONS

"THE SUBCONSCIOUS ATTITUDE OF THE SITTERS MEANS ALMOST EVERYTHING TO THE SUCCESS OF THE SITTING. TIME ELEMENT DOES NOT ENTER INTO MY EXISTENCE. IT IS POSSIBLE FOR ME TO BE IN THREE DIFFERENT PLACES AT THE SAME TIME AS EASILY AS ONE, (FOR INSTANCE, HOLDING LEONARD'S VEST, PULLING LEO'S HAIR, PULLING GILBERT'S HAIR, AND BRUSHING ACROSS HORACE'S FACE AND TOM'S HAND AT THE SAME TIME)..."

With great bravado we asked if our communicator would touch our hands. A rap informed us that he would. A mixture of excitement and apprehension electrified us as we waited in the dark. One by one my friends began to say that they felt their hands and forearms being touched in turn by the unseen entity. I couldn't stand the tension. I blurted out, "When it comes to me I'm going to grab it." Suddenly I felt a hard, stinging blow to my face, as if with a man's open hand. A loud crack resounded in the stillness. Len, sitting across from me with his back to the window, could make out my sudden grimace as my head flew back. I had been slapped, hard!

We jumped up and one of the guys turned on the lights. My cheek was red and I was rather dazed. We could hardly believe it: An open hand had struck me in the face!

That terminated the night's proceedings. We were all rather shaken by what had occurred, but with the resilience and intrepidity typical of teenage males our sense of excitement and curiosity about the phenomena brought us back together the following Saturday.

CHAPTER 4

BINDELOF'S BOYS

Having become accustomed to making legible marks on paper with pen, pencil, or crayon in a purely mechanical fashion, it is difficult to conceive that these messages, the originals of which I hold in my hands today, could have been produced as they were, namely by an "unseen hand" scribbling audibly away in a darkened room. I've put that phrase in quotes because later we did see the "hand" the way we see the earth's shadow in an eclipse. In those days, before the dangers of this type of radiation were known, some of us wore wristwatches with radium dials that glowed in the dark. A couple of times we were able to see an opaque form move over our hands, briefly obscuring our watch faces. Anyway, I examine these yellowed papers today in near disbelief because that's the way you react to mind-boggling phenomena. You question yourself: "Did it really happen? Can I trust my senses?" So it is with these sheets of ordinary old foolscap and with the photographs that resulted from the sittings. However, as an adult looking back at the content of the messages, it is easier to recognize that they were the productions of teenage minds–bright, mind you, but adolescent nonetheless.

In the message obtained on the last evening of September 1933, the pencil writes imperiously: "I WAS AND AM STILL AN ENTITY THAT IS ENTIRELY INDIVIDUAL. I CAN GOVERN THE POWER OF ANIMATION BY YOUR COMBINED EFFORTS. DO NOT QUESTION THAT POINT AGAIN." It went on to say that it has curative powers and that we can remedy any "muscular disease" with its aid. "The entity" displayed some rudimentary knowledge that we would have had, for example, calling cancer "a disease of uncontrollable cellular growth," but then said naively, "the retina muscles can easily be reshaped by the force." We were informed too, by the way, that the "patient" needed do nothing to prepare for the healing, not even remove his glasses.

Around this time some psychokinetic (PK) phenomena began to appear away from the "sitter group" setting. Larry's watch crystals began to crack and break with no apparent cause. His collar pins would disappear and show up in odd places. The most troubling occurrences were to follow. My stepfather, Eddie, got us a job working for the F.G. Montabert Company, a label manufacturer in the women's millinery industry. Our duties included taking orders from various companies on 38th and 39th Streets between Fifth and Sixth Avenues each morning. We'd take the freight elevator to the top floor, then walk down, stopping at each floor to pick up their orders for hat labels containing the names of the nation's big department stores. After picking up the orders we would take them back to the office, put the appropriate labels in little brown envelopes and deliver them after lunch to the customers. Not a challenging occupation, but we managed to fill in the day with visits to Gimbel's record department where we could listen to the latest symphonic recordings in a tiny booth without any cost to us. Our salary at the time was $12 a week.

Then the manufacturer began to get calls from the companies complaining that they had received the wrong labels. At first we thought it was just a mistake so we worked very carefully to make sure that we were filling and delivering the envelopes correctly, but again when the envelopes were opened, the labels had been switched. This happened several times.

At the following week's session, the communicator warned Larry that a "powerfully destructive elemental" was attaching itself to him and "weakly manifesting itself by destroying his watch crystals, removing articles from bags he places them in and seals, and the like." It continued, "To ward off this influence I prefer Larry to assume control of this intelligent force." In a later message at that same session, after "healing" had been done on the eyes of Tom and a fellow named Willie, in which they felt their eyeballs being manipulated (without having removed their glasses), the "entity" finally identified itself:

"THE QUESTION HAS BEEN RAISED AS TO WHY I SHOULD WANT TO DO THIS. I SHALL EXPLAIN . . . DURING MY PHYSICAL LIFE I WAS A DOCTOR. I LOVED MY WORK AS A MOTHER ADORES ITS CHILD. I DREAMT OF NOTHING DAY AND NIGHT BUT CURING THE ILLS OF HUMANITY. I ACHIEVED LITTLE FAME DURING MY LIFE AND MY HOPES WENT UNREALIZED. I SOON AFTER TRANSCENDED INTO THIS UNPHYSICAL EXISTENCE, AND ODDLY ENOUGH STILL POSSESSED THE INSATIABLE DESIRE TO AID YOU HUMANS. NOW I HAVE AT MY PERFECT CONTROL THIS TREMENDOUS FORCE WITH ITS BOUNDLESS HEALING POWERS. IT IS HUMOROUS INDEED TO OBSERVE YOUR DOCTORS FUMBLING IN THEIR CLUMSY ATTEMPTS TO CURE WITH THEIR SHINY PRETTY STEEL KNIVES AND THE LIKE, WHEN RIGHT BEFORE THEIR VERY NOSES IS A CURE THAT WILL SOON ROCK THE WORLD. MAY THE HONORS GO TO YOU FOR DISCOVERING AND

DEVELOPING IT. . . BELIEVE ME WHEN I SAY YOU HAVE BEFRIENDED A TRULY CONSTRUCTIVE PERSON WHO HAS THE INTEREST OF HUMANITY AT HEART. *My name is Doctor Bindelof. For convenience you may call me that in the future.* [Emphasis added] YOU HAVE A PANACEA. LET US PERFECT IT AND GIVE IT TO THE WORLD. YOUR RESULTS WILL LEAVE NO ROOM FOR DISPUTE. WILL YOU BE THE DISCIPLES OF A DEAD MAN?"

What romantic, grandiose claims! What dreams of potency and fame! We teenagers were awed. Who was this Dr. Bindelof? Was he a real doctor who had lived at one time? How should we address him? Quiet, dim Leo, who rarely contributed to these discussions, earnestly offered, "He said we should call him 'That.'" It was the comic relief we all needed.

We retired that night to the cafeteria full of excitement, enthusiasm, and wonder at our newfound benefactor and the possibilities he had presented to us. We were, as can be seen by the message, full of the desire to benefit mankind, but we were still normal, mischievous, teenage boys. Particularly Larry and me. In the next chapter, I'll let Larry to tell you his own story.

CHAPTER 5

LARRY'S STORY

I was living at home, which was on St. Nicholas Avenue between 158th and 159th Streets. I had a father who was a sweet man, very gentle, very withdrawn. I had two older brothers, a younger sister, and a younger brother who died when he was six. Tough. Then my oldest brother got deathly ill. My mother had two children in the hospital at the same time, one at Beth Israel and one at Monte Fiore. As soon as I came home from school or from Le Gallienne's, I would rush down to be with my buddies. After leaving school I'd be out in the morning and early afternoon job hunting. But it was the depths of the Depression and the theater was one of the most depressed areas of all. Broadway shows were down to about 30 a season and I had little chance of getting work. So I tried every other area: selling, making deliveries, and so on. During this time I made a few cents selling the *Saturday Evening Post*. I had a big white canvas bag that held the magazines that were delivered to us by a truck once a week. The magazine cost 5 cents a copy and we made 1½ cents a copy. After the champagne and caviar I still had enough to pay the chauffeur and the household staff.

Gil's home was a refuge to me. I stayed with his family and I ate with them. When they would go out to eat they would take me along with them occasionally. I loved them, I loved all of them. I spent more time with them than I spent with my own mother because she had to rush away. And not having any money—I used to walk down to 14th Street because I didn't have carfare to go to Le Gallienne's—to me this was great. Money didn't mean anything to me compared to knowing Gil and Dr. Bindelof. This was a whole new dimension, a whole new world I was discovering. I mean Gil and I were blood brothers.

But we were normal energetic teenagers. We got into all sorts of mischief, such as sneaking into an amusement park at night and getting lost in the house of mirrors. We went into business making signs. I would go to a neighborhood store, grocery, or meat market, and say: "Look we can make you much better signs. No matter what you're paying, we'll do it for less." I'd come home and say, "Gil, I have an order for 68 signs at 25 cents apiece." Meanwhile, Gil would have to paint the signs.

We started singing in the backyards of the large apartment houses along Riverside Drive. Gil played the ukulele and our repertoire included "Dinah," and "Ukulele Lady." We'd stand shoulder-to-shoulder and croon: "It was moonlight in Kaluah, Nights like this are very fine." We received many contributions hurled from windows, mostly 2 or 3 cents wrapped in pieces of newspaper. Once an African-American elevator operator beckoned to us from a doorway and motioned to us to follow him through the basement of his building. We had recently been reading about sex murders and were a little wary but we went with him anyway. He took us to where the lockers for the help were. He opened up his locker and we breathed a sigh of relief when he reached into his civilian jacket and handed us a dime. That was good money!

I wasn't with them, though, the night they went into the tomb. Gil, Leonard, Howard, George, Tom, and Leo decided to visit a Manhattan cemetery at night, maybe on a dare, or for the thrill of it; no one really remembers the reason. What they all remembered was that they stole into a mausoleum, and not long after they entered, they began to hear and then be pelted by stones which seemed to be "thrown" at them and dropped on them from inside the tomb, in other words from the walls and ceiling. They beat it out of there fast.

The appearance of stones falling from ceilings or pelting houses, inside and out, is a well known poltergeist phenomenon that Gil and probably Leonard had most likely read about. The outbreak may have been caused by the same spontaneous PK energy that caused my watch crystals to crack and the labels to dematerialize and rematerialize. It could be that the boys felt guilty because of their trespassing and that might also have contributed to a self-inflicted "stoning."

At the next session with Dr. Bindelof, on October 14th, we were admonished:

"TO CONTINUE THE SCEANCES IN THIS MANNER IS HOPELESS. I WAS TO HASTY IN MY CONCLUSIONS. THE HARMONY WHICH EXISTED AT THE PREVIOUS SITTINGS HAS COMPLETELY DISSAPEARED AND THE INCONSISTANCY OF THE SITTERS ONLY ADDS TO THE CONFUSION. GEORGES ABSENCE FROM THE LAST SITTING MADE THE AVAILABLE CURING FORCE VERY SLIGHT. WILLIES DISBELIEF ADDS TO THE DIFFICULTY. LEOS AND MONTES ABSENCE MAKE MATTERS WORSE. THE EDITION IS OF NO HELP IN REPLACING THE OTHER

SITTERS. IF YOU WISH TONIGHT I WILL GIVE YOU PHYSICAL MANIFESTATIONS FOR THE BENIFIT OF THE NEW PEOPLE. BUT MY DESIRE--CURING--HAS BEEN RENDERED IMPOSSIBLE. I REGRET CAUSING MONTE ANY INCONVENIENCE. LARRYS CONTINUED CONTROL OF THE SITTINGS WILL SOON DISCOURAGE THE ELEMENTAL. PERHAPS AT SOME FUTURE DATE WE MAY CONTINUE WITH OUR ORIGINAL EXPERIMENT THE CURING. I BEG OF YOU BOYS NEVER TO DO WHAT YOU DID IN THAT TOMB AGAIN. BELIEVE ME I HAD DIFFICULTY IN AIDING YOU THEN."

As you've noticed, the good doctor didn't believe in apostrophes and wouldn't have won any spelling or punctuation contests.

His reference to Monte had to do with the objections his parents were raising about Monte's attendance at these sittings. They were skeptical about the influence our group was having on him and were anxious that he should study diligently and get into medical school. At a subsequent sitting Bindelof advised Monte: "MONTE PLEASE DO NOT ARGUE WITH YOUR FAMILY. RATHER GIVE THIS UP." Monte, partly because of his private nature and partly because of his constant testing, then asked a mental question as to how he could convince his parents. The answer that came back was: "A NOTE FROM OVERSTREET."

This answer made no sense to anyone in the group except Monte. Unknown to the rest of us, he had written to a Professor Overstreet at City College asking for an interview. He interpreted the message to mean that perhaps a note from this Professor Overstreet might persuade his parents that this was a worthwhile endeavor.

At one sitting, instead of the familiar "drum roll" and crash of Bindelof's "staccato" signature announcing his presence, we heard five knocks. The pencil wrote out, in script rather than the familiar block printing, "I am a friend of the doctors. . ." The personality identified himself as a Dr. Rinchner. In later sittings, whenever "Dr. Rinchner" communicated, he wrote in script. Another very primitive "entity" also appeared much later. He called himself "Bad" and wrote in a kind of me-Tarzan-you-Jane Pidgin English.

We became less interested in levitation and more in getting "information" about a spiritual existence beyond the grave and about our own personal problems. We knew definitely now that the written messages couldn't somehow have been prepared in advance. Monte's question wasn't even spoken aloud, and most of the other questions asked were spontaneous and were answered immediately. Holding each other's hands on top of the small night table, our feet touching, our backs crammed against walls and furniture in the small room, we'd hear the pencil writing almost immediately in reply, sometimes with one- or two-word answers, but often with long, rapidly written responses that would have taken three or four times longer to write in the usual manner under the most favorable conditions.

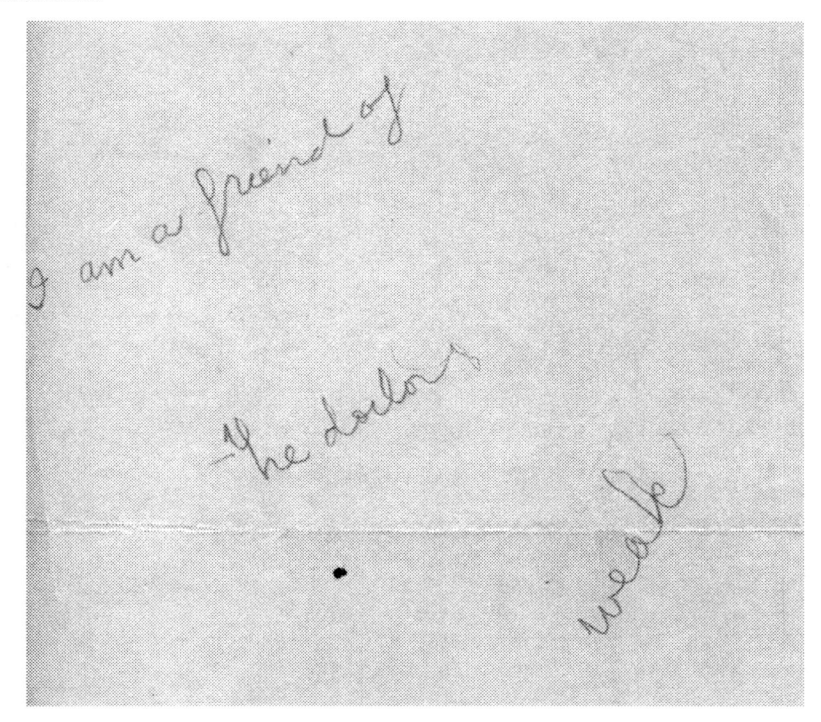

"I am a friend of the doctor"

Some of the messages received later on contained drawings and diagrams; a few were in mirror writing. Once or twice when several sheets of paper were placed on the shelf and were not exactly aligned, the message ran off the top sheet of paper onto the one beneath it.

The responses could be very literal. For example in one of the last sessions, when Lenny asked for clarification of a message, the same words appeared but this time were more clearly and precisely written. When we then asked the communicator to "elaborate on it," the same thing was written again, this time decorated with "elaborate" flourishes.

It's hard to describe the feeling I had during the days following Dr.

"Both gone me here bad"

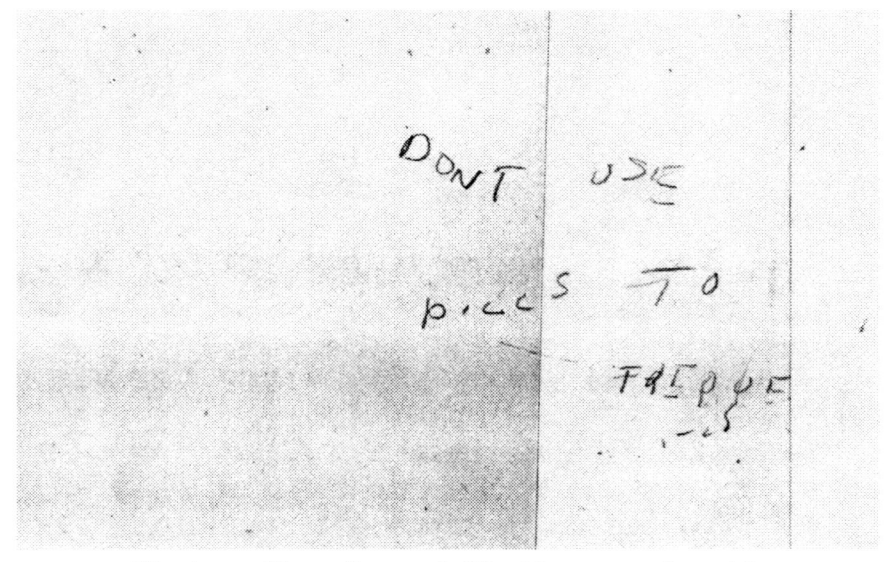

"Don't use pills too frequently." In this message the writing ran off the top sheet of paper onto the one beneath it. The last few letters were probably written on the table.

Bindelof's identifying himself and asking if we would be his disciples. It was as though a whole new universe had opened up. I would ride the subway and feel sorry for my fellow passengers because they didn't know what I knew. They hadn't entered into the amazing sphere where time and motion had completely different meanings. I wanted to stand up and tell them all that had happened, to assure them that life did not end with the death of the physical being. Although I could in no way comprehend what the Dr. had told us about his universe, I was secure in the belief that there was something beyond physical existence.

I tried talking to my mother and brothers about this wonderful new world, but my brothers ridiculed me. My mother tried to understand but without the actual experience it was beyond her ken. I soon realized that I had to keep it to myself when outside the magic circle.

Some months into the Bindelof experience I ran into Eva Le Galliene in Times Square. She remembered me as one of her apprentices and we chatted for a few moments. When she asked what I was doing, I inadvertently blurted out my experiences in the group. She reacted as though I had told her I had just flown in from the moon. It was a blow because I regarded her as someone special, but it was another indication of

Gilbert (on the left) and Larry around 1933 on the roof of 38 Ft. Washington Avenue and at the Cloisters.

LARRY'S STORY

how unready the average person is to even consider the subject. Despite my realization that sharing my experience required a special kind of person, I never wavered in my belief that the experience was real and proved the existence of some form of life after death. A belief I still hold.

One more comment before I go. For a long period of time, as I said earlier, I stayed over at Gil's, sharing meals and good times. Since he had only a single bed, we shared that on the nights I slept there. Monte admitted he always thought we had a homosexual relationship, and insists on it to this day. The laughable thing is, we were both sexually naïve. I didn't lose my virginity until 1934 when I was 18. What Gil and I shared besides Bindelof, was a love of music, a mad sense of humor, and a genuine fondness for each other. I always thought he was the most talented person I had ever known and still do. I learned many important and valuable things during those years.

Well, that's all for now. I'll turn this story back over to Gil.

CHAPTER 6

THE DOCTOR GETS ANNOYED

Larry still firmly believes that Dr. Bindelof was a real person who came to us in spirit to help us and others. But an indication that these messages may have been a product of our beliefs and imaginations is borne out by "communications" from other "entities." We got one message from Arthur Conan Doyle (who was known to be a spiritualist and whose sister was a medium), and, in response to a question about life on other planets, one from a man who lived on Mars. In those days it didn't seem as silly as it does today.

By November of 1933, there were inklings of some "trouble in Paradise." We had difficulty getting through to the Doctor: Other "entities" seemed to be "taking over." The pencil scribbled messages such as "HATE BINDELOF" and "YOU MAY NEVER AGAIN SEE BINDELOF," but eventually the dead physician prevailed and thanked us for sticking with him. He even sketched a kind of speaking trumpet, specifying its dimensions. He instructed that it be made from funnels and a rubber tube, which we could "construct at a nominal cost," so that he might speak with us.

A week later Bindelof seemed quite annoyed. The notes recorded that evening show that immediately upon "appearing," he reprimanded Thomas about something. Tom offered an eloquent and dramatic apology, which was not accepted, and when Larry, acting as spokesman, asked if we might proceed with the cures, the doctor answered no. We asked if we could try later, and he peevishly replied that he didn't care. On further questioning he wrote that he was "discouraged with the whole business." This brought forth a lot of comment by most of us, to which Bindelof replied, "YOU'RE ALL THE SAME."

We questioned him on the meaning of that last message and he scribbled, "WHERE ARE YOUR NOTES" and "I ASKED FOR A TUBE WHERE IS IT" (no punctuation). He was displeased that the asked-for apparatus had not been brought. Leonard inquired if it was his fault, and receiving an affirmative reply, promised to have it ready at the next sitting. Bindelof still refused to continue with the healing and reiterated that he didn't care.

Larry asked then if it was because we were "unscientific" and the answer came in one (affirmative) loud rap.

We turned on the lights and drew up a plan for conducting the séance, then returned to the sitting. Bindelof approved the plan and wrote a message discussing the conversation that had taken place during the interim. On Larry's suggestion, he listed conditions he wanted observed in the room, such as temperature, humidity, time, and a record of those present.

At this session we made an attempt to have "Dr. Bindelof" place a penny inside a locked wooden box; that is, the penny would have to dematerialize and then reconstitute itself inside the container. We heard noises from the lower shelf on which the penny and box had been placed. When the lights were turned up, we found the penny half way through a crack in the box--it evidently had been trying to crash its way in. Our notes say, "A second attempt at dematerialization [was made] after the bracelets were heard jumping around being banged together." None of us remembers these bracelets clearly. Perhaps we were trying to link the two metal rings without breaking either of them. At any rate, we obviously didn't accomplish our goal—perhaps because we didn't really believe we could do it—and quit the effort in this most colorful fashion.

Finally, we received a written comment: "THIS IS ASSININE" [sic].

> I CANNOT THANK YOU ENOUGH FOR THE WAY YOU AIDED ME LAST WEEK. LET ME WARN YOU THAT SHOULD THIS CHAP RETURN AGAIN AND FRUSTRATE MY ATTEMPTS TO SECURE CONTACT WITH YOU, DO NOT DISSOLVE THE SITTING UNTIL YOU HAVE ENABLED ME TO REACH YOU. IF YOU ACT CONTRARY TO THIS ADVICE YOU MAY ERECT A PERMANENT BARRIER BETWEEN US. I HOPE TOM WILL FORGIVE ME FOR NOT TREATING HIS EYES LAST WEEK BUT I WAS SO EXHAUSTED AFTER THAT ENCOUNTER THAT I DID NOT HAVE THE STRENGTH (YOU BOYS WERE ALSO MENTALLY FATIGUED) I SHALL TRY TO MAKE UP FOR IT THIS WEEK TOM. I SHALL SUGGEST A DEVICE WHICH YOU CAN CONSTRUCT AT A NOMINAL COST; SO THAT I MAY BE ABLE TO SPEAK WITH YOU.
>
> ○ — DIAMETER OF RUBBER TUBE
>
> SMALL FUNNEL ABOUT 3 INCH DIAMETER — RUBBER TUBE 5 FEET — LARGE FUNNEL ABOUT 8 INCH DIAMETER
>
> RUBBER BAND TO COVER HALF OF SMALL FUNNEL TUBE

In this message Bindelof provides instructions for a kind of speaking trumpet.

CHAPTER 7

TRUMPET FOR A DEAD MAN

Before the next meeting we adopted Larry's idea to form a society in order to comply with our "mentor's" wishes to be more scientific and systematic in our work. That Saturday, on November 25, Monte, who was now chairman of the Committee for Planning, submitted an agenda that included—in addition to the demonstration of the "talking apparatus" and "eye cures"—questions about the origin, evolution, and characteristics of the soul, and its relationship to the unconscious. Heavy stuff.

We also kept more formal minutes: "Society meeting. Roll called, all members present. Minutes of the last meeting submitted and accepted. The report of the Committee of Records and Appropriations proposed dues for this week of 25 cents. Report accepted. Committee on Planning presented a constitution which was also accepted. Apparatus (trumpet) demonstrated and approved."

After brief messages on the nature of the soul and some other business, we were instructed to place the apparatus on the lower shelf of the table. This position was found to be impractical so Bindelof suggested elevating it with a diagram marked, "LIKE THIS." So we adjusted it, only to receive a message reading, "FOR HEAVENS SAKE THE THINGS TO [sic] HIGH".

The minutes state that the doctor "attempted to speak but achieved nothing but a blowing sound. He was absent for a short time and finally wrote that the apparatus was too primitive and he was sorry but it could not be used." So much for that horn, but as you will see, as is usual in the development of these phenomena, effects do grow in strength if the participants persist, and we eventually achieved some success.

Despite our high-minded inquiries pertaining to the universe and the soul, we were still high-spirited teenagers not above some petty partisan behavior. One member named Willie confessed some skepticism and it was reported that he had "declared his intention to discontinue sitting," so he was voted unanimously out. Tom was thrown out, and then readmitted. Leo was also banished by vote, at least temporarily.

But it was poor Horace who took the brunt of our derision and pranks. Horace Joseph, you might remember, was a nerdy type who had been invited to sit in as a guest and then applied for membership in the society. He was accepted on condition that he pay dues but was not guaranteed admission to the sittings. He would not accept membership under those terms so we relented. We probably allowed him to become a member just so we could plague him. We would, in fact, sometimes take his dues but only allow him to sit in the living room while we conducted our séances in my bedroom. Perhaps because he was so lacking in color, or had what Larry called the personality of a turnip, Larry developed an irrational aversion to him. Horace was always asking what Larry considered "skeptical questions," and Larry was the one who was the most devout believer in Bindelof's reality. One day, in my kitchen, he must have asked a particularly nettling question while Larry was drinking a glass of water. Larry, in exasperation turned to him and tossed the rest of his drink into Horace's face. It dampened only his person, not his enthusiasm. Larry apologized and we continued with the sessions.

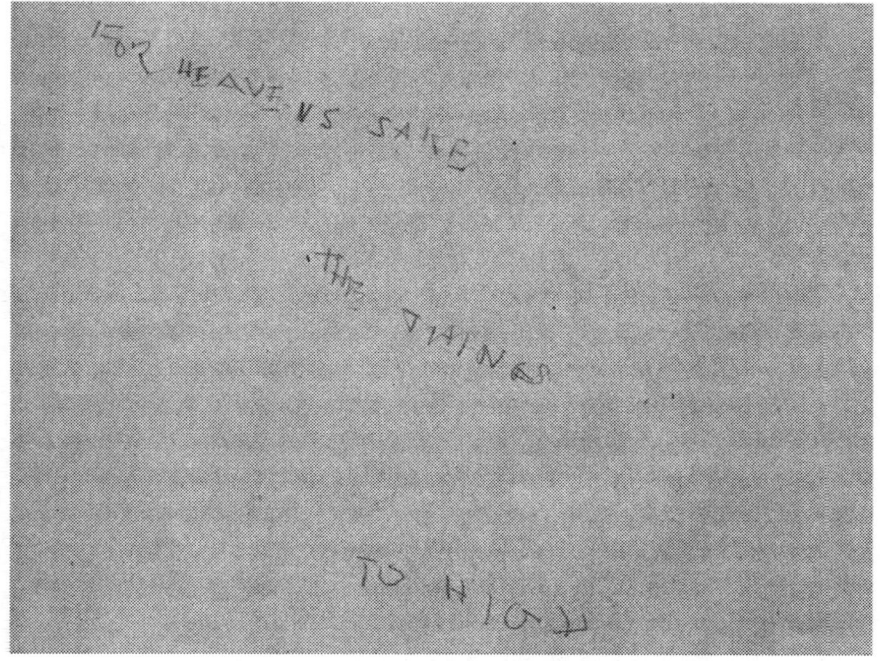

"*For heavens sake The things to high*"

CHAPTER 8

SEE ME, FEEL ME, TOUCH ME, HEAL ME

On the last Tuesday in November, Larry was suffering from a severe ache in the right lower jaw, supposedly caused by an abscessed molar. Since we couldn't get the guys together in the middle of the week for a special sitting we asked my mother to join us. Bindelof announced himself and Larry felt a massage and extreme pressure being applied *below* the diseased tooth. The treatment lasted about three minutes. Larry reported that he experienced immediate relief, that the acute pain disappeared during the treatment and that a dull residual ache remained for about ten minutes, after which "sensations were normal."

Bindelof also admonished him, writing:

"At the rate you are going you will lose every tooth in your head in about 5 years. The lack of calcium in your body is amazing. It is a wonder to me your teeth do not break when you chew. You must eat green vegitables, lettuce especially. Learn to like them. You must. You must have a dentist attend to your front teeth also."

Bindelof's "healing by touch" became a feature of the Saturday night sittings. In addition to the "regulars" who received treatments for ailments such as earaches, eye strain, or myopia, relatives and friends of the sitters presented themselves for treatment much as they would at a clinic. One of these was Lenny's mother, Mrs. Lauer, who, much to her son's surprise not only expressed an interest in the sittings but attended a few in the hopes of being relieved of "nervous insomnia." Bindelof's treatment for her consisted of "a massage of varying pressures across the skull, temples and nape of the neck." His written message informed us that "additional treatments depended upon results obtained."

Horace's mother, Mrs. Joseph, also sat in to relieve a stomach condition. In a statement she made in January 1934, she related that "Dr. B. then came to me and pressed heavily on the top of my head, the side of the head and then the forehead." She reported "great relief" on the following day from this condition that had troubled her for five years previously. "The second treatment differed from the first one," she continued, in that she felt no hand but "heard rumblings from within."

As I remember, an extremely loud and robust rumbling belch by the lady broke the intense concentration and stillness of the darkened room. We were convulsed with laughter, which we tried in vain to suppress. Nonetheless, Mrs. Joseph reported that the result was "beneficial" and that after a third treatment that "consisted of pressure on the head," the stomach condition was gradually improving.

Those who felt Bindelof's touch reported that it was human-like. In January 1934, George Kaiser attested in writing: "After lifting my hand from the table, with a warm moist trembling hand, the Doctor did the following. He flexed my wrist backward and forward, then with his thumb massaged first the back of my hand and then my wrist. This continued for a period of about 30 seconds and then he massaged the palm. Putting my hand back on the table, he then patted my head."

The affectionate patting or slapping often concluded the treatment. George's cousin Leo also recounted this kind of experience:

Dec. 30 [1933]

> As is the custom and order of proceedings, I took the place between Leonard and Gilbert for the continuation of the treatments the Doctor had begun about two months previous. The Doctor first put his hand on my head and moved it from there to my forehead. He pushed my forehead back and I, thinking that he wished to apply pressure to that region, resisted him. He then left my forehead and wrote that I should not resist him. The lights went out and I again felt his hand on top of my head. He then pushed my head back and I felt his fingers at a point upon the neck where the thyroid glands are situated. He left that spot after a few seconds. I felt his hand upon my head. He pushed my head down and then I felt pressure upon the top of my head. He mussed my hair up and then

when he was through with the treatment he brushed it back into place again.

Jan. 6 [1934]

The Doctor practically did the same this week as he did last, only he concentrated more upon the top of [my] head than upon my neck. When he finished he stroked the top of my head and then with a playful slap he left.

In many instances the treatments seemed to alleviate pain and other discomfort. One evening a special sitting was held to obtain Bindelof's help for my young aunt Ellie who had a severe toothache. What follows is an account that she wrote in July 1967:

> The following incident, although it took place more than 30 years ago is still fairly vivid in my mind. I had recently had a tooth filled and unaccountably one weekend it began to ache. Since I knew there was no hope of getting any medical help at that time I asked my nephew Gilbert if we could have a sitting and ask Dr. Bindelof to help me. There was a girl friend visiting at the time and since she had never been present at a sitting she was a bit nervous but agreed to sit with us. I believe my sister [Olga], who always refused to have anything to do with the sittings also agreed since we had no one else around to ask. I don't know why we considered numbers necessary, but apparently we did, probably since our usual sittings had at least seven. We used the small night table, which was always used and within a few moments after starting (joining hands and placing them on top of the table) I suddenly felt a

finger exploring the outside of my cheek. It did not feel the same as a human finger. Then I could feel it begin to go through my cheek, inside my mouth and touch the offending tooth. The pain stopped. I then asked to have the Doctor explain the cause of the pain. We placed a piece of paper and a pencil on the lower ledge of the table and within a few minutes could hear the pencil racing across the paper. This was a familiar sound--it always happened at our regular sittings. To the best of my recollection the explanation was something about air being trapped between the filling and gum etc. [Ellie's recollection is correct. The message written by "Bindelof" in that second week of January 1934 reads, "AIR SPACE BELOW FILLING."] I didn't know enough to know if this was a possible explanation and I didn't care. The tooth had stopped hurting and it never bothered me again. I seem to remember that the proceedings caused a bit of hysteria in the visiting friend, but she calmed down quickly.

In 1989, when she was visiting me and my wife, Marion, in New York, a visitor asked Ellie if she could remember what exactly the finger felt like, if not "the same as a human finger." She described it as feeling like a hot dog casing filled with warm air. And she definitely remembered it going through her cheek.

In December 1933 Howard Frisch also was treated. As he reported in a 1966 statement:

> I am sure that it was because I was jealous of the attention being paid to the other members of the group for their ailments that one evening I said I had been experiencing some pain in my

eyes, or perhaps it was a headache which I complained of. When the lights were out, the speaker (I believe it was always [Larry]) asked Dr. Bindelof if he could help me. There was a rap for yes. At this point you can well imagine my trepidation! I believe we had already experienced the 'slapping' of [Gil]. I had no desire for spirit hands to press my eyes, but I sat in silent suspense. Suddenly, I felt from behind, fingers coming over my forehead towards my eyes. They were so gentle that there was no cause for alarm, I realized, at all. Sometimes in thinking of this episode I have tried to remember whether the feel of the hands was as I had expected them to be--in other words whether or not I had self-hypnotized myself. I am afraid that I cannot remember that detail. I may add that I had then one doctor ... who remains our family doctor to this very day, in his eighties. His hands are gentle, but they are firm and masculine: the hands of Dr. Bindelof seemed almost feminine. They massaged my eyes for a few minutes, and I really think they caused me some relief, even though the headache was mostly imaginary.

Now incidental to possible fraud, I want to say that at the time the hands of Dr. Bindelof were placed over my head, I was sitting in such a way that it would have been impossible for anyone of the other sitters to approach me from behind. The room was so small, so crowded. I can even remember that I sat almost with my back to one of the walls.

Bindelof's message to Larry, "Thought I told you to go to the dentist."
Notice how the paper is crumpled and folded.

We were so crammed into the small bedroom that it would have been impossible for anyone to squeeze undetected--or be able to fit at all--behind another's chair in order to stroke or massage the patient from behind. In addition the room was never pitch dark, so that any gross movement by any of us would have been seen as well as felt. Even if someone would have been able to manage it, there is still the problem of fingers passing through cheeks and pressing from underneath a tooth.

CHAPTER 9

THE PORTRAIT

As I mentioned before, I had always been especially engrossed in music and fine arts. My interest in photography played a primary role in our early experiments with psychic photography using only photographic plates. It was inevitable that we would return to the subject.

Now that we were "in contact" with "Dr. Bindelof" we were curious as to what our spirit leader looked like. In December 1933, we asked him if we could obtain a photograph of him. The message printed rapidly in the dark of the December 16th séance gave us instructions on how to "photograph" him. We were to use a camera, this time, rather than just the glass plates in their metal holders. (As you will see later, we had been experimenting with a microphone and amplifier in an attempt to get spoken communication as well. This was one of the other experiments Bindelof alludes to in the message.)

"TONIGHT IN VIEW OF THE FACT THAT WE HAVE SO MUCH TO DO WE MUST NOT SPEND TO [SIC] MUCH TIME ON ANY ONE EXPERIMENT. THE PHOTOGRAPHY REQUIRING THE MOST ENERGY WOULD BEST BE DONE FIRST. LET ME EXPLAIN A LITTLE MORE IN DETAIL WHAT I WANT DONE. FIRST I SHALL ATTEMPT TO GIVE YOU A PICTURE OF MYSELF.

PROCESS: 1-USE FULL APERTURE IN TOTAL DARKNESS
    2-SET FOCUS FOR FIVE FOOT POINT, FOCAL CLARITY TO BE AT THE CENTER OF TABLE.
    3- SET PLATE. REMOVE COVER.
    4-OPEN LENS IN TOTAL DARKNESS FOR PERIOD OF 20-30 SECONDS.
    5-DEVELOP
SECOND: PICTURE OF COMMON FORCE
    1- FOCUS UNIVERSAL
    2- DISTANCE ENOUGH TO INCLUDE ENTIRE GROUP (SITTERS)

3- 75 Watts 20-30 seconds
4- you should observe lines of force
   with irregular spots on plate
Third: picture of outside identities
   1- Universal focus
   2- Darkness (intelligent entities cannot
      be photographed in light)
   That will be all for the photography.
If no results are obtained this time try again next week. Please remember this method."

Bindelof then discussed the circumstances surrounding Mrs. Lauer's experiences. He also referred to Tom's expulsion (because he "has become absolutely antagonistic") and to keeping Horace out but allowing him to sit in the room away from the table, or in the hall because "his mental vibrations unbalance the unit making communication difficult." Finally he instructed that all plate loading and developing was to be witnessed "so that it may be reported as such on the records."

We followed our spirit mentor's instructions faithfully. The minutes note that we spent a half-hour preparing the photographic apparatus and that the sealed package of plates was opened in the presence of "Gil, Howard, Horace, Mrs. Lauer, Len, and Monte." Later, they all witnessed my developing the plates in the very crowded bathroom. We were, however, rewarded with some remarkable photographs.

The first was the portrait of a distinguished looking, bearded gentleman whose wing collar would be quite fashionable in the nineteenth century. The picture is slightly out of focus but quite distinct. It is in three quarter profile and resembles more a portrait one would sit for than a snapshot. A half century later it still boggles the minds of the remaining members of the group that this image could have resulted from the short time exposure of an empty plate that was in a camera focused at the center of a table and taken in total darkness.

In the "picture of the common force" taken with illumination, some of us and the barometer on the wall can be seen but there are, as the message predicted, lines and irregular spots or blotches on them as well for which no known technical explanation could be found.

The third photograph, again, like "Bindelof's" portrait, taken in darkness, depicts strange forms that Leonard thought resembled "helmeted

Portrait of Dr. Bindelof

soldiers carrying long guns or rifles," and had the tone of a "real battlefield." This was supposed to have been the picture of "outside identities." Len speculated years later that since we boys considered them to be dangerous, I might have imagined them as soldiers carrying implements of destruction and projected this image. Could be.

Whatever the reason, it's obvious that the images produced on these plates were not what you'd normally expect under these conditions.

CHAPTER 10

SPEAK TO ME

Attempts to receive verbal communication from our mentor rather than just written messages must have been in our minds early on. Our first attempt to receive "direct voice" responses (for which there is much anecdotal evidence in the literature of psychical research) was made in early November 1933, when "Dr. Bindelof" drew a diagram of that "speaking trumpet," which we then constructed from rubber tubing, a funnel, and other odds and ends. We were disappointed that we got "only" blowing sounds from this primitive device, but thinking back, it was amazing that we got sounds at all.

At the end of that month, in part of a lengthy message (written on both sides of a sheet that was then folded four ways and crumpled into a tight ball), Bindelof told us that "THE ONLY METHOD BY WHICH I WILL BE ABLE TO SPEAK WITH YOU IS BY A MICROPHONIC AMPLIFICATION SYSTEM. THE FAINT VIBRATIONS CLOSE AGAINST THE DIAPHRAGM MUST BE MAGNIFIED TO BE AUDIBLE." He was so quaint!

We got the equipment and set it up the following week, December 2, 1933. The microphone was suspended from the ceiling so that it hung low above the center of the table. The amp was placed on top of the piano. During the experiment the microphone swung back and forth, from time to time touching the sitters. Towards the end of the experiment the microphone was carried around my head with the mike touching the back of my neck.

The minutes remind me that we excluded Leo from the society and admitted Horace unconditionally. At 9:25 pm we proceeded with the experiment to try to hear Bindelof's voice. Our very first attempt produced definite sounds but no distinct words could be made out.

At 10:15 pm, after a fifteen-minute rest, we resumed the microphone experiment with the sounds becoming more distinct. We left off and then got a message from Dr. Bindelof saying that he would improve with practice. It had been an exhausting evening. For the first 14 or 15 minutes after our second rest we got no results. Then when the Doctor finally arrived he petulantly refused to treat Tom but consented to treat Monte. We were told to rearrange our seating order and then got a feeble message saying "Leo in." Leo, who had been exiled earlier and was sitting outside the circle, again joined the group but again we got no results. We wearily tried again at 11:20 but, again--zilch. So we quit for the night.

On January 20, 1934, Bindelof began a long message (two pages of very small, tight printing) with an apology for his failure to use the microphone. "WE STARTED SO LATE IN THE EVENING," he continued, "THAT BY THE TIME I WAS READY TO USE IT YOU WERE ALL COMPLETELY EXHAUSTED. I SUGGEST WE LEAVE THIS EXPERIMENT AND THE PHOTOGRAPHY FOR A FUTURE DATE WHEN WE HAVE BETTER FACILITIES." He then added, "WHILE THEY ARE INTERESTING, THEY ARE QUITE UNIMPORTANT."

Bindelof then "explained" the phenomena involving the rapid writing and crumpling--but not the occasional folding--of the paper:
"I HAVE NEGLECTED TO TELL YOU WHY I SEEMINGLY CRUMPLE THE PAPER AFTER A MESSAGE SUCH AS THIS. THE EXPLANATION MAY CONFOUND YOU BUT I SHALL ENDEAVOUR TO TELL YOU ANYHOW. WHEN YOU HEAR THE PENCIL SCRATCHING AT THAT TERIFFIC SPEED YOU HAVE PRESUMED THAT I AM WRITING AT THAT SPEED. I AM ACTUALLY WRITING AT A NORMAL RATE--HERE IS WHAT HAPPENS[:] A TYPE OF FORCE (WHAT IT IS I DO NOT QUITE KNOW MYSELF) FORMS A SPHERE AROUND THE PAPER AND PENCIL WHEN I WRITE A MESSAGE THAT YOU APPROXIMATE WOULD TAKE ABOUT 20 MINUTES TO PRINT IT DOES TAKE ME 20 MINUTES BUT THE SPHERE REDUCES THE TIME FACTOR SO AS TO MAKE THE WRITING APPEAR TO HAVE BEEN DONE IN LESS THAN A MINUTE. IN OTHER WORDS 20 MINUTES WORK CAN BE DONE IN 20 MINUTES, YET BE DONE IN ONE MINUTE EVEN THOUGH IT STILL TOOK 20 MINUTES TO PERFORM. AS FOR THE CONSUMATION OF ENERGY--20 MINUTES OF ENERGY IS CONSUMED IN THE ONE MINUTE. WHEN THIS FORCE DISSIPATES IT DOES WHAT YOU MIGHT SAY--COLLAPSES OR CONTRACTS TOWARDS THE CENTRE OF THE SPHERE DRAWING THE PAPER IN WITH IT AND CRUSHING IT TO THE EXTENT YOU OBSERVE. STRANGLY ENOUGH THE QUALITY OF THE WRITING IS IMPROVED WITH THE USE OF THIS FORCE. IN THE SHORT MESSAGES YOU WILL NOTICE THAT THE PENCIL SCRATCHES AT A NORMAL RATE AND THE PAPER DOES NOT CRUMPLE. [Upon examining many of the originals I found this statement to be untrue. Several of the short messages, i.e., containing only a few words, were crumpled. Conversely some of the long messages were not.] THIS IS BECAUSE THE FORCE IS NOT EMPLOYED. TO USE THIS FORCE REPRESENTS A TERIFFIC DRAIN ON THE SITTERS THEREFORE IT IS ADVISABLE

TO USE IT ONLY ONCE AND AT THE BEGINNING OF THE SITTING. I DOUBT IF IT COULD BE DONE TWICE AT ONE SITTING. THAT IS WHY I HAVE REFUSED TO ANSWER MANY OF YOUR QUESTIONS BY WRITING DURING THE SEANCE ABOUT THE CURES."

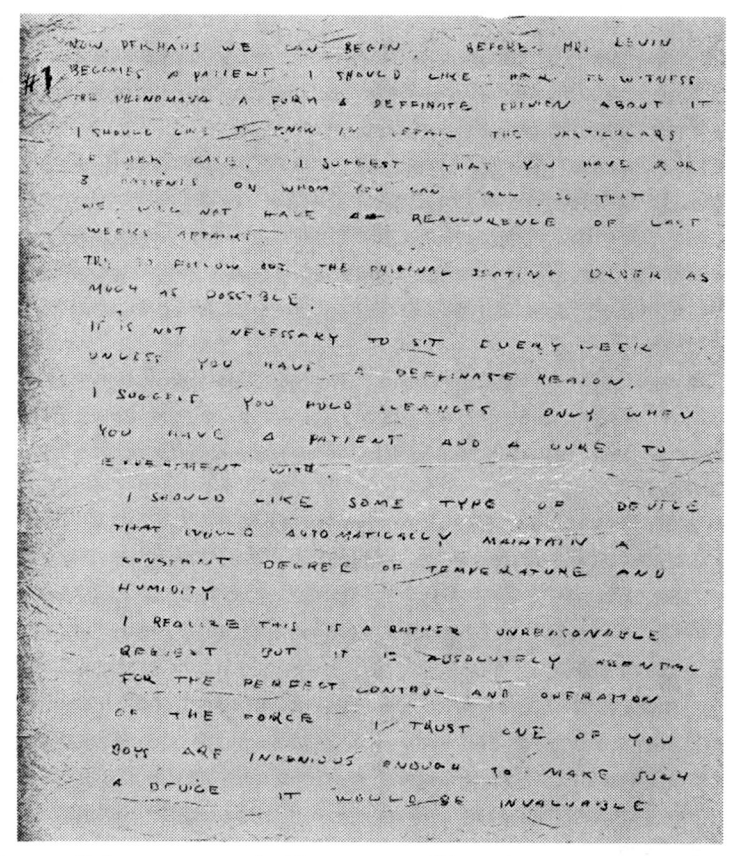

This is one of the most remarkable messages. Note the neat paragraphs and evenly spaced printing, the folding and crumpling, and the precise spelling.

The next part of the message had to do with Mrs. Joseph's treatment, a request for us to secure "a person with a definite ailment, preferably malignant," who is "harmoniously attuned to the entire idea (While a negative person can be cured it takes much longer)," and then added:

"AN INTERESTING POINT WAS BROUGHT UP THAT HAS ENTIRELY ESCAPED ME. A PERSON ON HIS DEATHBED MAY BY [SIC] REVIVED AND CARRIED THROUGH THE CRUCIAL PERIOD BE [SIC] EXCESSIVE HEART STIMULATION. (PERHAPS WE

CAN MAKE THE CIRCLE A PORTABLE MEDICINAL KIT.)" [The British spellings of some words may be attributable to the many volumes of works by British psychical researchers we read.]

Bindelof then admonished us regarding the "unexpected mid-week sitting" that had been held to alleviate the pain in Ellie's tooth that I told you about earlier. This fear expressed by Bindelof occurs almost as a theme throughout the sittings, no doubt reflecting our anxieties as well as those of the Victorian sitters we emulated:

"RATHER THAN LET ELLIE SUFFER ANY PAIN I MANIFESTED MYSELF BUT AT THE RISK OF LOSING FURTHER CONTACT WITH YOU. YOU OPENED THE DOOR WIDE FOR HARMFUL AND ALIEN IDENTITIES. WITH SUCH A SMALL CIRCLE THEIR PASSAGE IS MUCH FASTER THAN MINE, AND THEY MAY THUS HAVING ATTUNED THEMSELVES, PERMENANTLY INTERFERE IF NOT COMPLETELY RUIN OUR SITTINGS."

The message concludes with a reminder to Leonard and Ellie not to fall behind in their notes and a reference to a news item we had discussed regarding a sick infant that is conveyed with typical Bindelovian indignation:

"THAT BABY SHOULD HAVE BEEN IN THE INCUBATOR LAST WEEK. IT WAS SHEER LUNACY TO REMOVE IT FROM AN ENVIRMENT [SIC] THAT WAS SO OBVIOUSLY BENEFICIAL AND ON TOP OF THAT TO EXPECT A CHILD TO DIGEST A PROTEIN DIET WHEN IT WAS NOT FULLY DEVELOPED ENOUGH TO STOP THE SUGAR DIET -- THE MAN IS CRAZY."

In January 1934, Monte left the group to attend medical school. He had been keeping the minutes but they were now taken over by Marianne Meader. Ellie, who had met her in school, brought Marianne to our apartment. She was a dark-haired, blue-eyed German-American temptress whose voluptuous figure and sexy voice caused us all to sit up and take notice. Larry was immediately seduced by the enticing Fougere Royale perfume she wore and, as he put it later, fell madly in lust with her. Except for Howard, who seemed only to be turned on by books, we were all, with our galloping teenage hormones, a little in love with her. As it turned out, Lenny, the self-confident, no-nonsense, takeover person was the only one who really did something about it. But I'm getting ahead of myself again.

We attempted to obtain direct voice communication once more the following week on January 27, 1934, this time, finally, with success. In addition to Marianne, another girlfriend of Ellie's named Carlyn sat with us—it was her first time—and seemed to attract a good deal of attention from "Bindelof."

Another feature of these later sittings that I've neglected to mention was the recording of the room temperature and humidity, which Bindelof had requested some time before.

The first sitting began at 8:56 p.m. with ten sitters. We heard a series of unconnected knocks and received a message about the size of the group. One of the sitters was asked to leave the circle. At 9:04 the doctor's "staccato" was heard immediately and we got a second written message referring to the new girl, Carlyn's arm, which evidently was in need of healing. At 9:08 the doctor proceeded with Mrs. Lauer's treatment followed by Mrs. Joseph's final treatment. Another message informed us that he now was dismissing her case, "pending results to be observed in the future." As you can see we had a regular clinic going.

The following is a transcript of the rest of the minutes of that session. I have corrected obvious typographical errors and mistakes in punctuation and have inserted the contents of the messages referred to in brackets:

> Time 9:33. T. 70-Humidity 35%. It was suggested that the doctor should endeavor to develop talking by the same methods used in the "Margery case." Message #3 was received in reply.
>
> ["MEGAPHONE AT FIRST"]

The reference is to the celebrated case of the Boston medium "Margery," Mina Stinson Crandon, who was investigated in the 1920s by the American Society for Psychical Research. She was later suspected to have used fraudulent means to produce the phenomena in her séances. The case is still controversial.

> Time 9:40. T. 78-Humidity 32%. After an attempt to use the megaphone, (the doctor carried the megaphone around over the heads of the sitters) Mess.4 ["CARLYN DON'T BE SO NERVOUS SILLY"] was received in view of which Carlyn was asked to sit outside of the séance-room.

Poor Carlyn was freaking out. This was, after all, her first séance. Seeing the cardboard megaphone, which we had made on the spot, floating around our heads, hearing the various raps, especially Bindelof's loud "drum roll" from the table, and knowing that the pencil was writing with nobody guiding it, must have unnerved the poor girl.

The megaphone was carried around, touching several sitters. Short draughts of air, sometimes sharply interrupted, thus making a sound similar to the explosive "p," were clearly discernable. It is worth noting the fact that during the entire extent of this experiment the megaphone underwent much handling by the doctor. The mouth of the megaphone was found to be moist and somewhat creased. Message #5, referring to Carlyn's nervousness, was received. ["LATER (LET?) CARLIN COME BACK REAL SCARECROW"]

> Time 10:23. T. 72-Humidity 37%. Continuation of the meg. exp. Following a suggestion, the doctor attempted to say "Mamma." Although the sound produced clearly consisted of two syllables no true vowels or consonant values were present. In answer to direct questions the doctor stated that the megaph. was not satisfactory. Time was taken to construct a larger one.
>
> We sat again a little before 11 p.m., to continue the talking experiment with a larger megaphone.

Larry felt the end of the megaphone being placed against his ear and heard clearly pronounced whispers of "Larry, Leonard, do you hear me?" Larry asked, "Will you improve your talking with practice?" and the doctor answered orally, "Maybe." A lot of handling and manipulation of the megaphone accompanied all this. Then we got the sixth written message of the evening: "REST CARLIN NERVOUS."

When we sat again a little later to continue the talking experiment with the megaphone, there was further mentioning of sitters names: "Larry; Leonard; Howard; Gilbert; Murray. [The "Murray" referred to sat with us for a short time. He was later known as Peter Kalisher when he was a television news reporter. Many years later Larry looked him up in Paris. Kalisher denied remembering Larry or the Bindelof group.] In answer to direct questions Bindelof said that this method of communication, namely speaking, was more laborious than writing, however he would improve with practice and oral conversation would become easier. The doctor stated that he would like to look at Carlyn's arm. However the highly-strung, nervous condition of the girl's mind would not permit it. We got another message saying: "Perhaps you will have a little faith in me later Carlin?"

At about a quarter to midnight, Ellie, who had not been present at the séance, arrived and we sat down again in order that Ellie might hear the doctor speak. The megaphone floated up and was placed at Ellie's ear. She heard: "Hello Ellie. How are you? Sorry you couldn't be here."

I should note here that although the minutes use the words "speak" and "spoke," Larry and I remember only *whispered* words being heard.

In any case, the megaphone experiment was tried again at the next session on February 3, 1934, with "little success." The minutes note that the force seemed weak and scattered. The attempts at direct voice communication evidently ceased at that point for there is no further mention of them after this date.

CHAPTER 11

BINDELOF MISSING

The "interference" and difficulty in contacting Bindelof persisted in the following sessions. On February 10, 1934, the phenomena were slow in starting. A new participant named Jean took Leo's place as a guest and, as usual with a new person in attendance, no results were obtained in the first ten-minute sitting. Two messages were received from "Bad" reporting in his primitive style, "No doctor any more," and then, "No doctor any more me here please Bad No doctor any more."

Mrs. Lauer, Murray, and Marianne left the circle and another attempt was made to reach Bindelof, but only Bad answered again reiterating, "I now please doctor gone me now please doctor gone," in weak scribbles. Then more emphatically, sideways on another sheet, "Doctor no more here gone" (underlined three times).

Through Bad we were able to contact "Dr. Rinchner" who, in reply to our questions about Bindelof's whereabouts wrote, "Can not find him will see." Larry asked in what way the circle could be of use in the search, whereupon the message, "Don't resist any table movements" was written.

This message was followed by a great deal of rattling of the paper, table-movements, and levitations, supposedly as Rinchner "searched" for our mentor. A sixth message told us not to be nervous, and finally Rinchner wrote in a short seventh message, which was slightly crumpled, that he could not find him.

After a rest the group resumed sitting. Upon receiving Dr. Rinchner's five knocks—Rinchner's "signature"—he was asked if there was any hope of getting in contact with Dr. Bindelof again. The reply, in a more forceful script was, **"Get Thomas immediately."**

We took a break and tried unsuccessfully to locate Tom by telephone. We sat again without him and inquired of Rinchner whether stopping at this point would be advisable. Rinchner urged us to try a little longer, then told us, "You may feel contact during period outside forces—harmless do not fear them." During the ensuing search Lenny's watch was removed from his wrist and carried around the table. We could see its luminous dial shining in the darkened room. It was twirled around and toyed with, reset to read 3:16, and returned to Lenny's lap. Both of Larry's hands, one of Murray's, then Howard's and Leonard's were seized and placed on the lower ledge in that order. Several of us heard a faint staccato resembling that of Bindelof's. The contact was broken by some of the sitters' loud remarks, the hands were pushed away and no more results were obtained. We decided we needed a rest.

When we resumed again Rinchner "explained" in the eleventh message of the evening that the "Staccato built up from extreme concentration by hand not bindelof". By now it was past midnight and we were all tired so Lenny asked if we might stop the sitting. Rinchner answered affirmatively and promised to try everything in his power to locate Dr. Bindelof during the week, and also to thank "Bad" for his kind help.

The decline of interest and/or the draining of energy and distraction caused by the new members admitted into the circle took their toll on the production of the phenomena. Concentration on, or perhaps I should say allegiance to, the Bindelof-father figure also seemed to be declining.

The sitting of February 17, 1934, started slowly. Three attempts at sitting were made with no results in the first hour. Finally at ten o'clock we were able to obtain answers to direct questions by means of raps for "yes" and "no."

"Your not so wrong Larry"

Then Bad wrote "BOTH GONE ME HERE NOW PLEASE BAD." The minutes interpret this message as his not being able to find Rinchner and that he did not know Arthur Conan Doyle (obviously in reply to someone's inquiry). Bad's second message reads, "I LOOK AGAIN MEBY OBSORBED BY

COMMON FORC[E]." (On the back of this message is another, "TONGUE TIED IN LIFE," for which the minutes provide no explanation.)

At 10:23 Rinchner finally "returned" saying, "Have located Bindelof Tom in Peter out." We made the switch but were unsuccessful in contacting Bindelof. Two more messages from Rinchner instructed us to change the seating arrangements: "Try Tom in Mrs. L seat," and "Tom change with Howard Howard with Mrs. L."

There is reference to an article submitted, probably by Larry, because Rinchner writes, "Your not so wrong Larry." But the minutes say: "The reading of the message was made impossible by impatient knocks of Dr. Rinchner followed immediately by Dr. Bindelof's staccato." Finally we have Bindelof's message, upside down, in his distinctive printing, "WILL TRY TO EXPLAIN NEXT WEEK."

We tried to get treatment for Tom but we received messages telling us to "WAIT UNTIL WE HAVE A MORE PRECISE CONTROL." Larry was then treated for an earache and the messages "BE MORE EXACTING IN YOUR CHOICE OF GUESTS" and "GET THEM FIXED IN A HURRY" were printed, the latter probably referring to Larry's teeth, which were in poor shape.

Mrs. Lauer and Howard were treated with Howard being told, "EYE STRAIN TO MUCH READING," and at five minutes to midnight we "bid the Doctor good night."

There is no record of a séance the following week. There was a meeting however, the minutes of which follow:

> After a short conference with the officers, the chairman called the meeting to order at 11:35 and announced that a proposal had been made to disband and to return all money paid in form of dues. Reasons: Séances had been progressing rapidly until a short time ago, when new members had been admitted. Since then the results had been poor. Also nothing had been done in finding cases the Doctor had asked for.
>
> The floor was opened for discussion and then votes were taken, resulting in a 6:3 vote in favor of disbanding.

The meeting was adjourned, after announcement had been made that the money will be refunded on Saturday, March 3, 1934.

Respectfully submitted,
Marianne Meader

CHAPTER 12

THE NEW BINDELOF SOCIETY

On March 31, 1934, the first sitting of the "New Bindelof Society" was held at apartment 692 of the Ansonia Hotel in Manhattan. This was the apartment of Mr. and Mrs. George Meader, Marianne's parents. Mr. Meader was an American tenor who sang at the Metropolitan Opera House for a season or two. He was fairly short, balding, and had a thin moustache. He later got a Hollywood contract, not as a singer but as an actor playing supporting parts. You can still see him on TV in old films like *On The Town* in which he played the professor from the museum. And of course you can still see the stately, ornate Ansonia on Broadway at 72nd Street. It's now a historical landmark building, having housed many famous operatic and other theatrical performers.

Mrs. Meader was German. She was a tall, blonde older version of Marianne and, as we found out later, was an admirer of the strengthening Nazi party.

Although our sexual hormones were at their peak, most of us were sexually naïve, uninitiated, and idealistic. Once when Larry and I discussed what real love was, he said it meant seeing the one you loved nude and kissing her on the forehead.

Larry was completely infatuated with Marianne, and the few times they were alone, he confided later, were wonderful. They necked passionately but never progressed beyond the kissing stage. During these Ansonia sittings, Larry found out that she was also seeing Len. One day, on the upper deck of a 5th Avenue bus, Larry confronted her and demanded she choose either Len or him. Since, as we later found out, his rival had a more lusty definition of love and had been kissing her much below the forehead, she had no difficulty in choosing Lenny.

At any rate, the Meaders allowed us to use part of their spacious high-ceilinged apartment for the resumption of our sessions. In the minutes of this first meeting of the "new society," we dutifully recorded the date of the full moon (March 30) as well as the last quarter along with the times of the sittings, the "dry" and "wet" barometer readings, and the humidity.

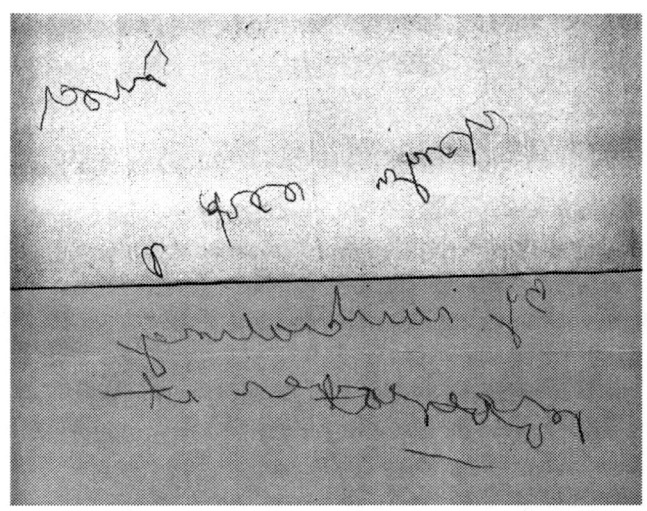

Two examples of mirror writing produced at the sittings. They seem to be short answers to spontaneous questions by the sitters.

Things were slow in starting, probably because of the break in meetings, but at the second attempt we got table movements and slight knockings "of more than one identity." The sitting was stopped, however, when the pencil was flung against a dresser in back of Larry.

Eighteen minutes later we tried again and this time the paper was crumpled by an "unknown identity." Finally, at the third sitting, we received an unsigned message from Bad announcing his presence: "ME HERE NOW PLEASE." We asked him to try to reach Dr. Bindelof whereupon the paper was crumpled and the table was levitated. Eventually we received: "FAINT OBJECTION IN AIR."

We inquired as to where the objection was coming from and were told that it seemed to be from the next room, where Mr. and Mrs. Meader were. Bad consented to continue searching for the doctor anyway and more table levitations and crumpling of paper ensued. After a time we got another written message that was illegible. We asked Bad what was meant but he could not give any explanation and made it understood that he had no special reason for writing it. He consented to take up the search again and finally a weakly written message appeared. It was in *mirror writing* (upside down and backwards): "BINDELOF NOT HERE LOOK AGAIN." After another short search Bad pleaded, "THEY ARE GONE WHY DONT YOU LET ME STAY PLEASE."

When the lights were turned off again, Larry explained that our reason for wanting Dr. Bindelof was because of the interest the group had in curing. Asked if he had curing powers, Bad hesitated and then rapped out the signal for "yes." The minutes state that this was "not understood by Larry because of the sitters who all said 'no,'" and when asked a second time, "the entity" rapped "no." Larry explained that we were sorry but couldn't let him stay and Bad consented to go on in his search for Bindelof. Presently we obtained the message, "I THINK I FOUND HIM TRY NO[W]." We resumed sitting instantly and shortly after got, "HESITATES TO COME BACK SPEAK TO HIM."

Larry took control, spoke to Dr. Bindelof and explained why the sittings had been broken up and the society disbanded. No results. Lenny then took over, reiterating what Larry had said. After a few seconds he was interrupted by Dr. Bindelof's "staccato." Lenny continued assuring the doctor that the society intended to take the work seriously and scientifically and begged him to take the part of leadership in this new society using the sitters as his "tools." The raps came back, "no." We then asked questions about his absence at the last sittings but he interrupted impatiently with his staccato knocks.

Larry tried to interest his mentor by asking him if he would consider taking on Mrs. Levin, Larry's mother, who had developed a tumor. The knocks were indecisive, yes and no. We took a break.

Just before midnight we sat once more and almost immediately received the distinctive staccato. After a brief question asking if Mrs. Levin could join us the following week, we received the doctor's answer: "NOT AS A PATIENT AS A SITTER."

The minutes of the new society's second meeting are the last recorded. It took place, just as the first, in the Meader's apartment at the Ansonia, on April 7, 1934, beginning at 9:17 p.m. Our first two attempts produced nothing but we found the pencil on the bed after the second sitting. At 10:03 we made a third attempt during which the pencil was thrown on the bed, paper was folded and thrown over Leo's head, and a pencil was taken from behind Lenny's ear and again thrown onto the bed.

At 10:31 Mr. Meader joined the group as a guest and we got some "controllable" table levitations. We conferred about our lack of success and attempted another sitting to ask what should be done. We succeeded only in getting what looks like an illegible weak attempt at script, after which the pencil broke in half. Another attempt produced a message in script

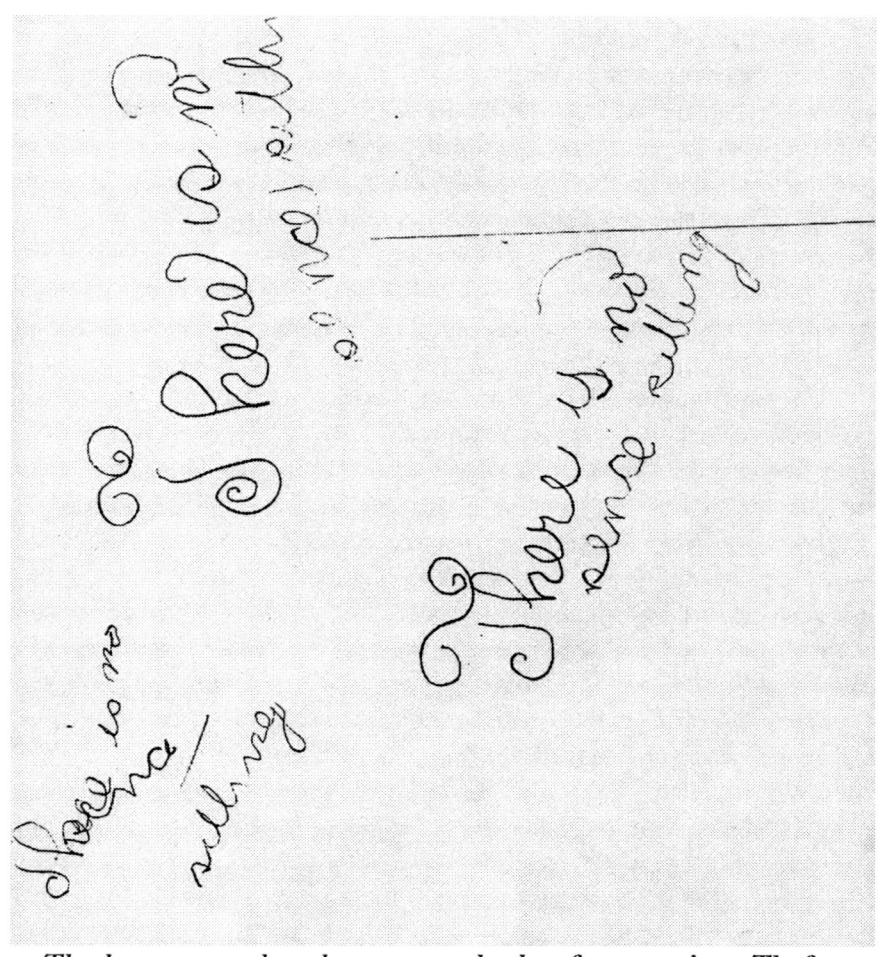

The three messages have been put together here for comparison. The first message is in the lower left; the "clarification" is on the right, and the "elaboration" above it.

whose words run into each other, saying, "There is no sense sitting." This is where, as I mentioned earlier, Lenny asked that the writer "clarify" and "expand" the message and amusingly the request was taken quite literally: the message was repeated, but this time the letters were farther apart and were more clearly written. Lenny then apologized for having caused the misunderstanding and explained that he wanted to know the reason behind the message. Larry asked the communicator to "elaborate" on the message. The final message contained the same words, but this time with even more elaborate spirals and flourishes embellishing it.

And that last message, I believe, pretty much summed up what we felt. Our interests were turning outward, toward living life, preparing for adulthood. Monte had long ago left for medical school. Larry had become involved with a small theater group that performed on Saturday evenings and was torn between his desire to perform and his devotion to the Bindelof sittings. There was also the scandal that caused dissention in the group. Lenny and Marianne's torrid affair resulted in an unwanted pregnancy. I'm sure the fact that Lenny was Jewish didn't help. Her parents felt that this would *not* be a blessed event and whisked Marianne to Germany for an abortion.

The undercurrent of conflict and anger, both conscious and unconscious, probably contributed to the violent and disruptive manifestations at these last sittings. Outside the séances Larry again experienced an event reminiscent of the disappearing labels. As he put it later, "Basically, I was very conflicted between my concern about life after death and the increasing imminence of Fascism. As a Jew, even a non-believer, I was frustrated about how little the so-called 'free world' was doing to stop Hitler. Combined with this was my personal confusion about sex, with Marianne Meader and Lenny. What was a poor precocious but naïve boy to make of it all? Plus the terrible conditions at home; illness, no money, and no real involvement with my parents or siblings."

Larry was living then with his family in a one-bedroom, furnished, ground-floor apartment in Sunnyside, Queens. His parents slept in the bedroom, his 12-year old sister Roslyn on a dinette bench in the kitchen-dining area, and his brother Sandy and he slept on a sleeper-sofa in the living room. When his eldest brother Arnold was home on one of his hospital passes, he slept on a cot in the living room. Larry had been dating a girl in the Bronx and one Saturday night had stayed late—he claims that it was just heavy petting, he was still a virgin. He didn't get home until about one a.m. and everyone was asleep. He put the small dental bridge for his front teeth (remember, his teeth were very bad) in a glass of water and, as usual, left it on the side of the sink before getting into bed. In the morning an empty glass greeted him. He searched high and low for his teeth, finally accusing his brothers of hiding them. They denied this vehemently. His mother felt he had somehow lost them at the girl's house and insisted that he call her. Cowed by his mother, as usual, he phoned the girl. His humiliation was increased by her ridicule--and that was the end of that romance. The teeth never showed up. Larry maintains that somewhere there is an elemental with a happy grin.

I was involved with some young woman, and I needed to prepare myself for my career in the arts. We drifted away from each other. We all needed to concern ourselves with "the real world" and our futures in it.

I don't think there is any doubt that I had been the source of the major occurrences in or out of the séance room, although I don't think I could have done it without the abundant energy of the others, especially, Larry and Lenny. After the breakup of the Bindelof group, I was the only member who occasionally dabbled in séances. There was always some ambivalence in my mind between staying clear of occultism and trying again to see if results were obtainable. I suppose it's somewhat like the alcoholic who swears never again to touch a drop and somewhere along the way takes a nip. Some people who knew of my background encouraged me. We wanted to see if it was still possible to achieve some results among a group of interested participants.

On one occasion, in the 1980s, my wife, Marion, and I met with some dedicated spiritualists in a refurbished old house in Hudson, New York that had a history of "odd occurrences." The room was large and in the center was a heavy oak table. About eight of us gathered around it in the dimly lit room. A small electric lamp in a corner afforded good visibility. We joined hands and waited. After a time of quiet the centerboard of the table began to rise, first slowly and then with considerable force as though it might take flight from the table. I became suddenly captivated, realizing that we had the beginnings of a remarkable demonstration. This was not to be. The group arose in panic. The board fell back into position and that was the end of the séance. After much talk and amazement we resumed the sitting but nothing more happened. My feeling was that perhaps, as it had in the past, a combination of personalities helped generate the force. But whatever had been generated apparently wanted no further part of the gathering. It's difficult to understand how and why such manifestations should occur on one occasion and not another.

Another striking example of the odd things that happen around me, usually produced unconsciously, occurred at a séance requested by Zella Merrit, the daughter of the late Paul Jonas who wanted to try to contact her father. Jonas, by the way, was the artist who made the dinosaurs for the Sinclair Oil exhibit at the New York World's fair in the 1960s. I agreed to sit with them. Again my talented wife, Marion, joined me and about eight to ten other people in Jonas's studio. We sat around a heavy table that was in the center of the wood-floored room. After a while the table began to move around the room, all of us traipsing after it. I felt that some of the group members were pushing it and, becoming annoyed with their behavior, stepped away from the moving circle. I turned to observe them and, suddenly, just as had happened when we boys trespassed in the tomb many years before, stones began to fall from some point below the ceiling of the room onto the party.

The spirit of Bindelof was not dead.

Amusing line drawing done by Gil many years later of the boys conjuring up a spirit.

PART TWO:
A BRIEF HISTORY OF PHYSICAL PHENOMENA

CHAPTER 13

IT DIDN'T BEGIN WITH THE FOX SISTERS

The Bindelof group was, of course, not the first of its kind. The levitation of tables seems to have been around as long as humans have—or at least as long as tables have. One of the earliest references to it appears in the works of the great Christian writer, Tertullian, who lived from about 155 to 222 AD. He chastised some pagans saying: "Do not your magicians call ghosts and departed souls from the shades below, and by their infernal charms represent an infinite number of delusions? And how do they perform all this but by the assistance of angels and spirits, *by which they are able to make stools and tables prophesy.*" (Emphasis added.)

Two hundred years later Ammianus Marcellinus, the Roman historian, described a kind of Ouija board used by certain philosophers of his day, which consisted of a pendulum swinging in a bowl around which were engraved letters of the alphabet.

We also know that some Jews practiced the skill in the seventeenth century.

According to Nandor Fodor, an ancient instance of table levitation was described in Samuel Brent's *Judischer agestreifter Schlangen Balg* of 1610 and was denounced as magic. In 1615 Zalman Zebi, a cabalist leader, replied in his *Judischer Theriak* that it was not magic but the work of the Lord for they sang beautiful hymns or psalms to the table and it could be no devil's work when God is remembered. (Later groups also found that singing songs helped facilitate table movement.)

The historical wellspring of the Bindelof group, however, arose just about a century and a half ago in upstate New York when, on March 31, 1848, the Fox family of Hydesville, New York heard knocks or "raps" coming from the table around which they were sitting. The sounds actually began to be heard a week or two before this date. In some instances they resembled the sounds of furniture being moved, but at other times they were loud poundings that echoed from the walls or floor causing violent vibrations in the house.

The Fox's two daughters, Maggie, aged 14 or 15, and Kate, 12, moved their beds into their parents' room because they were upset by the tumult of the previous nights. They went to bed around 7:00 p.m. but no sooner had they retired than the knockings began. This time, instead of exhibiting fear, the girls responded more intrepidly and lightheartedly. Kate snapped her fingers in imitation of the sounds and, to their amazement, the raps answered. Then Maggie clapped her hands asking for a reply. Again the raps answered. Their mother asked for 10 raps, which were obediently supplied, and then requested the ages of her children. Again the raps complied, with complete accuracy. (In a later chapter I describe how my ex-husband was able to do this with a transistor radio, getting it to make clicking sounds, also with complete accuracy.) They also "communicated" using the code of three tilts for "Yes" and no movement for "No," reciting the alphabet until a rap or tilt indicated the required letter (just as the Bindelof boys did at first).

The Fox sisters questioned the source of the raps, which spelled out that it was the spirit of a peddler who had been murdered and whose remains had been buried under the house. Somewhat frightened, Mrs. Fox sent for a neighbor who entered a skeptic but emerged a "believer" as the "spirit" accurately answered questions she put to it regarding her age and other personal facts. Needless to say the news of the rapping spirit spread quickly, and as the audience grew the "story" was developed: he had been a 31-year-old widower whose initials were "B.C.," came from Orleans County, and had left five children.

The rappings were heard for the first time in daylight about the third day. Some of those present made investigations and signed statements swearing that they could not find any apparent cause of the raps. The family moved to another house but the noises followed them.

The raps eventually spelled out the peddler's name but no trace of such a person or his five children was ever found. In retrospect, of course, it is easy to see that the raps originated with either one or both of the girls. The messages were either products of their suggestive unconscious or facts that they knew or were picking up telepathically from the townspeople, similar to those messages produced by the Bindelof group. The general populace, however, attributed the manifestations to communications from the dead

In April 1848 an editor named E. E. Lewis from Canandaigua, New York, obtained testimonies from the main witnesses, which he printed in a pamphlet offering $50 to anyone who could solve the mystery. Visitors flocked to their home in order to commune with the spirit world. The Fox sisters became world famous, and together with their older sister Leah, toured the country giving demonstrations.

The Rev. C. Hammond wrote the first recorded account of their "table tilting" after his visit to the Fox family at 8:00 p.m. on February 22, 1850. In it he describes sitting with Mrs. Fox and her three daughters at a large table on which a lighted candle was placed. As soon as they were seated

> sounds were heard, and continued to multiply and became more violent, until every part of the room trembled with their demonstrations. They were unlike any I had heard before. Suddenly, as we were all resting on the table, I felt the side next to me move upward—I pressed upon it heavily, but soon it passed out of the reach of us all—full six feet from me, and at least four from the nearest person to it. I saw distinctly its position—not a thread could have connected it with any of the company without my notice, for I had come to detect imposition, if it could be found. In this position it was situated when the question was asked, "Will the spirit move the table back where it was before?" And back it came as though it was carried on the head of someone who had not suited his position to a perfect equipoise, the balance being sometimes in favour of one side and then the other. But it regained its first position.

The sitting continued with Rev. Hammond reporting, among other occurrences, a transparent hand presenting itself before his face, fingers taking hold of a lock of his hair, and "a cold deathlike hand" being drawn over his face.

Later in their lives the two younger sisters fell upon hard times. By 1888 they were penniless widows who were rumored to be alcoholic to boot. A real soap opera. Maggie "confessed" that the rappings had been fraudulent but later recanted, saying she had succumbed to the temptation of a $1,500 bribe—quite a sum of money in those days—that she was given to do it. This "confession" led to the commonly held belief, widely disseminated by the professional "skeptics" or debunkers to this day, that the Fox girls had cheated by making the sounds by manipulating their toe bones or some such other nonsense.

Television shows on psychic phenomena will generally mention the Fox sisters as frauds as a preface to their programs, their writers just assuming that they were fakes. The "debunkers" have done a good job of deceiving the public. None of the other phenomena such as the levitations or the phantom hands are even mentioned. They don't explain how they could have produced sounds that shook the house or the accurate personal information they gave by manipulating their toe bones. Later the great Sir William Crookes tested Kate Fox's powers and found them to be genuine and quite spectacular.

Whatever their personal tragedy, the Fox girls were inadvertently responsible for the Spiritualist movement throughout the United States and Europe. (The basic principle of Spiritualism is that the spirit survives bodily death and that talented mediums can communicate with the spirits of loved ones to bring comfort to the living.) Within five years of the Hydesville happenings, thousands of mediums were practicing in the U.S. and Great Britain and hundreds of "magnetic circles" were established in major cities.

Mediums fell into two categories, mental and physical. The mental mediums merely communicated information from the dearly departed. Physical mediums, with whom we are primarily concerned here, produced physical phenomena through which the "spirits" communicated.

The craze spread to Europe, supposedly at first through passengers arriving on the steamer "Washington" in Bremen in March 1853. From the King of Prussia, who sat at satinwood tables in his salon, to the commoners who sat around kitchen and dining room tables, it was all the rage. Vienna and Paris soon followed, then Belgium and Holland, and across the channel to England where two mediums had already established themselves, having arrived from the U.S. some months before.

Even the famous Victor Hugo, during his exile in Jersey, became an enthusiastic sitter. At first skeptical, he and the intellectual group with which he sat soon received "messages" from the likes of Plato and Dante as well as "The Spirit of Criticism" and "The Shadow of the Tomb." Many of the communications were in verse and the spirit of Shakespeare, no less, challenged him to a poetry competition. What else would you expect from a gathering of erudite writers and poets?

Just as predictably, along with the many sincere and truly gifted mediums that surfaced, were a variety of self-deluded or marginally talented persons, as well as a host of out and out frauds eager to cash in on the craze.

CHAPTER 14

THE EXTRAORDINARY POWERS OF D. D. HOME

Religion has always been big business. Most people become horrified at the thought of personal oblivion after death and despondent at the loss of loved ones. They are eager to tithe or contribute in other ways to confirm their assurance that their souls will survive and that they will eventually be reunited with their other beloved mortals.

Spiritualism, too, became quite lucrative. Good mediums were in demand and could ask healthy fees, especially those who produced such spectacular phenomena as ectoplasmic apparitions of the sitters' loved ones, or direct voices, so that the living could converse directly with their dearly departed. Human nature being what it is, it was inevitable that phony mediums went into operation contriving "special effects" in the darkened parlors in order to bilk the credulous.

And so it came about that individuals and teams of investigators began to attend séances to uncover the frauds. The impostors used a variety of clever tricks and employed accomplices to assist them in their performances, though many were unmasked by these equally adept sleuths. In the U.S., the great escape artist, Harry Houdini, became a well-known debunker of bogus mediums after being burned by one of these fakes when he sought to communicate with his dead mother. Mediums eventually came into disrepute because of the many charlatans who invaded the séance rooms.

However, one person in particular, who was investigated extensively by expert debunkers and scientists alike, produced some of the most remarkable phenomena on record and was never found to be dishonest or fraudulent in any way. Even to this day this extraordinary man is considered by all (except, of course, those who choose to close their eyes to anything outside of their narrow, mechanistic world view) to be absolutely genuine.

Daniel Dunglas Home (pronounced "Hume") was the seventh son of a Scottish couple of modest means living in Edinburgh at the time of his birth in 1833. He was raised by his aunt, a Mrs. Cook, who immigrated to Norwich, Connecticut when he was a child. Evidently Mrs. Home had some psychic abilities that included clairvoyant and precognitive visions and, according to Home, his aunt told him that he too began having them at the age of four. His first memory of such an occurrence dates from a night in his thirteenth year, after he and his aunt had moved to Troy, New York. It seems that Daniel saw his friend, Edwin, whom he had left behind in Norwich, appear to him as a luminous cloud. Both boys were religious and one day as they were reading the Bible together, they made a pact promising that the first to die would appear to the other. Thus Home knew that Edwin had died. Four years later he had a similar vision in which he learned, to the exact hour, of his mother's passing.

In his autobiography, *Incidents in My Life*, published in 1863, he reported that shortly after his mother's demise he heard "loud blows" on the head of his bed, as if it had been "struck by a hammer." The following morning he and his aunt were startled by loud raps sounding from the breakfast table. His terrified aunt, jumping to the usual conclusion, believed them to be manifestations of the devil and summoned two clergymen to try to exorcise the evil spirit. Their efforts were in vain for not only did the raps continue but objects began to move about the room seemingly of their own volition.

It is interesting that while his aunt believed that the phenomena were Satan's doing, Daniel felt that they were demonstrations of God's goodness and that the knockings and movements reflected his prayers, or perhaps God's acknowledgment of them. He relates that once when his aunt tried to arrest a motile table by placing her Bible on it, "the table only moved in a more lively manner, as if pleased to bear such a burden."

Obviously his aunt was as firm in her opinion as he was in his, and finally, unable to tolerate these blasphemous displays of the Demon, she put her nephew out of her house. Home was eighteen.

By now, of course, word of the manifestations had spread and, although he never asked for direct payment or assistance, people came forward inviting him to live in their homes where he would hold séances and demonstrate his powers. These demonstrations must have been quite impressive in that they were nearly all conducted in good light with Home sitting among the observers rather than hidden behind the curtains of a "cabinet."

One notable sitting took place in Springfield, Massachusetts in 1852, for among the participants were a Harvard professor, David A. Wells, and the renowned poet, William Cullen Bryant. These men had come to investigate the medium. They reported on their findings in a published, signed statement that Home quoted in his autobiography:

> The undersigned... bear testimony to the occurrence of the following facts, which we severally witnessed at the house of Rufus Elmer, [a Home benefactor with whom he was living] in Springfield...
>
> 1. The table was moved in every possible direction, and with great force, when we could not perceive any cause of motion.
>
> 2. It [the table] was forced against each one of us so powerfully as to move us from our positions—together with the chairs we occupied—in all, several feet.
>
> 3. Mr. Wells and Mr. Edwards took hold of the table in such a manner as to exert their strength to the best advantage, but found the invisible power, exercised in an opposite direction, to be quite equal to their utmost efforts.
>
> 4. In two instances, at least, while the hands of all the members of the circle were placed on the top of the table—and while no visible power was employed to raise the table, or otherwise move it from its position—it was seen to rise clear of the floor, and to float in the atmosphere for several seconds, as if sustained by some denser medium than air.
>
> 5. Mr. Wells seated himself on the table, which was rocked for some time with great violence, and at length, it poised itself on the two legs, and remained in this position for some thirty seconds, when no other person was in contact

with it.

6. Three persons, Messrs Wells, Bliss and Edwards assumed positions on the table at the same time, and while thus seated, the table was moved in various directions.

7. Occasionally we were made conscious of the occurrence of a powerful shock, which produced a vibratory motion of the floor of the apartment in which we were seated—it seemed like the motion occasioned by distant thunder or the firing of ordnance far away—causing the table, chairs, and other inanimate objects, and all of us to tremble in such a manner that the effects were both seen and felt.

8. In the whole exhibition, which was far more diversified than the foregoing specification would indicate, we were constrained to admit that there was an almost constant manifestation of some intelligence which seemed, at least, to be independent of the circle.

9. In conclusion, we may observe that Mr. D. D. Home, frequently urged us to hold his hands and feet. During these occurrences the room was well lighted, the lamp was frequently placed on and under the table, and every possible opportunity was afforded us for the closest inspection, and we admit this one emphatic declaration: We know that we were not imposed upon nor deceived.

Wm. Bryant

B. K. Bliss

Wm. Edwards

David A. Wells

Despite his success and the admiration he received, Home's ambition was not to be a famous medium but a physician. Such was the esteem in which he was held that one of his devoted patrons generously financed his education. Fate stepped in, however, in the form of what was then called consumption, a term for what we know today as tuberculosis. Home had never been a robust child, and now the illness weakened him to the extent that he could not complete his studies. Contrary to the practice of the time, in which victims of this disease would seek out warmer, sunnier venues, his physician recommended that he move back to the British Isles. Consequently he arrived in England in 1855 with his few belongings and several letters of introduction to English spiritualists.

He became even more of a celebrity in England and in Europe where his fame spread rapidly especially among the upper classes. He performed for and hobnobbed with luminaries of the time such as the well-known writer, Sir Edward Bulwer-Lytton, and poet Elizabeth Barrett Browning, and with royal personages, among them the Queen of Holland, Napoleon III, Kaiser Wilhelm I, and members of the court of Csar Alexander II of Russia.

I mentioned only Mrs. Browning because, to use typical British understatement, Robert Browning was no friend of Home's. In July 1855, the Brownings attended a sitting in Ealing at the home of a Mr. J. S. Rymer in whose house D. D. Home stayed for several months and where sittings were held practically every day. In a letter to her sister written about a month later, Mrs. Browning reported:

> We were touched by the invisible, heard the music and raps, saw the table moved and had sight of the hands. Also at the request of the medium, the spiritual hands took from the table a garland which lay there and placed it upon my head. The particular hand which did this was of the largest human size, as white as snow, and very beautiful. It was as near to me as this hand I write with, and I saw it as distinctly. I was perfectly calm! not troubled in any way, and felt convinced in my own mind that no spirit belonging to me was present at the occasion. The

> hands which appeared at a distance from me I put up my glass to look at—proving that it was not a mere mental impression, and that they are subject to the usual laws of vision. These hands seemed to Robert and me to come from under the table, but Mr. Lytton saw them rise out of the wood of the table—also he tells me . . . that he saw a spiritual (so-called) arm elongate itself as much as two yards across the table and then float away to the windows, where it disappeared. Robert and I did not touch the hands. Mr. Lytton and Sir Edward both did. The feel was warm and human—rather warmer in fact than is common with a man's hand. The music was beautiful.

The music to which Elizabeth refers came from an accordion which Home would barely touch, usually holding a corner of the bellows with two fingers of one hand. The instrument would play by itself. Home was evidently quite musical and although his fingers were nowhere near the keys, the accordion would produce various melodies requested by the sitters.

It may be noted here, too, that the table around which the group sat at Ealing was an enormous mahogany dining table large enough to seat 20 and probably weighing about 100 pounds. Dutch researcher George Zorab, in discussing this group of sittings in a 1971 article in the *Journal of the Society for Psychical Research,* pointed out that it was necessary for the myopic Mrs. Browning to use her lorgnette in order to see the hands at the far end of the table distinctly. She may have been some three yards or more away. The length of the table would have made it impossible for Home to have manipulated spirit hands with his arms or legs or with some kind of instrument as some of his detractors had suggested. But even if that were possible, as Zorab noted, there is still the problem of how he could have "faked an active functioning human hand to pick up a garland from the table and place it on Mrs. Browning's head, right under the noses of herself and the other sitters." He might also have added the problem of the Lytton's contact with these "warmer than human" hands or the self-playing instrument that charmed Elizabeth Browning.

But Robert Browning was not charmed at all. An egotist, he must have been incensed that the garland, the poet's laurel crown, was placed not on his head but on his wife's. He might also have been jealous of the attention Home paid to Elizabeth. Whatever the cause, Browning developed an immediate hatred for Home. He penned the following note about the same sitting, which he enclosed with his wife's letter:

> Mr. Browning did, in company with his wife, witness Mr. Hume's [sic] performances at Ealing . . . and he is hardly able to account for the fact that there can be another opinion than his own on the matter—that being that the whole display of "hands," "spirit utterances," etc. were a cheat and imposture.

Browning didn't stop there: He wrote a long "report" about this sitting and published an insulting and derisive poem about a fraudulent medium, not mentioning Home's name, of course, but it was apparent to all to whom he was referring.

Of course the poet was not the only person who accused Home of fraud, but these claims were never found to be valid. And even those like Browning who refused to accept the reality of his phenomena could not explain the "earthquake" effect in which Home would cause the entire séance room, furniture and all, to tremble and move up and down as if an earthquake were occurring.

D. D. Home had a whole repertoire of mind-boggling physical phenomena. He could also cause dining tables replete with china, glassware, flatware, food, etc. to tilt to one side without anything sliding from the table. And he could decrease or increase the weight of the table so that it would first be raised easily (or would raise itself) and then be so heavy that several men could not lift it.

Fully materialized forms, lights, or luminous objects would variously appear in the room. As in the Bindelof group, touches, pinches, pulling on clothing, and other tactile phenomena would occur. Hands of various sizes, colors, and shapes would materialize, often ending at the wrist. Although these were quite solid, they would dematerialize while in full view of the participants, dissolving or melting into the air. Sometimes these hands would be disfigured or oddly shaped just as hands of the communicating "loved ones" had been in life.

Although we are focusing on physical phenomena, Home was also a "mental medium" through whom "spirits" would converse or otherwise communicate with the living. He was therefore an excellent telepath who, while entranced, would sometimes take on the mannerisms of the "dearly departed."

In addition to the accordion's sound, other music would be heard when there were no other instruments in the room. Voices and odors were also present without any seeming sources.

One of his more amazing feats of mind over matter was his ability to handle burning coals and to transfer this attribute to others. One sitter, a Mrs. Hall, wrote in a letter to Lord Dunhaven that Home went to the fireplace where he poked the fire

> which was like a red-hot furnace, so as to increase the heat; held his hands over the fire for some time, and finally drew out of the fire, with his hand, a huge lump of live burning coal, so large that he held it in both hands, as he came from the fireplace in the large room into the small room; where, seated round the table, we were all watching his movements. Mr. Hall was seated nearly opposite to where I sat; and I saw Mr. Home, after standing for about half a minute at the back of Mr. Hall's chair, deliberately place the lump of burning coal on his head! ... Some one said – "Is it not hot?" Mr. Hall answered – "Warm, but not hot!" Mr. Home had moved a little away, but returned, still in a trance; he smiled and seemed quite pleased; and then he proceeded to draw up Mr. Hall's white hair over the red coal. The white hair had the appearance of silver threads, over the red coal. Mr. Home drew the hair into a sort of pyramid, the coal still red, showing beneath the hair; then, after, I think,

four or five minutes, Mr. Home pushed the hair back, and, taking the coal off Mr. Hall's head, he said (in the peculiar low voice in which, when in a trance, he always speaks), addressing Mrs. Y, "Will you have it?" She drew back; and I heard him murmur, "Little faith, little faith." Two or three attempted to touch it, but it burnt their fingers. I said, "Daniel, bring it to me; I do not fear to take it." It was not red all over, as when Mr. Home put it on Mr. Hall's head, but it was still red in parts. Mr. Home came and knelt by my side; I put out my right hand, but he murmured, "No, not that; the other hand." He than placed it in my left hand, where it remained more than a minute. I felt it, as my husband had said, "warm"; yet when I stooped down to examine the coal, my face felt the heat so much that I was obliged to withdraw it... When Mr. Hall brushed his hair at night he found a quantity of cinder dust.

Home was a tough act to follow. He could not only levitate tables but himself as well. He was seen on many occasions, in well-lighted situations and by various witnesses, to stretch or elongate himself, growing taller then returning to his usual size, but he was also seen to rise bodily into the air. One such incident occurred at the home of a Mrs. Parkes, where witnesses saw him stretch up his hands above his head and rise into the air three feet from the floor. Mrs. Parkes, who was seated in a chair right next to him, "looked at his feet" just before he descended.

The eminent scientist Sir William Crookes also was present at a Home séance when the medium announced that he was rising and indeed did glide smoothly upward until his feet were about 6 inches from the floor. Crookes reported that he remained suspended for about 10 seconds before slowly descending. Just before his levitation Home had been holding an accordion out at arm's length. As the group watched—there were 9 people present in addition to Crookes and Home—the instrument expanded and contracted as it played a melody. Home then let it go and the accordion went behind his back and there continued to play. It was then that Home rose into the air. The medium's hands and feet were visible: two large spirit (alcohol or methyl alcohol burning) lamps illuminated the room. While he was levitated they heard the accordion fall heavily to the ground. It had been suspended in the air behind Home's vacated chair and about 10 feet away from the spot at which he was standing when he lifted off the floor. The instrument was then "both seen and heard to move about behind him without his hands touching it. It then played a tune without contact and floating in the air." Then as Home held the accordion out with one hand so that all could see it, Mrs. Crookes saw a light on it near the keys. Then they all "heard and saw the keys clicked and depressed one after the other fairly and deliberately, as if to show us that the power doing it, although invisible (or nearly so) to us, had full control over the instrument."

In that position the accordion played a "beautiful tune" after which Home placed the accordion under Crookes's arm, "the keys hanging down and the upper part pressing upwards against my upper arm. He then let go and the accordion remained there. He then placed his two hands one on each of my shoulders. In this position, no one touching the accordion but myself, and every one noticing what was taking place, the instrument played notes but no tunes."

There were also many raps that night, and a planchette (a device such as is used on Ouija boards and in automatic writing) moved with no one touching it. As in the Bindelof group, there was scribbling on paper and the touching of participants. A bell was taken from Crookes's hand under the table, rung, and given to a "Mrs. I" by a hand that she described as soft and warm. A wooden lath or board floated about, pointed at different times to various people, and later bobbed up and down vertically between the leaves of the open table. Lastly, the water bottle and a tumbler levitated about eight inches above the table and, while floating, tapped together to answer questions and moved back and forth from one to another of the circle.

The ectoplasmic manifestations were interesting in that some were seen by all present but others seemed only to be visible to Mrs. Crookes and to Home. For instance, Mrs. Crookes saw a hand and fingers touching the flower in Home's buttonhole, then remove it and give it to "Mrs. I." The others only saw the flower moving through the air. They all saw a finger protruding from the opening of the table and then more fingers coming up a second time and waving about.

Some of Home's ectoplasmic limbs must have been quite "normal" looking. Although the hand that crowned Mrs. Browning was white and large in size, other witnesses to Home's powers described a variety of different hands. A Mr. Frank L. Burr, editor of the *Hartford Times*, wrote that a hand he observed was a thin, pale, lady's hand, which was peculiar in that the fingers were "of almost preternatural length," set wide apart and unusually pointed. It also narrowed, he said, from the lower knuckles to the wrist, where it ended.

The writer relates how it then disappeared but reappeared shortly after a pencil fell on the table. The hand took the pencil and began to write. He bent his face down close to it as it wrote in order to examine it closely and it vanished. (The writing was said to be the name, in her own handwriting, of a relative of one of the sitters who had died some years earlier.) The editor ends by affirming that it was produced by no hand of anyone in the room, and that the hand returned once more to shake hands with each person present: "I felt it minutely. It was tolerably well and symmetrically made, though not perfect; and it was soft and slightly warm. IT ENDED AT THE WRIST."

At another sitting Burr describes shaking hands with another hand produced by Home, reporting that when the hand found that it couldn't get away, it yielded itself to him for his examination, turned itself over and back, and then shut its fingers and opened them. Burr then poked his finger through the hand forming a hole. The wound closed, leaving a scar before disappearing.

Other witnesses watched hands and arms forming. One such occurrence featured a luminous hand and arm that vanished only to begin to form again starting with the elbow. It materialized rapidly and steadily until the arm and hand rested on the table again as it had a few moments before. When the hand picked up a bell and brought it to the reporter, he described it as a "real" hand, soft and warm, with knuckles and fingernails, feeling much like an infant's hand except for its size. But as he held it, it melted in his grasp and disappeared.

CHAPTER 15

SIR WILLIAM CROOKES

At this point, in order for the reader to appreciate the import of his testimony, I must stop and introduce you more formally to the aforementioned Sir William Crookes.

If you look him up in any encyclopedia you will find that he was a highly respected scientist with a list of impressive achievements. (In your dictionary you may locate Crookes—or Crookes'—layer, Crookes space, and Crookes tube.) Crookes was born in London on June 17, 1832. At the age of 22 he was made superintendent of the meteorological section of Radcliffe Observatory in Oxford and the next year was appointed professor of chemistry at the Chester Training College. Four years later, in 1859, he founded the publication *Chemical News*, and in 1864 became editor of the *Quarterly Journal of Science*. Among his scientific accomplishments were the discovery of the element thallium (1861) and its atomic weight (1873). He invented the sodium amalgamation process for separating gold and silver from their ores and produced diamonds artificially. He developed "Crookes glass," an optical glass that protected the eyes of glassblowers and steel workers from dangerous radiation, and invented the radiometer. He was also the inventor of the spinthariscope, a device that makes the radiations from radium salts visible by impingement on a zinc sulfide screen, and the aforementioned "Crookes tube," which determined the magnetic deflection of electrons. It was used by Roentgen in the discovery of X rays, and was the forerunner of today's television picture tube. His work on radiation changed science's understanding of it, and at the turn of the century he was able to separate uranium from its active transformation product, Uranium X.

Between 1908 and 1912 he was at various times president of the Chemical Society, the British Association for the Advancement of Science, and the Institute of Electrical Engineers, as well as a member of many other international scientific organizations. Among his published works were *Select Methods of Chemical Analysis* (1871) and *Diamonds* (1909). He continued to publish articles on various scientific subjects until his death in April 1919.

During his lifetime he received many public honors including the Royal Gold Medal (1875), the medal of the Universal Exposition of Paris (1881), the Albert Gold Medal (1899), the Order of Merit (1910), and the gold medal of the Society of Chemical Industry (1912). He was knighted by the British Empire in 1897, an honor that was late in coming because of his investigation of psychic phenomena.

It was only with reluctance that Crookes undertook these investigations. As you can see by his achievements, he was heavily committed to his scientific work and not enthusiastic about pursuing an area he considered fruitless. He had already written a derogatory article entitled "Spiritualism Viewed by the Light of Modern Science" in which he had expressed the opinion that "The increased employment of scientific methods will produce a race of observers who will drive the worthless residuum of spiritualism hence into the unknown limbo of magic and necromancy."

Knowing his views and confidant of his critical acumen, he was approached by friends to undertake an investigation of these purported phenomena. He was most likely convinced, as were his friends and the press, that "With a man like Crookes conducting investigations into spiritualism, we will not have to wait long for the exposure of these cunning charlatans." And so he agreed, but only on the condition that he would be permitted to conduct the experiments in his own home, under his controls, and to subject the medium to whatever scientific tests he devised.

He chose Daniel Dunglas Home, thinking to made short work of exposing his tricks. To his surprise Home agreed to all the conditions. These experiments with Home convinced Crookes of the reality of the phenomena. They started a quest for the understanding of psychic powers that lasted the rest of Crookes' life and nearly ruined his reputation and his career.

After his first séance with Home, Crookes realized that what he experienced was an extraordinary phenomenon. Crookes must have been aware that men throughout history, men such as Galileo, have been persecuted for speaking the truth when it conflicts with the beliefs and worldviews held by the majority. Still he persisted, convinced (mistakenly, as many who have come after him have been) that if he demonstrated through controlled experiments, under his own stringent conditions, that Home's powers were real, the truth would be accepted. Fortunately for us he did persist, for his work with the medium, more than the testimony of the hundreds of other witnesses to Home's phenomena, proved that psychokinesis is a real and measurable force. (It was also fortunate that Crookes, as editor of *The Quarterly Journal of Science*, had a vehicle through which he could publish his findings. As many psychical researchers today have found out, no matter how impeccable your research, it will not get published in professional journals if your subject matter is contrary to the prevailing scientific worldview.)

It has been said that Crookes was conceited enough to believe that (1) his own reputation would serve to convince anyone of his competence in judging Home, and (2) that critics could not doubt his word. I don't totally agree because he didn't go it alone. He asked several eminent colleagues to assist him, although it is a testimony to his courage that he didn't reveal their names in publishing their findings, thus taking the brunt of the criticism upon himself.

One was Alfred Russell Wallace, whose essay, "On The Law Which Has Regulated the Introduction of New Species," put forth his theory of survival of the fittest. Wallace sent it to Charles Darwin who, having been thinking along the same lines, collaborated with him and they together formed the theory of natural selection. Wallace received the Darwin Medal of the Royal Society in 1890, the Royal Medal in 1898, and the Order of Merit in 1910 for this and other work.

Another collaborator in Crookes's endeavors was Cromwell F. Varley, who conducted elaborate experiments with photoelectric effects in relation to ionization. With Crookes he found that cathode rays consist of negatively charged particles. He also invented an electric accumulator, supervised the laying of the Atlantic cable, and was a highly regarded scientist and inventor to the end of his life.

As Gil Roller wrote in his own book, *A Voice From Beyond*, it doesn't make sense "to claim that men like Crookes, Varley and Wallace, whose scientific achievements represent brilliant deductive reasoning and laboratory techniques of the utmost finesse, were, along with other witnesses, naive victims of clever impostors. A man who can determine the deflection of electron streams by magnetic fields, and design the equipment necessary to make such determinations, is not likely to be the dupe of a string-pulling medium, especially in his own laboratory under his own test conditions."

Other participants included Sir William Huggins, an eminent physicist

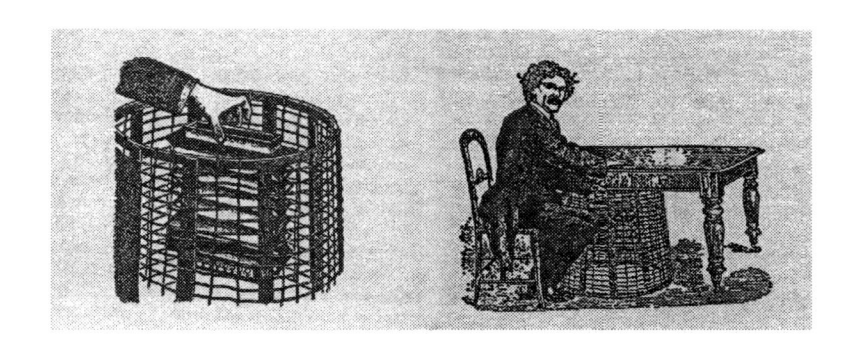

Drawings of Home with accordion in cage from Roller's
A Voice From Beyond.

and astronomer; Serjeant-at-law E.W. Cox, a prominent lawyer; a Mr. Gimingham, Crookes's chemical assistant; his brother, Walter Crookes; and the wives of both Walter and William Crookes.

Some of the experiments were elegantly simple. For instance, Crookes devised a wire and string mesh cage supported by wooden laths, just high enough to fit under his dining room table but too close to allow a hand to reach into its interior or a foot to be pushed underneath it. A new accordion, purchased by Crookes, was placed in the cage.

The room was well lit with a gas lamp and in Crookes's words: "For the greater part of the evening, particularly when anything of importance was proceeding, the observers on each side of Mr. Home kept their feet respectively on his feet, so as to be able to detect his slightest movement..."

Crookes relates that the cage was pulled out and the accordion was pushed in with its keys downwards, then pushed back "as close as Mr. Home's arm would permit but without hiding his hand from those next to him." (The accompanying woodcut, above, shows Home's right hand on the table, his left seemingly caught between the bottom of the table and the cage so that just his fingers are inside the device.) Those on either side soon observed the instrument waving about followed by sounds and then notes coming from it. His assistant, under the table, reported that the accordion was expanding and contracting but that Home's hand, still holding the top corner, was quite still. The instrument then began "oscillating and going round and round the cage, and playing at the same time." It continued to play a tune as they held Home's feet and watched him carefully.

As such a result could only have been produced by the various keys of the instrument being acted upon in harmonious succession, this was considered by those present to be a crucial experiment. But the sequel was still more striking, for Mr. Home then removed his hand altogether from the accordion, taking it quite out of the cage, and placed it in the hand of the person next to him. The instrument then continued to play, no person touching it and no hand being near it.

> . . . I and two others present saw the accordion distinctly floating about inside the cage with no visible support. This was repeated a second time, after a short interval. Mr. Home presently re-inserted his hand in the cage and again took hold of the accordion. It then commenced to play, at first, chords and runs, and afterwards a well-known sweet and plaintive melody, which was executed perfectly in a very beautiful manner. Whilst this tune was being played I grasped Mr. Home's arm, below the elbow, and gently slid my hand down it until I touched the top of the accordion. He was not moving a muscle. His other hand was on the table, visible to all, and his feet were under the feet of those next to him.

Having achieved such success they then turned to a second experiment. Crookes had constructed a balance apparatus to try to test Home's ability to alter the weight of an object. He used a mahogany board a yard long and about 9 inches wide that was suspended at one end from a spring balance. The balance was furnished with an automatic recording device. The other end of the board rested on a table so that the board lay horizontally. Home sat at the table placing his fingers lightly on the end of the board while Crookes and Huggins sat on either side of it. As Crookes reported:

> Almost immediately the pointer of the balance was seen to descend. After a few seconds it rose again. This movement was repeated several times, as if by successive waves of the Psychic Force. The end of

the board was observed to oscillate slowly up and down during the experiment.

Mr. Home now of his own accord took a small hand-bell and a little card match-box, which happened to be near, and placed one under each hand, to satisfy us, as he said, that he was not producing the downward pressure. The very slow oscillation . . . became more marked and [Huggins], watching the index, said that he saw it descend to 6 1/2 pounds. The normal weight of the board as so suspended being 3 lbs., the additional downward pull was therefore 3 1/2 lbs. On looking immediately afterwards at the automatic register, we saw that the index had at one time descended as low as 9 lbs., showing a maximum pull of 6 lbs. upon a board whose normal weight was 3 lbs.

In order to see whether it was possible to produce much effect on the spring balance by pressure at the place where Mr. Home's fingers had been, I stepped upon the table and stood on one foot at the end of the board. [Huggins], who was observing the index of the balance, said that the whole weight of my body (140 lbs.) so applied only sunk the index 1 1/2 lbs., or 2 lbs. when I jerked up and down. Mr. Home had been sitting in a low easy chair, and could not, therefore, had he tried his utmost, have exerted any material influence on these results. I need scarcely add that his feet as well as his hands were closely guarded by all in the room.

Crookes published his findings in the journal he edited, but instead of appreciation from his fellow scientists for his efforts and for the light he had shed on the sometimes extraordinary abilities we posses, those who before had expressed such confidence in his critical acumen now responded to his reports with a barrage of denouncements and ridicule.

I will quote Crookes's angry reply to his critics, although the passage is somewhat long, not only because of its eloquence, but because it is as timely an answer to today's devout skeptics as it was to Crookes's contemporaries.

> When I first stated in this journal that I was about to investigate the phenomena of so-called Spiritualism, the announcement called forth universal expression of approval. One said that my "statements deserved respectful consideration"; another expressed "profound satisfaction that the subject was about to be investigated by a man so thoroughly qualified as," etc.; a third was "gratified to learn that the matter is now receiving the attention of cool and clear-headed men of recognized position in science"; a fourth asserted that "no one could doubt Mr. Crookes' ability to conduct the investigation with rigid philosophical impartiality"; and a fifth was good enough to tell its readers that " if men like Mr. Crookes grapple with the subject, taking nothing for granted until it is proved, we shall soon know how much to believe."
>
> These remarks, however, were written too hastily. It was taken for granted by the writers that the results of my experiments would be in accordance with their preconceptions. What they really desired was not the truth, but an

additional witness in favour of their own foregone conclusions. When they found that the facts which that investigation established could not be made to fit those opinions, why—"so much the worse for the facts." They try to creep out of their own confident recommendations of the enquiry by declaring that "Mr. Home is a clever conjurer, who has duped us all." "Mr. Crookes might, with equal propriety, examine the performances of an Indian juggler." "Mr. Crookes must get better witnesses before he can be believed." "The thing is too absurd to be treated seriously." "It is impossible, and therefore can't be." "The observers have all been biologised [hypnotized] and fancy they saw things occur which really never took place," etc., etc.

These remarks imply a curious oblivion of the very functions which the scientific enquirer has to fulfill. I am scarcely surprised when the objectors say that I have been deceived merely because they are unconvinced without personal investigation, since the same unscientific course of a priori argument has been opposed to all great discoveries. When I am told that what I describe cannot be explained in accordance with preconceived ideas of the laws of nature, the objector really begs the very question at issue, and resorts to a mode of reasoning which brings science to a standstill. The argument runs in a vicious circle: we must not assert a fact till we know that it is in accordance with the laws of nature, while our only knowledge of the laws of nature must be based on an extensive observation of facts. If a new fact seems to oppose what is called a law of nature, it does not prove the asserted fact to be false, but only that we have not yet ascertained all the laws of nature, or not learned them correctly.

Unintimidated by his detractors, Crookes continued his investigations with Home and others. It was the next major investigation he conducted, however, that jeopardized his professional career, brought accusations of the most sordid nature upon him, and delayed by many years his recognition as a major contributor to science by the crown.

Although I have focused on Home's primary phenomena, there were many more remarkable occurrences at his séances, many of which were catalogued by Crookes. The scientist prefaced his inventory of Home phenomena by reminding his readers that darkness was not essential at these demonstrations but that bright light "exerts an interfering action" on some of the phenomena. He also reminds us that with the exception of cases specially mentioned, these occurrences took place in his own house, in the light, and with only private friends present in addition to the medium.

Pauline, Princess Metternich-Sandor, made an observation I consider very important in her book *Geschehenes Gesehenes Erlebtes* (*Happened Viewed Experienced*). She reported that a candlestick was placed on a small table with the candle lit. "Now this small table started moving, raising, dancing, then tilting sideways so that under normal circumstances every object on top would have fallen down. Yet . . .the candlestick did not fall down, moreover the flame, instead of burning vertically upwards, inclined by the same angle as the table." This phenomenon illustrates, as do many of his other feats, that Home must have been altering the gravitational field in some way.

Crookes cites first movements of (sometimes heavy) objects without physical contact by the medium. These and other phenomena "are generally preceded by a peculiar cold air, sometimes amounting to a decided wind." He relates how he witnessed pieces of paper blown around by this icy breeze that also lowered a thermometer by several degrees. At other times, although there was no apparent movement of the air, the cold was so

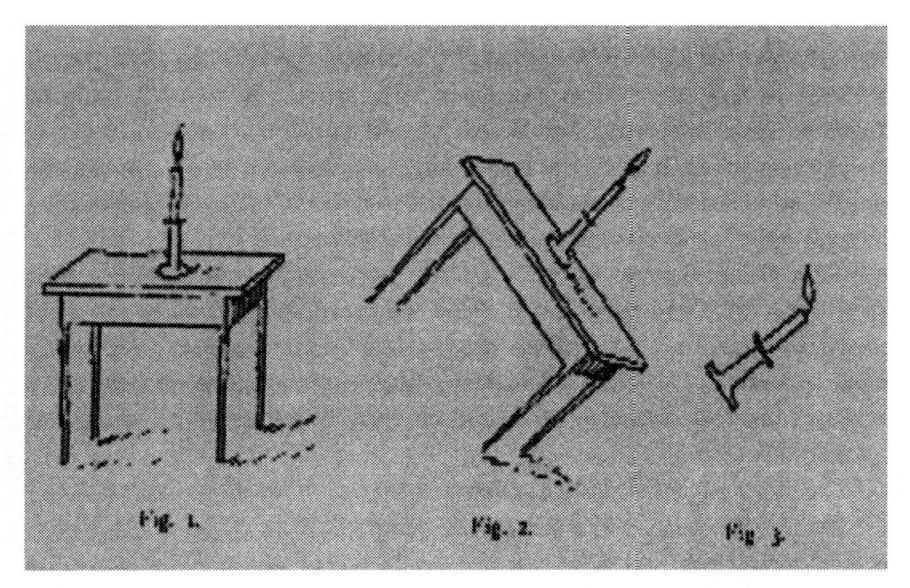

The candle flame should not tilt when the table does.

intense that he "could only compare it to that felt when the hand has been within a few inches of frozen mercury."

In his second "class" of phenomena Crookes notes that the term "raps" gives a very erroneous impression. The sounds he heard varied, he reported, from "delicate ticks, as with the point of a pin" to a "cascade of sharp sounds as from an induction coil in full work" and loud detonations. While Home's sounds were very varied, they were not as powerful and certain as those produced by America's Kate Fox. Crookes met her and tested her as well. It seems that Miss Fox had only to "place her hand on any substance for loud thuds to be heard in it, like a triple pulsation, sometimes loud enough to be heard several rooms off. In this manner I have heard them in a living tree—on a sheet of glass—on a stretched iron wire . . .and on the floor of a theatre." Again, actual contact wasn't necessary. Crookes states that he tested these sounds in every way that he could devise, "until there has been no escape from the conviction that they were true objective occurrences not produced by trickery or mechanical means."

He also cites the levitation of heavy tables without contact and the levitation of others besides Home. On one occasion he witnessed a chair, with a lady sitting on it, rise several inches from the ground and on another "the lady knelt on the chair in such a manner that its four feet were visible to us. It then rose about three inches, remained suspended for about ten seconds, and then slowly descended." He also witnessed two children, on separate occasions rise from the floor with their chairs, in full daylight, under what he felt were "satisfactory conditions; for I was kneeling and keeping close watch upon the feet of the chair, and observing that no one might touch them." His account does not make clear who was causing the levitations, the children themselves or another person.

The most spectacular phenomena, he claims, were Home's own levitations. Crookes tells us that there were at least a hundred recorded instances of Home's rising from the ground "in the presence of as many separate persons." He himself observed this phenomenon three times, once while Home was sitting in an easy chair, once kneeling on his chair, and once standing up.

Another intriguing phenomenon is that of "luminous appearances." These were produced by Home and, as you shall see later, by another man as well. They consisted of points of light darting about and settling on the heads of different people, and bright lights that answered questions by flashing a desired number of times in front of Crookes's face. There were also sparks of light rising from the table to the ceiling, and again falling upon the table, striking it with an audible sound. There was a luminous cloud which floated upwards to a picture, and a "solid self-luminous body, the size and nearly the shape of a turkey's egg" that floated noiselessly about the room, "at one time higher than any one present could reach standing on tip-toe, and then gently descend[ed] to the floor. It was visible for more than ten minutes, and before it faded away it struck the table three times with a sound like that of a hard solid body. During this time, the medium was lying back, apparently insensible, in an easy chair."

Of necessity, in order to see faint luminous objects, the lights had to be extinguished or greatly reduced, but Crookes claimed to have maintained "the strictest test conditions." Under these conditions he experienced more than once, "a solid, self-luminous crystalline body placed in my hand by a hand which did not belong to any person in the room." And "In the light, I have seen a luminous cloud hover over a heliotrope on a side table, break a sprig off, and carry the sprig to a lady; and on some occasions I have seen a similar luminous cloud visibly condense to the form of a hand and carry small objects about."

This last occurrence leads him into the category of ectoplasmic hands and arms, luminous and otherwise, some "icy cold and dead," others warm, solid, and lifelike, one of which he held on to as it gradually turned into vapor and disappeared.

Crookes witnessed direct writing somewhat like that obtained by the Bindelof group. The medium was Kate Fox, and the circumstances were very much the same as the New York boys experienced. Said Crookes:

> I have had words and messages repeatedly written on privately-marked paper, under the most rigid test conditions, and have heard the pencil moving over the paper in the dark. The conditions—pre-arranged by myself—have been so strict as to be equally convincing to my mind as if I had seen the written characters formed. But . . . I will merely select two instances in which my eyes as well as ears were witnesses to the operation.
>
> The first instance . . . took place, it is true at a dark séance, but the result was not less satisfactory on that account. I was sitting next to the medium, Miss Fox, the only other persons present being my wife and a lady relative, and I was holding the medium's two hands in mine, whilst her feet were resting on my feet. Paper was on the table before us, and my disengaged hand was holding a pencil.
>
> A luminous hand came down from the upper part of the room, and after hovering near me for a few seconds took the pencil from my hand, rapidly wrote on a sheet of paper, threw the pencil down, and then rose up over our heads, gradually fading into darkness.

The second instance he cites was a "good failure," which he notes often teaches more than the most successful experiment. It was in a lighted room, in his house, with only a few friends and Mr. Home present. Since the medium seemed "strong" that evening, Crookes requested that he attempt a written message. An "alphabetic communication" informed them, "We will try." A pencil and paper had been lying on the table. "Presently the pencil rose up on its point, and after advancing by hesitating jerks to the paper, fell down. It then rose, and again fell. A third time it tried, but with no better result." After three unsuccessful attempts, a wooden lath lying nearby slid towards the pencil, rising a few inches. The pencil rose up again, propped itself against the lath, and "the two together made an effort to mark the paper. It fell, and then a joint effort was again made. After a third trial the lath gave it up [in disgust, I suspect] and moved back to its place. The pencil lay as it fell across the paper, and an alphabetic message told us—"We have tried to do as you asked, but our power is exhausted."

Crookes also cites, under "Miscellaneous Occurrences of a Complex Character," an incident where Miss Fox was responsible for the dematerialization of a small hand-bell belonging to Crookes that he had left in his library. The bell re-materialized in the dining room where Kate was giving a séance. The door between the two rooms was locked and, in addition, the library was brightly lit and was occupied the whole time by Crookes's two sons. They reported that no one had entered the room and that they were sure it was there after the adults had repaired to the dining room because one of them had been playing with it until admonished by his brother to stop.

Crookes's eleventh classification was "Phantom Forms and Faces," which he called "the rarest phenomena" he had witnessed. I think it best to let you read his actual words:

> The conditions requisite for their appearance appear to be so delicate, and such trifles interfere with their production, that only on very few occasions have I witnessed them under satisfactory test conditions. I will mention two of these cases.
>
> In the dusk of the evening, during a séance with Mr. Home at my house, the curtains of a window about eight feet from Mr. Home were seen to move. A

dark, shadowy, semi-transparent form, like that of a man, was then seen by all present standing near the window, waving the curtain with his hand. As we looked, the form faded away, and the curtains ceased to move.

The following is a still more striking instance. As in the former case, Mr. Home was the medium. A phantom form came from a corner of the room, took an accordion in its hand, and then glided about the room playing the instrument. The form was visible to all present for many minutes, Mr. Home also being seen at the same time. Coming rather close to a lady who was sitting apart from the rest of the company, she gave a slight cry, upon which it vanished.

CHAPTER 16

THE PHANTOM OF KATIE KING

I have emphasized these last experiences because they explain to some extent why Crookes was not put off, but rather was most likely eager to investigate the mediumship of a young woman named Florence Cook. Miss Cook, who was born in 1856, was fifteen when she attended a séance with her mother and, having demonstrated some psychic abilities herself before that time, determined then to become a medium. After a few séances, witnesses claimed that phantom faces would appear at the curtains of her cabinet, the enclosure or curtained off corner of the room in which many mediums isolated themselves while they were entranced. The phantom form of a woman then appeared beside the entranced girl and walked about the room. The phantom that materialized called herself "Katie King," claiming to be the daughter of John King, the spirit contact of another medium, Eusapia Palladino, about whom you'll read more later.

Florence was accused of trickery and supposedly attempted to prove herself genuine by having herself tied with cords, their knots sealed with wax, and placed in a tiny niche that restricted her movements.

She also volunteered to be tested by physicians and researchers. Three who investigated her were a Dr. J. E. Purdon, an American physician living in Britain; Dr. James Gully, a prominent English physician; and Alexander Aksakoff, an internationally known Russian aristocrat and the foremost Russian psychical researcher of that time. All three men experienced her phenomena and were convinced of their genuineness.

Aksakoff's testimony is particularly convincing. At Florence's first séance he attended (at her parents' home), the medium was bound so that she could not rise from her chair without pulling at a string that was fastened to a table in the room. Aksakoff reported that Katie chattered away in a low whispery voice demanding, "Do ask me questions, reasonable questions that is!" He asked if she could show him her medium, to which she replied, "Yes, certainly, come here very quickly and have a look!"

He immediately got up and drew back the curtain, which was no more than five steps from his chair. Florence, clothed in a black dress, was still seated in her chair, and Katie had disappeared.

As soon as he was seated, Katie again materialized, standing next to the curtain. She asked if he had a good look and he replied, "Not so good because it was rather dark behind the curtain."

"Then take the lamp with you and go and have a good look immediately!"

He found himself "alone and facing the medium who, in a deep trance, was sitting on a chair with both her hands bound fast behind her back. The light shining on the medium's face started to produce its usual effect, i.e. the medium began to sigh and to awake. Behind the curtain an interesting dialogue started between the medium, becoming more and more awake, and Katie who wanted to put her medium to sleep again. But Katie had to give way. She said "goodbye" and then silence followed.

The séance ended and he tested the bindings finding the knots and wax seals still intact. When he cut the medium free, he said it was only with difficulty that he could get the scissors under the tape, so tightly were her hands bound together.

The Medium Florence Cook   *Phantom Katie King*

Florence resembled her phantom, Katie King, but there were significant differences.

Aksakoff attended the second séance about a week later, on October 28, 1873. This sitting was held at the home of J. C. Luxmoore, who had presided over Florence's séances and was the person who generally bound her. Aksakoff was a friend of William Crookes and, probably at his recommendation, Crookes attended this demonstration. Again, other scientists and critical observers such as Dr. James Gully, Alfred Russel Wallace, Cromwell Varley, Serjeant-at-law, E.W. Cox, a Mrs. Florence Marryat, and others, including his wife, assisted Crookes. Crookes must have been impressed enough to invite the young girl to his home where he could study her mediumship in a controlled setting. She agreed to submit to his conditions and they embarked on a series of experiments that was to last three years.

"Katie" looked remarkably like Florence Cook but with significant differences. For one thing, she was several inches taller than the medium, especially when she floated above the floor. (She would glide around sometimes because her feet had failed to materialize.) When her feet were there, she would often be requested to stamp them (they were bare) on the floor to make sure she wasn't standing on tiptoe. Her hands were also larger, her fingers longer than Florrie's and, more importantly, Katie had perfectly formed fingernails while Florrie bit hers down to the nubs. The medium had pierced ears; Katie didn't. Their hair color was different: Florence had dark brown, nearly black tresses, while Katie, who had once given Crookes a lock of her hair, after he had checked to see that it really grew from her head, had golden auburn hair.

There were other differences such as Florence having a rough large blister on her neck whereas the phantom's neck was smooth. Later, when photographs were taken of Katie, she posed with Crookes. Later he had himself photographed again, this time with Florence dressed up to look like her phantom. In comparing the photos the two images of Crookes are identical in stature, but Katie is half a head taller than Florence and "looks a big woman in comparison with her."

I am citing these dissimilarities because one of the accusations made by detractors was that the phantom was Florrie herself draped in white muslin. It was also alleged that Katie was one of Florence's sisters, but no critic ever explained how an accomplice could have infiltrated the Crookes house, let alone the carefully scrutinized room the medium used as her "cabinet," whose windows and doors were carefully locked and sealed. Nor was it explained how Florence or her sister/accomplice could appear not fully formed or disintegrate in front of witnesses' eyes. Reports had been printed as early as the spring and summer of 1873, before Crookes met her, that when the medium's power was running low, Katie would gradually disintegrate, her body melting away or evaporating to form a kind of cloud. Her head would speak to the assemblage from the floor where it was resting before it too disappeared.

But perhaps I'd better be more specific about what transpired chez Crookes. The scientist and his colleagues took elaborate precautions to insure that no fraud could be perpetrated. With the aid of Varley and Wallace, Crookes set snares that made Florence an isolated prisoner during the séances.

Before beginning, Florence was inspected by a female member of the investigators to ensure that she had nothing on her person but the clothes she was wearing. She was then admitted to the Crookes's library where she would remain throughout the session. The room was thoroughly searched; windows were locked and sealed with thread secured by wax, which was imprinted with a signet or seal over the knots. The door to the library was closed, locked, and secured in a similar manner. Next, Florence, seated on a couch, or later on, lying on the floor, her head on a pillow, was wired by each wrist with a fragile platinum wire that ran from a battery source to a galvanometer in the adjoining laboratory. Any movement of the wire over the skin surface, or its removal, would change the resistance of the current flow and would be immediately detectable. Sometimes she was bound, hand and foot, with cord in addition to these other precautions. The curtained entrance to the lab was crossed with fine wire, making it impossible to pass through without breaking a circuit connected to another galvanometer. Lastly, the windows and doors to the laboratory room were sealed in the same way and each investigator searched the room.

According to Varley:

> The medium was treated like a telegraphic cable. An electric current passed from her right wrist along her arm to her left wrist, as well as another circuit across the door into the laboratory. Despite all this the half-materialized form of Katie King appeared down to the waist only, the remainder of the body being missing or invisible. I held the hand of this strange

being, and at the end of the séance, Katie told me to go and awaken the medium. I found Miss Cook entranced as I had left her, and all the wires intact. I then awakened Miss Cook.

The question has been raised, "Why use a 'cabinet' at all? After all it only seems to increase suspicion." The answer may be that although Home didn't require one, most mediums (perhaps especially female mediums) had to feel secure to achieve the necessary trance condition, and most likely felt more comfortable with privacy—this was Victorian England after all. At any rate the arrangement seemed to facilitate the generation of the force. Florence allowed Crookes, whom she trusted, to enter the library with Katie King where he saw, and eventually photographed, both the medium and the apparition at the same time. I quote again from Crookes's writings:

> I have for sometime past been experimenting with a phosphorous lamp, consisting of a 6-oz. or 8-oz. bottle, containing a little phosphorised oil, and tightly corked. I have had reason to hope that by the light of this lamp some of the mysterious phenomena of the cabinet might be rendered visible, and Katie has also expressed herself hopefully as to the same result.
>
> On March 12th, during a séance here, after Katie had been walking amongst us and talking for some time, she retreated behind the curtain which separated my laboratory, where the company was sitting, from my library which did temporary duty as a cabinet. In a minute she came to the curtain and called me to her, saying, "Come into the room and lift my medium's head up, she has slipped down." Katie was then standing before me clothed in her usual white robes and turban head-dress. I immediately walked

into the library up to Miss Cook, Katie stepping aside to allow me to pass. I found Miss Cook had slipped partially off the sofa, and her head was hanging in a very awkward position. I lifted her on to the sofa, and in so doing had satisfactory evidence, in spite of the darkness, that Miss Cook was not attired in the "Katie" costume, but had on her ordinary black velvet dress, and was in a deep trance. Not more than three seconds elapsed between my seeing the white-robed Katie standing before me and my raising Miss Cook on to the sofa from the position into which she had fallen.

On returning to my post of observation by the curtain, Katie again appeared, and said she thought she would be able to show herself and her medium to me at the same time. The gas was then turned out and she asked for my phosphorus lamp. After exhibiting herself by it for some seconds, she handed it back to me, saying, "Now come in and see my medium." I closely followed her into the library, and by the light of my lamp saw Miss Cook lying on the sofa just as I had left her. I looked round for Katie, but she had disappeared. I called her, but there was no answer.

On resuming my place, Katie soon reappeared, and told me that she had been standing close to Miss Cook all the time. She then asked if she might try an experiment herself, and taking the phosphorus lamp from me she passed behind the curtain, asking me not to look in for the present. In a few minutes she handed the lamp back to me, saying she could not succeed, as she had used up all the power, but would try again another time. My eldest son, a lad of fourteen, who was sitting opposite me, in such a position that he could see behind the curtain, tells me he distinctly saw the phosphorus lamp apparently floating about in space over Miss Cook, illuminating her as she lay motionless on the sofa, but he could not see anyone holding the lamp.

Crookes tells next of a séance held the evening before he wrote this letter, which is dated March 30, 1874. Although it contains valuable information, it was rather ill advised, for its somewhat naive candor prompted immediate and violent repercussions in this straitlaced Anglo-Saxon society. Crookes was accused of sexual involvement with the young medium, a charge that threatened Crookes's reputation, resulted in the long delay in his attaining knighthood, and is still a subject of debate a century later.

Crookes reported that on that occasion the medium's power was very strong and that Katie took his arm while walking through the laboratory. Alluding to an incident that had occurred the previous December, in which a rival medium's henchman had grabbed the phantom unexpectedly, Crookes candidly admitted that he was tempted to repeat it. "Feeling," he said, "that if I had not a spirit, I had at all events a lady close to me, I asked her permission to clasp her in my arms . . . Permission was graciously given, and I accordingly did—well, as any gentleman would do under the circumstances." He verified that "the 'ghost' was as material a being as Miss Cook herself," a statement that I'm sure came back many times to haunt him. (Pun intended.)

The more important part of the report, however, follows:
Katie now said she thought she would be able this time to show herself and Miss Cook together. I was to turn the gas out, and then come with my phosphorus lamp into the room now used as a cabinet. This I did, having previously asked a friend who was skillful in shorthand to take down any statement I might make when

in the cabinet, knowing the importance attaching to first impressions, and not wishing to leave more to memory than necessary. His notes are now before me.

I went cautiously into the room, it being dark, and felt about for Miss Cook. I found her crouching on the floor. Kneeling down, I let air enter the lamp, and by its light I saw the young lady dressed in black velvet, as she had been in the early part of the evening, and to appearance perfectly senseless; she did not move when I took her hand and held the light quite close to her face, but continued quietly breathing. Raising the lamp, I looked around and saw Katie standing close behind Miss Cook. She was robed in flowing white drapery as we had seen her previously during the séance. Holding one of Miss Cook's hands in mine, and still kneeling, I passed the lamp up and down so as to illuminate Katie's whole figure, and satisfy myself thoroughly that I was really looking at the veritable Katie whom I had clasped in my arms a few minutes before, and not at the phantasm of a disordered brain. She did not speak, but moved her head and smiled in recognition. Three separate times did I carefully examine Miss Cook crouching before me, to be sure that the hand I held was that of a living woman, and three separate times did I turn the lamp to Katie and examine her with steadfast scrutiny, until I had no doubt whatever of her objective reality. At last Miss Cook moved slightly, and Katie instantly motioned me to go away. I went to another part of the cabinet, and then ceased to see Katie, but did not leave the

> room till Miss Cook woke up, and two of the visitors came in with a light.

This last passage again gives proof that there could have been no hidden accomplice. In one of the forty-four photographs taken during the experimental period, Florence Cook is seen slumped over on the couch, while towering over her is the expanded form of Katie King now distorted but still recognizable.

The phantom, or what some would call a "thought form," that is, an ectoplasmic form created from the medium's mind as well as his or her biological matter, was a fascinating phenomenon. At times it was completely lifelike: Crookes was able to take her pulse, a steady 75, while Miss Cook's a short time later was "its usual rate of 90;" her heart was heard beating rhythmically in her chest and her lungs were found to be "sounder than her medium's, for at the time . . . Miss Cook was under medical treatment for a severe cough." Yet at other times she was "less than corporeal;" once when Crookes's assistant, Dr. Tapp attempted to take Katie's pulse, his fingers went right through her wrist.

As in the cases of others, these manifestations took their toll on the physical health of the medium. Florence had to take rests from the experiments periodically to recover her strength.

Several people wrote of the last appearance of Katie King, most importantly, of course, Crookes himself. I quote from it in part because it reveals Florrie's reluctance to part with her alter ego/phantom who could do so many things that a Victorian teenager perhaps could not, and to illustrate the strong Florrie/Kate dual personality that seemed to exist. Crookes asked Katie if he could "see the last of her," and she invited him into the cabinet and allowed him to stay there to the end:

> After closing the curtain she conversed with me for some time, and then walked across the room to where Miss Cook was lying senseless on the floor. Stooping over her, Katie touched her, and said: "Wake up, Florrie, wake up! I must leave you now." Miss Cook then woke and tearfully entreated Katie to stay a little time longer. "My dear, I can't; my work is done. God bless you," Katie replied, and then continued speaking to Miss Cook. For

several minutes the two were conversing with each other, till at last Miss Cook's tears prevented her speaking. Following Katie's instructions I then came forward to support Miss Cook, who was falling on the floor, sobbing hysterically. I looked round, but the white-robed Katie had gone. As soon as Miss Cook was sufficiently calmed, a light was procured and I led her out of the cabinet.

Crookes concluded with a public acknowledgment of the debt he owed Florence Cook for her selflessness in this work. He defended her character and affirmed again the genuineness of the phenomena.

Although Crookes reported positively on the mediumship of Eva Fay in 1875, he drastically reduced his involvement in psychical research in order to concentrate on his primary, mainstream scientific work that eventually made him famous and wealthy.

Many years later in an address to the British Association in 1898 he stated that he had nothing to retract, that he adhered to his published statements and expressed optimism and confidence that science would eventually unravel the mysteries of psychic phenomena.

Florence Cook did not fare so well. She continued to give séances producing other phantoms, but her powers waned and perhaps she was unable to find someone whom she could trust and who would protect her interests as Crookes had done. In 1880 she was caught impersonating her phantom, "Marie." The cabinet was opened and her clothes were found strewn around her empty chair. It turned out that the man who was supposed to have tied her, deliberately left the knots loose enough to be slipped. In trance, a medium may unconsciously cheat if she is able, so that some experts, like George Zorab, have argued that this was most likely a case of unconscious fraud. At another séance that year Mrs. Marryat testified that she was herself tied to the medium inside the cabinet while "Marie" appeared outside it.

Florence, like the Fox sisters, took to drink after her powers waned, and supposedly "confessed" to a young suitor that "Katie King" was a hoax to cover her adulterous affair with Crookes. The "suitor" made his revelation some 56 years later, after all the parties directly involved were dead. Those who are aware of all the facts give his testimony little credence.

Certainly the details of Florence Cook's mediumship, the observations of so many witnesses and researchers before as well as during the Crookes investigations, and the integrity of a man of Crookes's character, devoted to finding the truth, overwhelmingly give more weight to the genuineness of the case than any "confession" that might have been made by a sad and aging former celebrity trying to attract a younger man, detracts from it.

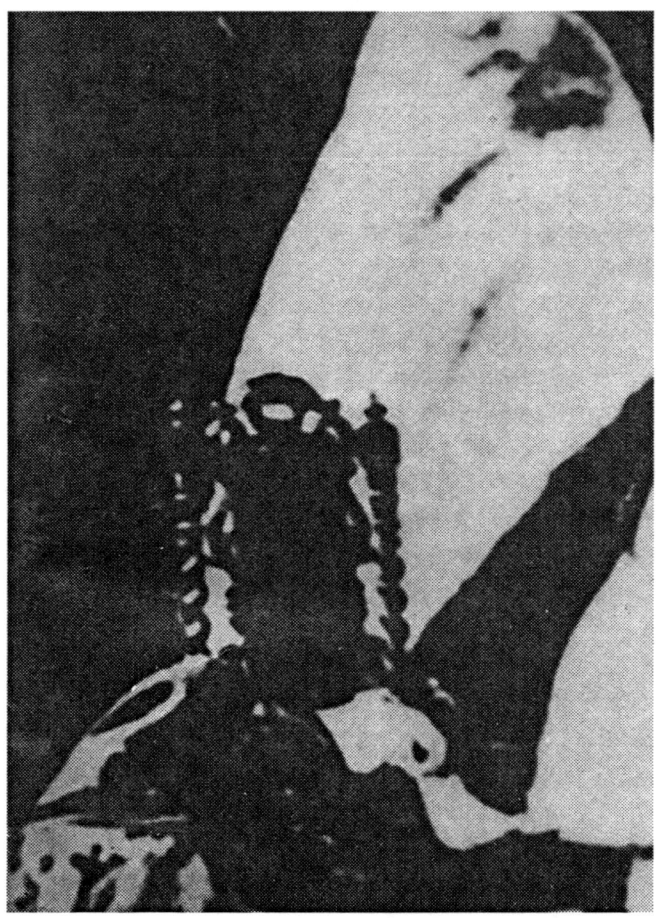

Sir William Crookes took this photo of Florence and Katie together during his investigation of the case. The medium is seen slumped over on her left side. The phantom is distorted and enlarged, either forming or dissipating.

CHAPTER 17

THE NEAPOLITAN WONDER

There should be no relaxation of scientific strictness . . . We must resign ourselves to earth-conditions. Metapsychic phenomena should be treated as problems of pure physiology. Let us experiment with these rare, privileged and wonderful persons and remember that they deserve to be treated with all respect, but also that they must never be trusted.
— Professor Charles Richet, *Thirty Years of Psychical Research*

Both D.D. Home and the young Florence Cook were delicate, sensitive people who could rub shoulders with the finer elements of society. Home, especially, as we saw, was a refined, intelligent, gentleman who hobnobbed with royalty and well-heeled celebrities. Eusapia Palladino was another story. (There is some discrepancy as to the spelling of Eusapia's name. Some researchers contend that it is spelled "Paladino," with one l. I am using the double-l spelling used by most English-speaking scholars.)

Palladino was born in Bari, in southern Italy, in 1852, two years before Florence Cook. Her mother died when she was an infant and Eusapia was entrusted to a neighbor to raise. When she was 12 her father was murdered and the orphan was shipped off to Naples to adoptive parents. She was a handful. Evidently the family tried in desperation to civilize her, to get her to perform basic acts of hygiene, and to educate her. They didn't succeed. Eusapia wound up with another family at age 13.

It was in this temporary home that she manifested her first phenomena. Word quickly got around and it wasn't long before she was giving séances. In 1872 a Signore Damiani took her under his protective wing and began to promote her talents, but she didn't come under the scrutiny of scientific investigators until the 1880s.

At about that time Cesare Lombroso, a respected professor of psychiatry at the University of Turin, came across an intriguing phenomenon in one of his female patients. He found that the young woman, whom he diagnosed as having "hystero-epilepsy," could "read" with her eyes shut. Now Lombroso was known as an expert in criminology—he had devised a method of "determining" a person's character from physical features. He was antagonistic to spiritualism but, perhaps with his world view somewhat expanded by his patient's ability, he agreed to investigate La Palladino. He had been publicly challenged to do so in an open letter to a Rome newspaper written by Dr. Ercole Chiaia, an ardent though amateurish investigator.

After two sittings with Palladino, Lombroso declared himself "converted." His report resulted in a gathering in Milan of more psychically sophisticated investigators to study her on a scientific level. Among them was Professor Charles Richet of the Sorbonne and Alexander Aksakoff, the Russian who introduced Crookes to Florence Cook.

The most well-known of these investigations was held in the summer of 1894 on Richet's own little island off the French coast, Ile Roubaud. English parapsychologists, F. W. H. Myers and Oliver Lodge were introduced to Palladino at this meeting. These two men were astute, experienced psychical investigators. Myers had been to hundreds of séances and knew every trick in the book employed by fraudulent mediums. Their expertise was crucial to these sittings because Eusapia was a notorious cheater.

Lombroso described her as a "crafty" trickster, both in and out of trance. She was observed freeing one of her hands held by incompetent or inexperienced controllers in order to move objects or make touches, lifting the legs of the table with one of her knees and one foot, pretending to adjust her hair while slyly pulling out one strand to put over the balance tray of a letter weigher in order to lower it, surreptitiously gathering flowers that would appear as "apports" later on, etc.

But Stephen Braude, in his book *The Limits of Influence*, makes an important point, often overlooked by historians, that Palladino was certainly not "crafty" in her cheating. She could never be accused of sophisticated or clever trickery because, "Nothing about Eusapia was sophisticated or particularly clever. Her tricks were discovered precisely because they were clumsy and elementary." He notes that she only cheated when she felt she could get away with it, or when she was entranced and was allowed to slip her fetters or controls either through incompetence or design.

She was never found resorting to trickery when subjected to tight controls by expert observers who knew how to thwart attempts at deception. Besides, even her cheating could not account for the majority of her phenomena.

But perhaps we had better pause here to discuss the problem of deception as practiced by mediums—you remember the scandal of Florence Cook, who at one séance was found impersonating her phantom, "Marie." Although Home never did so, mediums have been known to fake effects either consciously or unconsciously when not restrained. Palladino was known to do this, especially when she disliked her investigators. She was, however, an "honest cheat," especially with those she respected, in that she would warn observers to hold, tie, or restrain her because while in trance she would attempt to do what they wanted by normal means if she could, rather than to exert her paranormal powers.

Some researchers, especially an English group led by Richard Hodgson dismissed out of hand anyone found cheating. (The late D. Scott Rogo called Hodgson an egomaniac and, in many ways, he was an incompetent researcher more interested in enhancing his prestige as an exposer of frauds than in searching for scientific truth. There are still a few of these types around today.) The group never seemed to comprehend, as many of their contemporary counterparts still don't, what the European investigators understood: as Arthur Koestler once noted, it's not a matter of either/or, but one of "how much genuine, how much charlatan."

The Europeans had known for years of this fraudulent element in Palladino's mediumship. Like many others she was a strange combination of genuine medium and trickster, a principle that most of today's scientists still don't seem to grasp—or don't care to.

Richet, Myers, and Lodge used their prodigious experience and skills to foil the trickster element and bring out the true medium. Richet's house was the only one on the island so they were guaranteed privacy. Still, they took precautions. The door to the ground floor room in which the sittings were held was usually locked and the window shutters, although partially opened, were fastened. A note taker, either M. Bellier, Richet's secretary, or another researcher, the Polish investigator Julian Ochorowicz, sat outside one of the two windows recording the observations called out to him by the men in the room.

Once the medium and the investigators were seated around the table, the lamps inside the room were extinguished. The only illumination came from moonlight or the note taker's lamp outside the window. On the night of the first sitting the moon was particularly bright; they opened the shutters wide so that the room could not have been very dark. Eusapia was at the head of the rectangular table with Richet and Myers respectively to her right and left. Lodge and Ochorowicz were at the far end. Richet controlled both her arms and one hand while Myers held both feet and her other hand.

Richet felt a hand move over his head and rest on his mouth for a few seconds, during which time he spoke with a muffled voice. A round table moved toward them and Richet felt his head stroked from behind, just as the Bindelof boys had experienced. Richet then held both the medium's knees with one hand. Probably one of her hands was on her knee while Myers secured the other hand. The round table continued toward them in jerky movements. Then a small cigar box fell onto the table, and something was heard rattling in the air.

Richet now held her head and right hand, while Myers raised her left hand into the air holding it lightly by the tips of its fingers, but with part of his own hand free. A saucer containing small shot (bird-shot) that had been in another part of the room was placed into his hand in the air. Next a covered wire from an "electric battery" came onto the table, wrapped itself around Richet's and Palladino's heads and was pulled until the medium called out.

Now Lodge came and secured her right hand while Richet held her head and body and Myers had hold of her left hand and both feet. Eusapia made several spasmodic movements, each "accompanied or followed by violent movements of the neighbouring round table."

An accordion that had been on the round table and had moved unobserved to the floor began to play single notes (the scribe, Bellier, stopped counting after 26). While it was playing, Eusapia's fingers made movements in the researchers' hands, as though she were pressing the keys with difficulty. Lodge said he felt the quick notes with "singular precision." If her finger touch failed to get a response, there would be an "interval of silence and rest."

A few minutes later Myers heard a noise on the round table next to him and turned to see a white object detach itself from the table and move slowly through the air between his head and the medium's. (He could see it crossing the painted colored stripes on the wall so the light must have been adequate.) Lodge saw it coming past Myers's head and settling on the table. It was "the lamp-shade coming white side first." The round table moved away and "blows" or raps were heard from it. Then Lodge felt his back being touched while Richet saw both of Eusapia's hands, one of which he still held. Her body was also visible.

A music box on the round table began to play and then they saw it float through the air and settle on the large table against Myers's chest. It moved to the middle of the table and played there, moved again to the floor between Richet and Palladino, still playing, until Richet said "enough of that music," and it stopped either from obedience or because it needed winding.

Myers was "repeatedly and vigorously" shoved from behind. Lodge changed places with Ochorowicz to see what was pushing him but saw nothing visible, although Myers kept feeling the shoves and complained that "things which pushed like that must be visible."

Eusapia came out of her trance and the session ended. During the second half of the sitting, she had taken one of Myers's fingers and drawn some scrawls with it outside Richet's jacket, which was buttoned up to his neck. Myers had said, "She is using me to write on you," and they thought no more of it. After the sitting, while Richet was undressing, he found on his shirt front, which had been covered by the flannel jacket and a high waistcoat, "a clear blue scrawl," which he immediately ran out to show to the others.

At the third sitting, with similar tight precautions and controls, Lodge suspended the music box from the ceiling so that it was hanging at least two feet beyond Eusapia's reach. He made sure that it was completely run down so that it couldn't play unless it was wound. He arranged the room exactly as he wanted it and kept guard over it to make sure no one entered or tampered with it, then locked it immediately after the sitters came in.

Again there were movements of furniture, loud raps, touchings, pinchings, etc. In her trance, the medium's head was leaning over onto Lodge away from the direction of the music box, her hands and feet held securely. They heard the suspended box being wound partially three times, with short pauses, taking about four seconds in all, according to Bellier, the note taker, who also heard it. It then began to flap as if its door was trying to open, and then to play and emit raps. While it played, Palladino's hands waved Lodge's in time to the music. It stopped, was immediately re-wound, and went on playing again. While this was going on, it began to swing and they heard the string break, but instead of dropping to the floor, it was gently placed on Myers's head and then on the table.

For the fourth sitting, the conditions were the same except that

Ochorowicz took the notes, replacing Bellier, who had left. They experienced startlingly loud, frightening bangs coming from the tables in the room. They also saw a small bright light moving rapidly above the table, and the table rising high into the air and remaining there--Eusapia only barely touching its top—while they counted to eleven. An armchair about four feet behind the medium began to move. They could all see it since it had been near the window, the shutters were open, and it reflected the sky-light overhead. Not only did it move, but it tilted in reply to questions.

They heard the sound of a key fumbling in the door and Ochorowicz called in asking who was unlocking the door. No one was near the door and Eusapia was well controlled. Then loud blows on the door were heard and the key appeared on the table. It disappeared again and now they heard it replacing itself in the lock and locking the door. The key then returned to Richet's hand on the table and remained there. Richet reported that he saw a black seemingly square object that seemed to extend the key to him when it was returned. He contended that it was light enough to see the position of everyone's hands at all times and that they were sitting about four or five feet from the door.

Myers was grabbed from behind while standing, and pulled and shaken roughly. The four of them were standing holding hands around the table when a loaf of bread and other objects from a nearby buffet were transported to the table, including a pile of five plates. Perhaps Eusapia was hungry.

Then Eusapia led them near a writing desk in the corner and made "three little movements with her held hand." The desk tilted backwards after a short interval. She moved further away and repeated the action. The bureau tilted again but "with more delay." The third time she was about two meters away and more time elapsed between her gesture and the desk's movement, "perhaps," Lodge reported, "as much as two seconds."

Lodge and Myers were so impressed by what they had witnessed that they beseeched two colleagues from the (British) Society for Psychical Research to come to the island. Mr. and Mrs. Sidgwick were antagonistic and distrustful of physical mediumship, having exposed many clever fakes in the past, but they reluctantly agreed to come. With great expertise, they assisted in controlling the medium in eight sittings and came away begrudgingly admitting that what they had witnessed indeed seemed to be genuine.

Of course the ever-skeptical Hodgson attacked the report, giving some ridiculous "explanations" for how Palladino accomplished these feats, such as alleging that she must have tied cords to the bureau, which she pulled to get it to tilt. He didn't explain, however, how she sneaked the "cords" into the room that had been so carefully arranged and guarded by Lodge, or how she could have attached them to the piece and "pulled" them without being detected. Nor did he explain how she could "pull" them so that the bureau tilted backward, away from her!

It was this same Hodgson who sabotaged the sittings Palladino gave in England. She was invited for further testing to Myers's home in Cambridge in July, 1895, a year after the Ile Rubaud investigations. Eusapia probably sensed Hodgson's hostility toward her and no doubt responded in kind.

As Rogo pointed out, Hodgson had displayed an alarming ineptness and bias in "debunking" other mediums. He was also "an egomaniac [who] rushed to England, not to sit with Palladino with an open mind and see her phenomena for himself, but to 'protect' Myers and Sidgwick from the fraud, and at the same time expose Palladino, thereby increasing his own prestige."

His scheme worked all too well. He deliberately loosened the controls and then denounced her when she did what he must have known she would from the European investigators' reports. There are incidents in Hodgson's dealings with other psychics that point towards a certain incompetence on his part, but it seems more likely here that his disregard for the warnings of previous investigators was a deliberate attempt to discredit the "vulgar Neapolitan peasant" and to add another notch to his gun. But what can be said of the Sidgwicks, who could not be accused of incompetence? Didn't they realize what he was doing? Whatever their motives, they and Hodgson contended that all the phenomena produced at Cambridge were fraudulent, and that since she had cheated there was no reason to believe that any of her phenomena were genuine. The SPR refused to have any more to do with her.

Eventually they were forced to give in to pressure from the continent, and thirteen years later, in 1908, the SPR assigned three arch skeptics (who Brian Inglis called "The Fraud Squad") to travel to Naples to settle the matter, fully expecting that their "triple threat" would finally unmask this fake.

The trio was eminently suited to the job. The Hon. Everard Feilding was an extreme skeptic who, according to another doubter, E. J. Dingwall, was one of the "keenest and most acute critics" that England had produced.

Palladino levitating a table.

Feilding had vast experience, and had exposed many frauds. He was, however, open minded and would not accept critical comments unless they were accompanied by "properly adduced evidence."

The second man was Hereward Carrington, whom you may remember from the first part of this book was called in by young Gil's stepfather, Eddie, to look into the poltergeist outbreak and suspected that Gil might have been causing the disturbances. Carrington was an amateur magician as well as a psychical researcher. He had just written a book on physical phenomena that mostly exposed and analyzed the trickery used by bogus mediums.

The third member of the "squad" was W. W. Baggally, an expert at conjuring who claimed to have investigated almost every British medium after Home "without finding one who was genuine." Dingwall affirmed that Baggally, who was almost as skeptical as Feilding and just as eager to be a detective on the psychic bunko squad, knew more about the methods of trickery than Feilding and could therefore better concentrate on essentials.

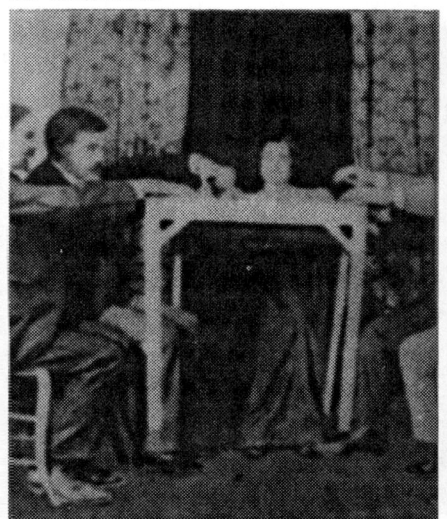

On the left, Palladino, in a controlled experiment causing a table to levitate. On the right, Houdini, demonstrating how it could be faked—if credulous witnesses allowed him to perform under his conditions.
Source: **A Voice From Beyond.**

Baggally arrived in Naples after Feilding and Carrington had already had four sittings with Eusapia. He found two shaken men. Their skepticism and confidence that they would easily expose this trickster had gradually given way to wonder as they were forced to realize that what they were experiencing did not fit into their material world view. After a few sessions with the medium, Baggally too was converted.

They had obtained three adjoining rooms on the fifth floor of the Victoria Hotel, which no longer stands. The sittings were held in the middle room (Feilding's). Palladino supplied the curtain and a small table for the "cabinet," both of which were thoroughly inspected by the men. In fact, before each séance, the room was thoroughly examined—remember these men were experts in conjuring and knew every technique employed by the cleverest magicians of their day.

After the room was inspected and secured, one investigator would go down and escort Eusapia back. The outer door would then be locked, as were the connecting door to Baggally's room, next to which the cabinet curtain was hung, and the hall, and the other door connecting Carrington's room with another guest's.

The room was illuminated by electric lights that could be dimmed but, as they reported, the most numerous phenomena occurred when they were most vigilant and when the light was the strongest. The strength and number of phenomena seemed to depend more on Eusapia's mood and health than on the conditions.

The men also treated her with respect and never relaxed their controls, which must have pleased the medium. They were also refreshingly surprised that, instead of imposing conditions that would make trickery easier, Eusapia actually made it more difficult for cheating to occur. For instance, she would often call their attention to something that was about to occur (rather than diverting their attention as a magician would do) and caution them to properly secure her hands and feet.

Because of their rigid controls and the illumination of the room, the three investigators were convinced of the reality of her phenomena. The tables levitated numerous times, various objects moved about, and hands and heads of different sizes, shapes, and complexions appeared both in and outside the cabinet. The men were touched and grabbed by phantom hands, which they all attested were "human" in every respect, complete with fingernails. They were not Eusapia's or anyone else's present, and by their feel and action could not have been produced by some contraption. (Besides, the medium allowed them to search her and no such device was ever found.)

The investigators, profoundly changed by their experience, reported that they found no cause to suspect that the phenomena were anything but genuine. As Baggally noted, no mechanism was detected, no accomplice was present, and the three men were experienced investigators who had previously detected fraud after fraud: "I find it impossible to believe that Eusapia could have been able to practice trickery constantly during the many hours that the séances lasted and remain undetected."

But, as seems to be inevitable in the never-ending search to find some way of disproving these mind-boggling phenomena, the 1908 Naples investigations have again come under attack recently, almost 90 years later. The contemporary doubter maintains that the trio of experts didn't specifically say that they tested the connecting door of Baggalley's room for a hidden panel through which an accomplice could sneak behind the curtain. The reader, in looking over the above facts will see how ludicrous the accusation is. It is made even more ridiculous by the fact that these men were experts at false paneling for just such a purpose, and to imagine that they would not have checked for these devices, just because they didn't specifically say so, is not to be in touch with reality. Besides, even an accomplice hiding behind a curtain would not "explain" the many levitations, phantom body parts, and so on, that appeared, in good light, in the room outside the cabinet. There are none so blind.

CHAPTER 18

THE CASE FOR ECTOPLASM

I have alluded before to this "blindness" that prevents people from accepting the evidence of reliable witnesses and, indeed, of their own senses. The late Brian Inglis coined the word "skepticemia," a disorder characterized by a readiness to believe the worst: "to accept the word of skeptics that, say, a medium has been exposed, without pausing to wonder whether the skeptic may not be even more tempted to cheat than the medium." The Hodgson-Sidgwick fiasco was a good example of the "germ" that set off an outbreak of this disorder in the SPR, a plague that has yet to be erased.

What antidotes can we offer? More cases of extraordinary phenomena? As Inglis and others have noted, these occurrences have been reported since the beginning of recorded history and from every corner of the world. There has never been such an extensive body of accumulated evidence, attested and sworn to by so many witnesses from every stratum of society that has been so completely rejected by so many.

Inglis also coined the phrase, "retrocognitive dissonance" based on psychologist, Leon Festinger's concept of cognitive dissonance. "Retrocognitive dissonance" may be explained this way: "I saw a person levitate in my living room and I am sure there was no way of faking it. But people don't levitate. I saw a magician "levitate" on the stage, so what I saw earlier must have been a trick after all." But, as Inglis pointed out, time alone can account for retrocognitive dissonance. For example, Richet, in thinking back over his earlier investigations of Palladino wrote:

> At the moment when these facts take place they seem to us certain, and we are willing to proclaim them openly, but... when we feel the irresistible influence of our environment, when our friends all laugh at our credulity: --then we are almost disarmed, and begin to doubt...

> May I not have been grossly deceived ? .
> . . And we end up by letting ourselves be
> persuaded that we have been the victims
> of a trick.

Our human minds cling tenaciously to the familiar, concrete, everyday world. We resist anything that threatens our safe, comfortable, reality—that's why earthquakes are so frightening; we have nothing stable to cling to, our solid foundation literally crumbles away.

In the case of ectoplasmic manifestations and other phenomena that collide with our perception of reality, Inglis noted that skepticism often leads into "grotesque distortions of the evidence," as in the writings of some of Palladino's later critics.

Of course, some phenomena, by their very nature, strain the credulity of even those whose "boggle thresholds" have been stretched nearly to infinity, especially since these phenomena sometimes take on bizarre characteristics, produced as they most likely are through the same distortions of reality our unconscious mind creates in our dream material. They are also subject to the psychological idiosyncrasies of individual personalities, and may at times be influenced by what Carl Jung called the "joker" or "trickster" aspect of our psyches.

One case in point was that of Marthe Beraud (referred to as "Eva C." by her investigators), who was tested by many researchers including Baron von Schrenck-Notzing, Dr. Gustav Geley, and the Nobel Prize winning psychologist and physiologist Professor Charles Richet in the early 1900s. (Either he or Geley coined the word "ectoplasm.")

The entranced Beraud would exude a white substance, usually, but not always, from her mouth, which would take on the appearance of gauze or muslin, generally developing extensions or pseudopods, then hands or arms, and gradually gaining in consistency. Richet noted two phases of its development: a rudimentary or "rough draft" phase, and a second "building up" from the first indistinct "cloudy" phase. In 1906 he described the exuded material as forming various streams or "arms" as it descended to the floor, some of it forming branches that climbed over the arms of the chair. There appeared

> swellings in it like an empty snake skin
> while the two masses, B and X, seem
> to swell and get fuller. Slowly the mass
> X mounts up and the mass B descends,

so that X is on Marthe's knees and B below it, the latter becoming the base on which the whole formation rests, for it spreads out like an amoeba on the floor, and takes the form of a split base (two feet?). While these two parts continued to flatten out on the floor I had plenty of time to look very closely into the greyish, gelatinous, and barely visible mass X. . . It then slowly divided into clefts at its extremity, resembling a hand, in embryo, but sufficiently clear for me to say that it is a left hand seen from the back.

Another change sets in: the little finger separates from the rest, and in the grey, cloudy mass a hand can be clearly seen from the back, the fingers closed, the little finger extended, and a swelling resembling the carpal bones appeared, like [an X-ray] of these bones. Soon the cloudy mass disappears and I see an ill-formed hand like a cast in plaster. I think I see the folds and creases in the skin slowly form. I am holding both Marthe's hands, and can see them.

In 1910 Geley independently witnessed very similar occurrences.

From Eva's mouth a band of white substance about two fingers' breadth slowly descends to her knees. This ribbon takes varied form under our eyes: it spreads as a large, perforated, membranous tissue, with local swellings and vacant spaces; gathers itself together and retracts repeatedly. Here and there from the mass appear prolongations, a kind of pseudo-pods, and these take for a few seconds the form of fingers and rudimentary hands, returning into the general mass. Finally the cord turns on itself, lengthens on Eva's knees and, raising its end, moves towards me. I then see its end thicken, and this kind of bud expands into a perfectly modelled hand. I touch it, and it gives me the feeling of a normal hand; I feel the bones and the fingernails. Then it retreats, diminishes in size, and disappears in the end of a cord.

The Beraud investigation is important on at least two counts: First, she was carefully examined and controlled as perhaps no other medium ever was—she should have received the Croix de Guerre for her beyond-the-call-of-duty ordeals. Before and after each séance, the cabinets, whose curtains were usually left open anyway, were thoroughly searched. The medium was also completely searched as well: hair, armpits, nose, mouth, and knees were examined and at times she was subjected to rectal and vaginal probings as well. She was completely undressed and reclothed in a specially made garment that she was literally sewed into. The ends of the arms had tulle extensions stitched over them enclosing her hands. Her head was also enclosed in a hood of fine netting sewed onto the neckline.

In addition she was administered syrup of bilberries (a dark blue berry known for its coloring powers) so that anything she might bring up from her stomach would be stained. (Her exudations were never discolored.) In at least one session with Schrenck-Notzing she was given emetics to cause her to vomit up the contents of her stomach after the séance. Laboratory results showed that her stomach had contained the remains of her dinner in various stages of digestion, plus the wafers in which the emetic powders were enclosed—this was before the days of capsules—but nothing resembling material, paper, or any other substance that she could have swallowed and regurgitated to simulate ectoplasm.

In spite of these severe precautions some continued to maintain that she was regurgitating the substance. They ignored the facts—that the material would extrude through the veil covering and return back again through it to the medium's body, that it sometimes came from other parts of her body, that it moved, changed shape, and was sometimes felt to be solid and flesh-like, and it sometimes disappeared.

But the real criticism came when the ectoplasm began to take on flat, two-dimensional forms. The figures and faces looked as if they had been cut out of paper or thin cloth, complete with wrinkles or folds, and pinned or hung up on the medium. They looked especially phony in the photographs taken by the experimenters. As Inglis noted, it was as if some joker was at work creating suspicion by ensuring that the effects in the photos looked like fakes.

Even more suspicious was the fact that some of the materializations seemed to be influenced by things Beraud's read (as one might expect with unconscious manifestations). In one photograph the letters MIRO had appeared on an extrusion from Marthe's head. When the photograph was published a Parisian writer pointed out that the letters formed part of the masthead of the journal LE MIROIR, and that some of the forms and faces Marthe had produced were merely cut-outs from back issues of the journal altered to disguise their original source.

The seemingly damning evidence was refuted by Schrenck-Notzing when he obtained experts who attested that the photographs were taken at the sittings under the usual precautions and that the materialized portraits were not touched up magazine photos but almost parodies or variations on them. In other words, it was another indication that the form the ectoplasm took was governed by the workings of the medium's unconscious. What she produced were in fact ideoplasms, forms molded by her mental processes, using for raw material waking experiences, such as images she had seen in magazines, just as we do in the creation of our dreams.

At any rate, the photographs were misleading because they seemed to show fixed forms, paper cutouts, which appeared to be attached to the medium's hair or clothing. The witnesses pointed out, however, that although they looked that way in the photos, in reality they had moved and acted alive at the séance, and that the flat, two-dimensional ectoplasmic hands would move around and touch or grip sitters.

Evidently even the famous magician and debunker Harry Houdini got into the act, but instead of discrediting "Eva," he came away impressed. In a 1920 letter to Sir Arthur Conan Doyle, he reported that Eva had been asked to eat cake and drink coffee before being sewn into tights and having a net secured to cover her face. Still she extruded a "froth-like" substance, a white, plaster-like object, which appeared over her right eye, and something resembling a miniature face, about four inches in diameter. He reported that she later produced a "rubberish" substance that then suddenly vanished.

As we saw in the Bindelof group, and as you will see later in the discussion of Ted Serios, psychokinesis can affect photographic film directly, creating images originating in the conscious, but more frequently in the unconscious mind. Something of the sort was probably going on in Beraud's séances. In a 1920 sitting she produced a small photo of ectoplasm that appeared in the area of her chin. Upon examination with a flashlight the sitters observed a "rough drawing, as if crudely sketched in chalk." But when a photo taken of it was developed, they saw, much to their surprise, a picture that in no way resembled what they had seen. It was now a "much more finished and artistic product" with "a human face which has something calm and even dignified about it."

This same photo caused some temporary suspicion two years later when H. D. Taylor, in a journal article, described it as a picture of the medium, lying back in her chair with the small photograph gripped in place by her chin which was pressed tightly against her chest. But how she could secrete the picture despite the precautions taken, manage to whip it out, unfold it and tuck it under her chin under the watchful eyes of her examiners who were holding her hands firmly all the time was not explained.

Fortunately, this was one of the rare occasions with good results in which two cameras were used simultaneously to create a "stereoscopic," or 3-D, picture. Taylor, examining them with a stereoscope, realized that the picture was not clenched under Beraud's chin but that it was semi-transparent and her chin showed through it.

Cameras and photographic film are sometimes a great help in psychic research but at other times can be problematic. Psychokinesis can produce strange effects on film and sometimes will cause cameras to jam. (More about this is later chapters.) My ex-husband jammed cameras when he was nervous about having his picture taken: either the shutter would not function or the flash would not work. Once, when one of his "admirers" wanted to take a few candid snapshots of him, the camera worked perfectly except that the two pictures containing his image had a mark across the bottom-half of the photos resembling a miniature lightning bolt or a flash of static electricity. The rest of the negatives on the roll were perfectly normal and the persons we contacted at Kodak films could give no explanation for the anomaly.

We don't know what the mechanism is that enables certain individuals to produce images on film any more than we know what causes the

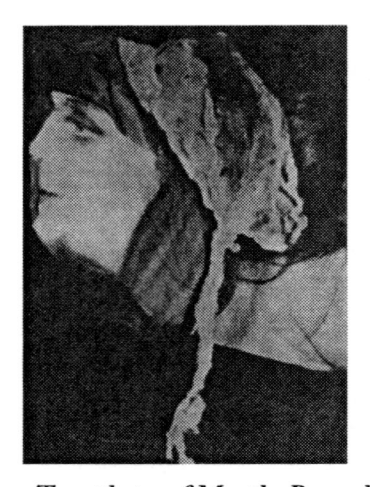

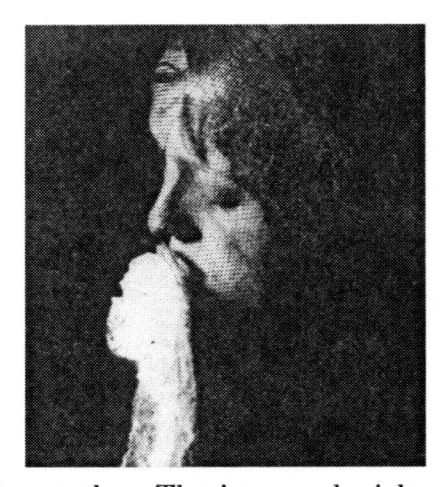

Two photos of Marthe Beraud producing ectoplasm. The picture on the right shows the substance extruding through the veil hood sewn on to her dress. On the left, a face, which looks two-dimensional in the picture, is forming in the vicinity of her right ear. The medium's chin and neck are on the lower right.

production of ectoplasm, or in fact, what ectoplasm is. The material that made up the phantom Katie King was analyzed and consisted of protein and fats, but often Katie deteriorated or "vaporized" and sometimes flowed back to where the medium sat entranced. Palladino and Beraud produced pseudopods or limb-like extensions that issued from their bodies. The Bindelof group felt pullings and touchings, some of which penetrated into their bodies, but they saw what was probably ectoplasm only once, when a "shadow" obscured their luminous wristwatch dials while passing over their hands in the dark.

In Home's case, although many witnesses saw and felt the solid forms (hands, full figures) that he produced, at times they were visible to only some of the sitters, as when Mrs. Crookes saw fingers playing the accordion but her husband could not. These forms, like Katie, were sometimes solid and sometimes transparent or vapor-like. In addition, no one saw connecting "threads" or "rods" between the medium and the apparitions.

William Jackson Crawford, a Doctor of Science and lecturer in mechanical engineering who died tragically in 1920 at the age of 39, made a valuable contribution to understanding ectoplasm. While lecturing on mechanical engineering at a university in Belfast, he investigated the physical phenomena produced by a 17-year-old medium named Kathleen Goligher, the eldest daughter of a family of dedicated Spiritualists.

When Crawford first witnessed a table "floating" in the air his mechanical engineer's mind immediately wondered if the reaction was on the floor immediately below the table, if it was on the medium herself, or in neither of those places. Once he satisfied himself that none of the sitters, generally members of her family, were touching the table around which they sat holding hands or with their hands on their knees, he set about answering the questions he had raised.

In sufficient gas light for Crawford to see that none of the sitters' feet were touching the table, he had the medium (who generally sat with her feet on the rung under her chair) placed on a large commercial scale borrowed for the occasion. He found that when a table or a stool levitated, Kathleen's weight increased by nearly—usually a few ounces less—the weight of the object. (The stool, by the way, floated up so high that Crawford reported, "if I had bent my head I could have walked right under it from one side of the room to the other.")

So that he could control conditions, many of the experiments were conducted in Crawford's home. Phenomena were usually produced immediately upon his request and were maintained long enough for measurements to be made. During one such session, Crawford entered the sitters' circle attempting to push a powerfully levitated table down vertically to the floor. He reported:

> I felt an elastic resistance. . . I then thought of pushing it inwards towards the medium. I was much surprised to find that the resistance to push it in that direction was not an elastic one, but one of quite a different order. The resistance was a solid or rigid one, and as a matter of fact the table appeared to be "locked."

Crawford theorized that a sort of cantilever structure was created by the ectoplasm and anchored in the medium. His "rod theory" proposed that a rod of material particles temporarily projected from the medium's body extended at an angle to the floor under the table or other object to be levitated and then upward.

His work in regard to the raps Kathleen produced is particularly intriguing. By having her sit on the weighing machine while the raps were produced he found that Kathleen progressively got lighter. The weight loss continued until the loudest, strongest blows were heard. At that point her weight had dropped eight pounds but would then return to normal when the raps stopped. He found that the weight loss was directly proportional to the intensity of the raps. By placing one of his hands near the place where the raps were taking place he concluded that each psychic rod, near its end, was solid but that "From a distance only a few inches from its extremity right up to the body of the medium, all appearance of solidity vanished and nothing could be felt in the line of the structure but a flow of cold, spore-like particles." However, even though the rod was made up mostly of a "gaseous body," it "operated exactly as if it were wholly solid from the body of the medium outwards."

These findings are somewhat similar to observations made by the English physicist Oliver Lodge in 1894 after witnessing Palladino's phenomena, which he described as being caused by "vitality at a distance." He said he had been touched and had seen others being touched by a "prolongation or formation" that he experienced "as if the connecting link, if any, were invisible and intangible, or as if a portion of vital or directing energy had been detached, and were producing distant movements without any apparent connexion with the medium."

It appeared that most of the ectoplasm responsible for the levitations came from the medium, but that a small percentage emanated from one or more of the other sitters. In Crawford's experiments he found that the sitters each lost a small amount of weight—no more than a few ounces—at each séance. The medium generally lost the least amount of this "permanent" weight. He came to conclude that a physical medium could supply temporary quantities of what he called "structural matter"—read ectoplasm—whereas good sitters could supply the "psychic energy." (This theory fits in well with the Bindelof group's results. The primary source of the "structural matter" was most likely Gil while the teenage sitters, at the height of their libidinal and psycho-physical strength, supplied quantities of energy, thus producing such powerful effects.)

But Crawford also observed that Kathleen's body, especially her thighs, became thinner while she was producing ectoplasm, returning to their former size afterwards. Other investigators have noted mediums' bodies shrinking in size or partially dematerializing as well. For example, Home, Kluski, and others were often weakened and debilitated after materializations and Palladino was reported by several investigators to appear shrunken and changed, her eyes dulled and her face diminished to half its usual size. One of her early examiners claimed that her lower limbs disappeared and Professor Haraldur Neilsson in Iceland witnessed the entire disappearance of Indride Indridason's left arm for a half hour.

I cannot cover all the material Crawford gathered from his many experiments with the Golighers and reported on in three books, but another finding that I think is important involved the use of clay and a red powdered carmine dye. Crawford tied Kathleen's ankles to the back rail of her chair and placed a dish containing extremely soft clay under the table. The "spirits" caused the raps to be made on the clay leaving various marks on it. After these demonstrations Crawford discovered a considerable amount of clay on Kathleen's shoes and stockings, and on the cord with which her ankles were tied. Minute pieces of matter identified as coming from her stockings and the furry lining inside the tongues of her shoes were also found deposited on the clay in the dish. These and other experiments drew Crawford to conclude that when the "plasma," as he called it, emerged from the medium and made impressions on the clay, it brought with it particles of matter from her clothing and then took with it tiny amounts of clay which it deposited on her shoes and stockings upon returning to her body.

He thought the emanations came from her ankles until a magnifying lens detected almost microscopic clay particles on the tops of her stockings. Crawford began using powdered carmine, which he had discovered would adhere to the plasma and leave a colored track. With the assistance of his wife, dampened carmine was placed on Kathleen's clothing. By placing it on her underwear it was established that the substance issued and returned to her trunk, at "the join of the legs." In addition, when carmine was found in Kathleen's shoes or boots, particles or small patches of it were often found on the table legs, the floor, or on "articles touched by the structures. As a rule the amount of carmine so deposited was slight and not comparable to the quantities on her stockings."

Crawford also cleverly used a stain, actually soot from an oil lamp this time, to learn about the shape of the ends of the "rods" and about their methods of gripping the table. He would cover the table legs and under-surface with soot and found that there were two methods by which levitation occurred. From the marks on the table he could tell that when the table was lifted by the legs, the plasma wrapped around them like a vine or tentacle.

Crawford was able to photograph the "plasma," although it was difficult because of the adverse effect light would have on the medium.

After six months of trying in vain, they finally achieved success: Twenty-six photographs showed the material extending from Kathleen to a table in either single or double rods or columns. Crawford explained that the material was photographed in an unstressed state because the combination of the strain of levitating a table combined with the light source needed to take the photographs would have been too taxing for the medium.

Needless to say, the photographs came into question because photographs don't do justice to ectoplasm. A more serious doubt was cast when, on July 30, 1920, just before the publication of his third book, Crawford committed suicide. There was nothing to tie his suicide to his investigations, in fact, he stated in a letter written at the beginning of that month that he was satisfied with his work of that year, especially with the results of the photographs. He wrote on the 14th that there would be a month's break "so that everyone concerned may have a good rest," and, on the 26th, four days before his death, he disclosed: "I have been struck down mentally. I was perfectly all right up to a few weeks ago. . . It is not the psychic work. I enjoyed it too well. I am thankful to say that work will stand. It is too thoroughly done for any material loopholes to be left." It would seem then, that the cause of Crawford's psychic pain lay elsewhere.

A Dr. Fournier d'Albe conducted about twenty séances with the Golighers in an attempt to confirm Crawford's findings but came away disappointed, saying that he saw nothing paranormal. Because of inadequate illumination he felt that he couldn't be sure that someone was not manipulating the table. Other researchers, however, reported that at the sittings they attended the light was adequate for them to detect any kind of fraud. In fact, a Mr. F. McCarthy Stephenson continued the work, photographing successfully some ectoplasm between Kathleen's feet and attesting to the reality of the phenomena.

Kathleen's husband, S. G. Donaldson, also took photographs in infrared light in the 1930s at sittings attended by friends. These also showed ectoplasm forming around the medium's feet. The sometimes gauzy, sometimes stringy material seemed to emerge from beneath her dress.

Infrared also proved invaluable with the Austrian medium, Rudi Schneider, who had produced psychokinetic feats similar to Palladino and the others. Around the same time as Donaldson was photographing Kathleen, a scientist named Eugene Osty tested Schneider in Paris. Osty used the infrared beam to detect any fraudulent movements the medium, now with his power declining, might make. The rays were designed to turn on overhead lights and activate cameras if the beams were interrupted. Time after time the mechanism was activated but Rudi still sat slumped, entranced, in his seat. They finally realized that an invisible stream or rod of ectoplasm was occluding the rays as it made its way towards the target to be levitated. When tested, the material was found to produce an absorption of one to seventy percent, and sometimes had the consistency of smoke.

What are we to make of all this? If Crawford and Osty were correct, then ectoplasm, visible or not, is the mechanism behind the raps, as well as the levitations and other phenomena. But is it responsible for all these phenomena? Could a medium affect a radio via ectoplasm when it is three thousand miles away, as we will read about later? It doesn't seem likely. Perhaps we are still blind men examining the elephant. Or is it that we are observing different animals altogether?

Another question raised by the Crawford experiments is whether or not the medium was unconsciously influenced by the investigator's preconceptions of how ectoplasm might function and "complied" by causing the substance to conform to his expectations. This concept is called ideoplasty. In other words, an experimenter's theory is confirmed because his or her beliefs affect the medium, who in turn shapes the phenomena. Thus Crawford's training in mechanical engineering might have affected the form of Kathleen's ectoplasm.

Ideoplasty might also have been at work when Richet examined Marthe Beraud. He reported that ectoplasm emerged as a kind of liquid or pasty jelly from her mouth or breast. With the physician Schrenck-Notzing and others looking on, he said this "paste" spread on his knee and slowly took form "so as to show the rudiments of the radius, cubitus or metacarpal bone whose increasing pressure I could feel on my knee. The ectoplasmic cloud would seem to become living substance while at the same time veils develop around it that conceal the mechanism of its formation into ephemeral living tissue." Remember, Richet was a renowned physiologist.

CHAPTER 19

THE UNIQUE POLE

A well-bred gentleman, dignified banker, journalist, and poet named Teofil Modrzejewski, who was born in Warsaw in 1883, produced not only ectoplasm but an astounding array of phenomena. This literate upper-class gentleman was not only an economic correspondent for a Warsaw newspaper, a writer of satirical songs and poems for sophisticated cabaret theatre, a translator of novels (from Italian), and the author of a volume on linguistic research, he was also one of the most spectacular stars in the galaxy of known mediums.

Modrzejewski began his mediumship in 1918 when he attended a séance given by a well-known Polish medium named Jan Guzik. After Guzik left, the sitters agreed to continue the séance to see if they could get phenomena without the medium's presence. Much to everyone's surprise, luminous visions formed around Modrzejewski.

The séance's organizer, a physician named Sokolowski, tested him and discovered that when Modrzejewski held a magnet, violet flashes were observed emanating from both poles (with a small "p"—no pun intended). Another D. D. Home had been discovered.

Those who have studied the man note that he had deep feelings about social injustices, hypocrisy, and oppression but tended to mask his ardor with flippancy. His interest and involvement in his psychic gift was serious and profound but this, too, he treated flippantly, choosing the pseudonym under which he performed as a medium, Franek Kluski, Kluski being a common pasta favored by the working-class. As Zofia Weaver notes, it depicts someone clumsy and dull. Luckily for us it's also easier to pronounce than Modrzejewski.

I referred to Kluski as a Polish D. D. Home. Like Home, he was never found to be fraudulent and produced a great variety of large-scale, indisputably distinct phenomena, which, like Home's, often took place spontaneously and beyond his reach or at a distance from his person. Like Home, too, he was of very delicate health and developed tuberculosis. His childhood was marked by illnesses and both his brother and sister died at an early age.

Kluski wrote that he had an imaginary playmate called the mole. From a shawl draped over two chairs he would make a tent in which he would "visit" with the mole and his dead siblings. At night he would have out-of-body experiences and pass through a luminous "slit" in reality to the mole's domain.

All this was not really unusual for the child since his paternal uncle, a priest, was mediumistic and had frequent telepathic visions. His father, too, was prone to spontaneous phenomena; he was often visited by the spirit of his own father, who would materialize and scold his son for drinking too much and slap him if he showed any disrespect. Normal daily life chez Modrzejewski!

It is no wonder then that he began having precognitive visions and perceiving "phantoms," which he accepted as living beings, as a small child. At around 5 or 6 years of age he had a whole entourage of "spirit" friends with whom he conversed. He called up visions of his dead siblings in front of other children and learned to control his out-of-body experiences.

Like Home, he lost a friend in his teenage years who later appeared to him. She was a girl he had fallen in love with and whose sudden death when he was sixteen deeply affected him. For the next four years he was haunted by visions of her lying in her coffin, until she materialized as she had looked in life and they made their farewells.

After that he led an ordinary life. He married and fathered children and was too busy with everyday activities to bother much with visions until that fateful evening when his powers were recognized after the Guzic séance.

Kluski began to develop as a medium after that evening. He generally demonstrated his abilities for friends and acquaintances who were not preoccupied with controlling for fraud but interested in obtaining evidence of an afterlife. However, he sat in many European cities and was witnessed by many people of varied backgrounds, university professors, businessmen, physicians, lawyers, etc. as well as psychic investigators such as Feilding, Geley, Richet, and others.

Even though the locations were randomly chosen and conditions varied with each sitting, strong phenomena occurred at each of them. His friend, Norbert Okolowicz, who was in charge of most of the séances and who chronicled them in a book, claimed that the most skeptical witnesses came away convinced of the reality of his phenomena. A well-known

THE UNIQUE POLE

magician of the time, Geo Lange, observed Kluski on three occasions and was satisfied that the effects could not be produced by tricks.

As is usually the case, Kluski began with "simple" movement of objects and then developed more complex manifestations. In some of the earlier sittings objects would pile up on top of each other. Large objects such as chairs, tables and other furniture were heaped precariously without regard to the laws of gravity.

But he became famous for the apparitions and lights that appeared at his séances. The lights, which from the descriptions must have been spectacular, were of many forms, shapes, and sizes. Some looked like illuminated soap bubbles, but others were elliptical or triangular, flower- or star-shaped, or, in one case, resembling an open mouth with teeth. Some lights surrounded or appeared around Kluski, others manifested yards away, often swinging or dancing in the air. They were of various colors, most often green or yellow, but sometimes red or blue. Some phosphorescent hazes developed into apparitions.

About a fifth of the phantoms he produced glowed from within, illuminated by their own light, but most were seen by the light of screens coated with phosphorescent paint, by "lighted discs" paranormally produced by the medium, or, in a few instances, by light coming in through a window.

The apparitions themselves deserve special scrutiny. Generally they were phantoms of deceased friends or relatives of the attendees. They would gradually develop from a kind of haze, slowly becoming more distinct, and acquiring clearer individual features, such as facial lines or mustaches, and various textures, such as the silk or other fabrics of their clothing, metal buckles, or leather gloves.

Many of the apparitions were of animals or birds, and some were of Kluski himself. His "ghostly double" would sometimes stand next to him; it was reported once to look lively and well while the real entranced medium seemed stiff and lifeless. At another time the phantom Kluski was bearded just as the medium, now clean-shaven, had appeared a few days before.

Like Florence Cook's "Katie King," the other apparitions often resembled the medium, until his friend Okolowicz mentioned this fact to Kluski. Immediately after that each apparition produced was totally unlike the medium.

The apparitions could change in what seems to be a phenomenon similar to today's computer-generated metamorphosis of faces. Okolowicz noted that in a few instances a face would become more masculine, then more feminine, as if several faces were superimposed over one another. Kluski's apparitions would pass through him at times but always seemed to go around the other participants. They would interact with the sitters and generally do what was requested of them, although they would at times display annoyance or independent behavior.

Most communication apparently took place by saying the alphabet aloud with raps indicating the letters of the message. Sometimes, however, this tedious method was bypassed and the phantoms were reported to have spoken.

One instance in which one of these apparitions spoke is rather amusing and illustrates that in a trance, as in a dream state, an image will carry over from one dream or trance to another. At one séance a phantom appeared and was identified by a sitter as his son. At the following séance, which the man did not attend, the apparition returned, moved to the spot where his father had been the time before, and kissed the hand of the stranger seated there. Realizing its mistake, the "spirit" backed off in confusion, saying "Father's not here."

Evidently numerous phantoms would appear simultaneously at Kluski's séances, moving around, making sounds, and touching those present. It was reported that the self-illuminated ones were often difficult to distinguish from the living participants. (And some of them were more interesting than the "live" ones.)

In addition to complete apparitions there were, it seems, quantities of "parts," that is, limbs of various shapes and sizes, sometimes seen extruding from Kluski, at other times floating in midair. Gustave Geley and others used basins of melted paraffin to preserve or display demonstrable proof of their existence.

Geley used blue-tinted paraffin and weighed it before and afterwards to make sure it was all accounted for (and no more added). In addition, in collaboration with Richet and Tocquet, another scientist, he secretly added a substance called cholestrin or cholesterol to it, which, when tested with chloroform and sulfuric acid turns red then brown, enabling them to detect any substitutions. (By the way, they never did: All the molds proved to contain the cholesterol.) As usual the liquid paraffin would be placed on the tables, the phantom hands--or an occasional foot or face--would be dipped in it, then withdrawn, with the paraffin cooling and hardening immediately. The phantom limb then would dematerialize and the delicate thin mold of cooled paraffin would be left, intact, on the table.

Upon examination the molds showed all the lines and creases, all the anatomical detail of human hands. Geley reported that he observed perfect, seamless, molds of different hands being formed. They were different from Kluski's hands and the fingerprints were not the medium's. Geley also noticed that when the medium was tired, the molds would be smaller than usual. These diminutive molds turned out not to be those of children's hands, but miniature adult hands. In addition, the hands were generally in positions from which no hand could be extricated without destroying the mold, such as with the index finger pointing and the others curled downward, the thumb curving around the middle finger. Geley made plaster casts from some of these molds, which are still on view at the Society for Psychical Research's library in London and the Institut Métapsychique International in Paris. Oh yes, expert modelers have testified that these are primary casts, originals, with such fine details and signs of active muscular contractions and skin folds that they could not be obtained without the use of a "living" hand. They have been at a loss, however, to determine how that living hand could withdraw while leaving the mold intact.

An incident that took place at one "controlled" sitting is worth noting in that it demonstrates, as in Palladino's séances, the determination of an entranced medium to accomplish what is asked of him or her—if not by paranormal means then by the easiest normal method. Generally, at Kluski's séances, a dim red light illuminated the room at the beginning of the session. Kluski would psychokinetically turn it off once he was in trance and ready to produce his phenomena. At this sitting the experimenter asked him to switch off the light. After three requests, during which the light remained on, Kluski, deep in trance, hauled himself out of his chair, dragging the two men "controls" with him, switched off the lamp, and returned, satisfied, to his chair.

Like other psychokinetically active people, Kluski's phenomena were not confined to the séance room. Spontaneous phenomena plagued him wherever he went. Raps would be heard (which actually caused him some pain) as well as other sounds such as footsteps, papers rattling, and furniture moving. Untouched typewriters would begin clicking away. Apparitions would be seen moving about in daylight, particularly if Kluski was taking a nap.

His electrical phenomena in the séance room were spectacular. He produced illuminated discs and glowing apparitions from whose hands beams of phosphorescent light would shoot out. But in his everyday life light hazes were noticed around him, too, and there were reports of "little fires" being seen inside his mouth. When he was emotionally moved light spots appeared on him, and once on a business trip a colleague who shared his hotel room told of hearing strange noises and seeing lights around him while he was asleep. Once he created havoc with the display of compasses in a store; they started spinning crazily when he leaned over the counter.

He also suffered from electrical discharges; blue flames emitted from the ends of his fingers. He was frightened of electrical storms, refused to conduct séances during these times, and suffered the same depletion of energy after a storm as he did after a séance.

Another phenomenon that pursued him outside of the séance rooms was the absorption and emitting of odors. During sittings participants would notice most frequently the smell of ozone, a form of oxygen usually formed by a silent electrical discharge and often associated with psychokinetic manifestations. But other odors, such as the scent of roses or the unpleasant stench of animals or disease, would also be sensed at times. These would linger on him for long periods afterwards. He seemed to absorb odors and then release them for hours, sometimes days. It is said that when he walked through a street bordered with lime trees, he arrived at his destination with his whole body—not just his clothes—reeking of lime trees.

The séances sapped his energy. A colleague reported after one sitting that it was painful to watch Kluski. His face would swell, his eyes were unfocused, and he coughed up blood into his handkerchief and had to be assisted from the room by a physician. Often his senses were so dulled that he could not tell the difference between water, tea, or alcohol, and sometimes he would have difficulty recognizing people.

Kluski finally had to give up his mediumship in 1925 because of the debilitating effects it had on his already fragile health. (He also suffered from a heart condition owing to a bullet lodged in his chest from a duel he fought around the turn of the century.) He died in Warsaw in 1943 from the tuberculosis that had plagued him for much of his life.

CHAPTER 20

INDRIDI INDRIDASON OF ICELAND

In 1883, the same year of Kluski's birth, another male child destined to mediumship was born to a farmer and his wife in a remote area of Iceland. In 1905, when Indridi Indridason was 22, he moved to "the big city," Reykjavik, to become a printer's apprentice. By chance the wife of the family with whom he was staying invited him to join her in a newly formed group that was experimenting with table tilting. As soon as he was seated, the table began to shake violently. Indridi made for the door.

Obviously they convinced him to come back. The leader of the group, Einar Kvaran, wrote that he invited the young man to his home and, again, as soon as he sat down, the table started to behave violently, trembling, shaking, and moving furiously about the room, overturning and nearly breaking.

Six people—Kvaran; Rev. Haraldur Nielsson, later a university professor; Indridi Einarsson, a playwright; Bjorn Jonsson, a journalist who later became prime minister of Iceland; and two other men, a High Court judge, and a psychiatrist—founded the Experimental Society in order to study Indridason. They held twice-weekly sittings from September to June for which they paid him a yearly salary. They even built him a small house two years later, in which he could live and where they could better observe him. He agreed to give séances only with the Society's permission and indeed they supported him until his tragically early death in 1909 at the age of 29, even though he had been forced to give up experiments two years before because of illness. He had contracted typhoid fever and it was later discovered that he also had, like Home and Kluski, tuberculosis.

In the five years that he was able to "perform," Indridason produced many varied phenomena, including sounds, lights, odors, materializations, apports (solid objects that would appear from nowhere), playing of musical instruments, direct voices, direct writing (with a pen rather than the Bindlovian pencil), and levitations of large objects and of himself. As the phenomena developed he seemed to induce a combination of these mediumistic phenomena and violent poltergeist-like attacks often directed at his own person. Members of the Society took turns guarding him around the clock.

In 1907 a bizarre incident took place while two members, named Oddgeirsson and Thorlaksson, were with him. Evidently they were experiencing some alarming poltergeist disturbances and decided to vacate the house. They lit an oil lamp in Indridason's bedroom and three candles in the adjacent living room. Indridason was standing up on his bed beginning to dress when Thorlaksson saw him suddenly hurled down on the bed. As he ran towards the medium to help him, a bowl that had been standing on a chest of drawers in the room flew towards him. It sailed past him, changed direction, and smashed against a stove in the corner of the room.

Thorlaksson returned to the outer room and Indridason continued to get dressed. Again they heard him scream for help and this time when Thorlaksson rushed in he saw him "balancing in the air with his feet towards the window." Thorlaksson grabbed him, pulled him down onto the bed and tried to pin him there but almost immediately felt both of them being lifted up.

Thorlaksson shouted to Oddgeirsson for help. As the man entered the bedroom a chair flung itself at him. He dodged it—it landed next to the stove in the next room—and joined Thorlaksson who was lying on Indridason's chest. As he sat on the medium's knees a bolster was thrown into the air while at the same time the candlesticks from the outer room came flying into the bedroom.

Skeptics expressed the usual doubts and derisive remarks and of course there was a raging controversy in the newspapers. The Society invited highly placed people to witness the séances, among them the Bishop of Iceland, the British Consul, and a magistrate who later became a Supreme Court Judge.

Enter Professor Gudmundur Hannesson, a highly esteemed scientist and medical and anthropological researcher who had founded the Icelandic Scientific Society and was an honorary member of the Icelandic and Danish Medical Associations. In 1908 Hannesson requested permission to investigate Indridason and chose an ophthalmic surgeon named Bjorn Olafsson to assist him.

In a paper presented to the Parapsychological Association in 1991, parapsychologists Erlendur Haraldsson and Loftur Reimar Gussararson reported on one of those sittings, which was held during the winter of 1908-1909 in a large meeting hall. The hall contained rows of benches, like a church, with the entry at the rear. In front was an empty space containing a small harmonium, a pulpit-shaped lectern in the middle of the wall, flanked by two chairs and a table.

The experimenters placed trumpets and a music box on the table and divided the empty area from the benches by nailing down a floor-to-ceiling, wall-to-wall net. The net was constructed of strong yarn or string and fastened on all sides with wooden strips threaded through the mesh and screwed firmly to the walls, ceiling, and floor. In the center, close to the floor, a narrow slit was cut to provide the only entrance.

Hannesson and Olafsson searched the hall thoroughly before and after the séance, and when Indridason arrived he was asked to undress and his clothes and person were examined. The door at the rear of the hall was locked and sealed.

Five people were in attendance: Hannesson, Olafsson, and Kvaran sat outside on the bench side of the net, while Indridason went through the slit into the "empty space" with Nielsson who was there to serve as a "watchman" or guard for the medium. The investigators did not allow music or singing so that they could hear any footsteps or sounds that might prove suspicious.

The lights were extinguished and the medium fell into a trance. A "spirit control" spoke through him warning that this might be an unusually noisy session because some uninvited visitors or spirits had arrived. Other voices were then heard speaking and swearing. Objects began to fly violently around the space and the medium's chair was "pulled" out from under him and thrown to one corner. When Nielsson moved to support Indridason, his chair too was snatched and flung.

The guard called to the others to retrieve the chairs so that he wouldn't have to let go of Indridason. Hannesson reported that he went in through the slit illuminated by a single lit match. He could see the two men standing in the center and all the articles inside the net. The chair was lying in a corner and despite the dark he immediately found it, but at the instant he turned around with it he was struck "a heavy blow in the back" as though someone had punched him with a closed fist. He then brought the chair to the men who were still standing in the spot where he had just seen them a moment before.

It seems that Hannesson returned to his place outside the net and immediately Nielsson shouted again, saying that the medium had been pulled up into the air, head downwards, feet towards the ceiling, and that the watchman was having difficulty hanging on to Indridason's shoulders. They could hear a lot of struggling and shifting about, the poor guard reported that he could barely hold him, the pull was almost too strong for him. Finally, the pull slackened, the medium sank slowly down, and Nielsson was able to seat him in the chair.

Suddenly the commotion started again, and again voices were heard. The chairs were snatched away time after time and finally shattered. Indridason was pulled into the air this time with so much force that Nielsson claimed he was repeatedly almost lifted off the ground. He had to struggle mightily to keep the medium from flying up into the air.

The scuffle moved towards the lectern and they suddenly heard the watchman cry out in alarm that they were in a dangerous predicament: Indridason's legs had been quickly pulled down into the lectern while the small of his back was resting on the edge. He was afraid the man could have his spine injured because while he was pulling at the medium's shoulders with all his might, the "others" were tugging on his legs. I don't know how this episode ended, but I assume they succeeded in preventing any injury.

Sometimes Hannesson acted as watchman with Nielsson but the phenomena continued. In 1924 he reported that he attended the séances for a whole winter, usually trying to detect fraud, but while there were some occurrences that he considered suspicious and would be especially vigilant concerning that particular aspect at the next sitting, he was never able to ascertain any deceit. On the contrary, he attested that the bulk of the phenomena were, as far as he could judge, genuine, although he qualified his confirmation somewhat by admitting that he had no means of investigating certain phenomena and so could pass no judgment on them.

Unfortunately, there remains little documentation by investigators of this tragically short-lived medium's work. However, there is one bit of speculation I should add here. Home, Kluski, and Indridason all suffered from tuberculosis, or "consumption" as it was called in the nineteenth century. Always on the lookout for any facts that might give clues to the enigma of these awesome physical manifestations, my eyes widened when I read part of an article in a copy of *The New York Times* one Sunday in 1993. In it a Dr. Paul Sledzik was being interviewed on old-world superstitions regarding tuberculosis. He stated that although consumptives could be seen wasting away, they would also have great bursts of energy and were known for a powerful sex drive.

Libidinal energy has often been associated with psychic or psychokinetic powers. We know for certain that budding sexual power flowed through the teenage Bindelof kids. They didn't have tuberculosis, but–who knows?– perhaps the illness shared by those three mediums added to their already prodigious ability

PART THREE:
TWENTIETH CENTURY MEDIUMSHIP

CHAPTER 21

LAST OF THE OLD TIME MEDIUMS?

At the same time as Gil, Larry, Len, and the other Bindelof Boys were holding their Saturday night sittings, a Scottish housewife named Helen Duncan regularly gave rather spectacular séances throughout Great Britain. Duncan stood astride the 19th and 20th centuries. She was born Victoria Helen MacFarlane in the small town of Callander in Scotland on November 25, 1897, to a master cabinetmaker and his wife. (In many books, Duncan's date of birth is given erroneously as 1898.) At the age of twenty she married Henry Duncan, another cabinetmaker, who was injured and disabled during the First World War. She had six children, half her number of pregnancies. In order to make ends meet she worked in a local bleach factory during the day and, having shown psychic abilities from a young age, gave Spiritualist sittings at night.

Duncan was a materializing trance medium in the tradition of Florence Cook and Franek Kluski. As a Spiritualist she believed in providing comfort to the living by bringing proof of survival to them from departed loved ones. In her case this took the form of materializations, that is, producing ectoplasmic apparitions of these dead relatives and friends that, like Katie King, would appear in the sitting room, converse with those attending, and then disappear, usually "melting" onto, or into, the floor.

A well-known mental medium named Lucy Hale who practiced in the UK for about 60 years, recorded a statement in July 1990, about four years before she died, which tells of two Duncan séances she attended that probably took place during the Second World War. Her accounts give an idea of what a typical Duncan sitting was like. The first séance was in a "small room" containing about 30 people: The church where they usually met was being redecorated. A "cabinet" was fashioned out of black curtains suspended from the ceiling by ropes, and a wooden chair was placed in it for the medium. The room was illuminated by a red light.

After they sang a hymn and said a prayer, the curtains were closed around Duncan. After about a minute the spectators observed a white flat band about a foot and a half wide slide out from under the curtain and slowly rise and thicken until it was about 4 feet high. Hale reported that it seemed to her that two arms came out of the sides of this white column, pushed aside some of the ectoplasm, and revealed the face and head of a young man with brown eyes and hair. A woman in the first row identified the figure as her husband, a Royal Air Force pilot who had recently been killed. The "husband" and wife conversed for a while, the pilot bid his wife good-bye, and the white mass sank back to the floor and retreated back under the curtains.

Duncan's "guide," Albert, then said a few words, according to Hale. Albert was a tall slim fellow who spoke in an educated Oxfordian manner, not in Duncan's thick Scotch brogue.

The ectoplasmic ribbon emerged and disappeared subsequently about 10 more times, each time resulting in figures distinct enough to be recognized by a person in the room. Some only revealed their faces; others displayed their heads and shoulders. Albert spoke between apparitions, sometimes introducing the next visitor (with phrases such as "This woman died after experiencing pain in the lower abdomen"), sometimes telling a joke to lighten up what must have been a rather heavy atmosphere.

The account of the second séance Mrs. Hale attended gives us some information about preparations for the sittings. Hale and another woman were appointed to act as "invigilators," what we might call "proctors" or people delegated to watch over proceedings to make sure no hanky-panky is going on. The women accompanied Duncan to an anteroom where they looked on as she stripped and donned black clothes. Hale states that there was no possibility of Duncan secreting white muslin or cheesecloth on her person and came away convinced of the medium's genuineness.

Duncan was later accused of being an accomplished trickster with an amazing ability for swallowing, regurgitating, and then re-swallowing, or concealing in some other way, huge quantities—we're talking *yards* here— of cheesecloth and passing the stuff off as ectoplasm. These accusations are not borne out by the many reliable eyewitness accounts, including the first reports from the London Psychical Laboratory, the research arm of the London Spiritualist Alliance.

In early 1931 this group reported that Mrs. Duncan had agreed to sit for them in London and published the conditions under which the lady sat. First, in the presence of two witnesses, all her clothing was removed and her "hair, ears, mouth and surface of body were examined." For the first three sittings, special clothing was provided, which included a "vest, pair of knickers and sateen overall." Dressed in this charming getup she was then placed in a heavy sack with only her head protruding.

In the last four sittings they changed the clothing to a kind of one-piece jumpsuit with the bottoms of the legs "fashioned as boots" and the long sleeves fitted closely at the wrists. After she had stepped into it, the back was sewn up from the waist to the neck. Attached to these coveralls were strong tapes at the neck, wrists, and ankles.

As they accompanied Duncan from the dressing room to the séance room, her inspectors held her hands so that she would have no opportunity to handle anything. She was then placed in the chair in the cabinet and the neck and wrist tapes were tied to the chair and sealed. Sometimes her feet were also tied and sealed. She therefore could move only three or four inches in any direction.

The room was illuminated with a red light bright enough for members to read the time "by small wrist watches." They sat in a semi-circle in front of the closed curtains, which stretched from curtain rings on a brass rod a few inches from the top of the ceiling to the floor. The "cabinet" was only a corner of the room. The cabinet provided privacy and darkness, which was thought beneficial to producing ectoplasm, but it also supposedly concentrated the medium's energy and further enhanced the output.

The curtains had openings in the center and at the sides adjoining the walls. There were no mechanical devices for opening and closing them.

The report states that ectoplasmic formations appeared sometimes in the center and sometimes at the sides but that each manifestation was corroborated by two or more witnesses and occasionally by all of them. Among the various manifestations they listed were: movements of the heavy velvet curtains; the "quality" of the control's voice (he answered to the name "Albert Stuart and displayed intelligence by making original observations and answering questions"); and the extrusion of ectoplasm in "various masses, shapes, movements and texture" and its rapid disappearance. They also noted the appearance of one "roughly resembling a human form, on one occasion over six feet high," probably Albert, and another one not more than two feet high with a childish voice, swaying rhythmically with the music.

Mr. Duncan, who would man the phonograph in another part of the room, probably supplied the music. Skeptics have noted that Mr. Duncan was at all of his wife's sittings, implying that he was an accomplice in tricking the audience. It hardly seems likely that her investigators overlooked this possibility and that precautions were not taken to control his whereabouts during the sessions.

At the first sitting something "dramatic" happened. During the sitting, Mrs. Duncan, "in deep trance," walked out of the cabinet dressed in her special séance outfit, but without the sack. She walked across the room trailing a band of ectoplasm about four inches wide and three yards long. She paused about eight inches from the light where "the substance was clearly seen to emanate from her nostrils."

At the end of the sitting the sack was found attached to the chair with each of the three seals unbroken "including the one at the neck."

They had also provided a rope about four yards long. At the end of two sittings it was found tied around the medium. Once it was wound twice around her neck with a "running noose," twice around her waist with several knots, then around her ankles, and finally up the back, tied very tightly around her wrists, "binding the back of one hand into the palm of the other." The rope was so tight that they had to cut it quickly in order "to release the Medium from discomfort and pain."

The other time the binding occurred while Duncan was still enclosed in the sack with only her head sticking out. It had been tied and knotted around her body *inside* the sack. Each time the seals were found to be unbroken. If this was trickery, this middle-class obese housewife was as adept at escape as Harry Houdini.

Another brief report printed in the spring of 1931 reiterated that ectoplasm "in copious amounts and active in manifestation" had been frequently witnessed. The forms produced claimed to be children as well as adults, and "Albert" occasionally showed himself "*with the Medium in view* [emphasis added], he standing six inches taller than Mrs. Duncan."

Then something went wrong. The London Psychical Laboratory declared Duncan a fraud. They claimed that the ectoplasm consisted of paper, cloth, and "such everyday materials" mixed with an organic substance similar to coagulated egg white. Another specimen consisted of surgical gauze. They note that on May 29, Mrs. Duncan left a sanitary "towel" or napkin behind in the dressing room; it was made of the same kind of gauze.

On that day, too, when asked to come out to demonstrate the emergence and reabsorption of ectoplasm, she came out–and while others held her hands–opened her mouth and extruded "ectoplasm" by "obvious movements of the mouth and throat muscles." It was about two inches wide and about eight inches long. Then she "sucked it back in again" by lip and throat movements. They noted that the material looked like it had been folded by compression. During the same sitting the entranced Duncan put out her tongue, which was claimed by "Albert" to be ectoplasm.

Obviously the woman was having more than a bad-hair day. What is not fathomable is the reasoning of people who believe that the "clever fraud" who produced yards of billowing material at one séance, would then stoop to so ridiculous a ruse as sticking out her tongue and trying to convince her examiners that *it* was ectoplasm. Or why this supposed wily lady would do something so foolish as to submit a piece of gauze from a "carelessly" left sanitary napkin for laboratory analysis.

They also implied that she was lying when she told them that she thought the production of ectoplasm was related to the fact that her urine was abnormally full of albumen. When they tested several urine samples by acidifying and boiling them, they found that they always coagulated and "the total specimen solidified." A medical report had stated that she did have nephritis at one time, which was accompanied by the presence of albumen in her urine. But because her blood pressure tested during the sittings was found to be subnormal and a urine test taken in a chance visit to a hospital turned out to be normal, they took the results as signs of deceit. They then assumed that the specimens she had previously submitted were "faked" by the addition of egg white.

But then what is ectoplasm made of? Schrenk-Notzing took a small sample from a medium with whom he worked and found that it was composed of protein, fat, and other organic substances. Other researchers analyzed samples of the stuff and determined that it was made up of organic substances such as leucocytes, and epithelial and other cells. They agreed that it was *albuminous* and resembled lymph and chyle but was not identical to them.

An eyewitness account given in a letter to the editor of the *Journal of the SPR* of a 1949 Duncan séance, which I will quote more fully later, is quite meaningful in this context. In this letter the author, Mrs. Denise Iredell, describes Duncan's ectoplasm as a "milky substance spilled from her nostrils" that would ebb and flow "to and from the floor" and would "snake out across the floor to the ankle level" of the sitter who had been called by Albert. She compares it with "the *movement and solidification of eggwhite* which spills from a broken egg in a pot of boiling water" [emphasis added].

She further describes that it concentrated and intensified into a "blob" between four and six feet above the ground but with a "misty substance swirling around the lower levels," and smaller putty-like blobs, which formed on the head of the emerging figure and then refined into features.

Albumin? Could be. Cheesecloth? I don't think so.

In their defense, the Committee did end their report by stating that in the first sittings there was no justification for anything other than the "supernormal." However, they were not all agreed that all of the manifestations in the later sittings were genuine, "although nothing had occurred *upon which a definite accusation of deception* (conscious or unconscious) could be based."

In his 1959 book, *This Is Spiritualism*, Maurice Barbanell, former editor of the paper *Psychic News* and friend of Mrs. Duncan, tells of an experimental séance of hers he witnessed in which ectoplasm "streamed" from her. He claims that it "billowed and flowed in swirling masses" so that even he, an experienced Spiritualist, was astonished at the display. Barbanell also witnessed materialization *inside* the cabinet where he saw the ectoplasm "exude from the medium's nostrils, mouth and ears in waving billows of luminosity that gradually solidified into the six-foot figure of her guide."

He describes, too, the shrinking size of ectoplasmic forms outside the cabinet, dwindling until they "resembled small globes of light" before disappearing as if through the floor. Several times he was invited to handle some of the substance right after it had been produced. He states that it was always "bone-dry" and had a stiff "feel," making it seem unlikely that it could have been regurgitated.

The London Committee had reported that the time they gave Duncan a blue dye to swallow she produced no ectoplasm. Barbanell relates, however, that he conducted the same experiment, having everyone in attendance ingest tablets of methylene blue. This time she did produce materializations—and they were in their usual white color.

If Duncan were the only medium to be examined in this way we might be more skeptical, but Marthe Beraud was similarly tested by several investigators, including Richet, and Geley whose credentials, like those of Crookes, were impeccable. Geley described her ectoplasm as developing 'entirely under my eyes." He described a "membrane" forming between her two thumbs, which were touching. It stretched and elongated as she moved her hands apart, but contrary to what an elastic band would do, it thickened and broadened at the same time that it lengthened. He wrote: "I see, in the middle of the ectoplasmic mass, two fingers appearing. These two fingers, an index and middle finger, are well formed and have nails. Anatomically they are perfect; their colour is rather dark. I touch them curiously. They are colder than normal. They are living fingers, and make movements of bending and stretching out. While I observe them, and without any apparent reason, I see them suddenly, in a space of a moment, melt and vanish. Total duration of this phenomenon—15 minutes."

In another eyewitness report emailed to me by Arthur Oram, author of the book, *The System in Which We Live* (1998), Oram told of a Duncan séance he attended in Swindon on September 14, 1942. In that sitting he saw a materialized form, which had been standing alone inside the circle of sitters, dematerialize. Like Katie King it seemed to melt into the floor, sinking down so that the head was the last part to disappear.

Regurgitated cheesecloth doesn't act that way.

So despite the London fiasco, Duncan went on giving successful séances until one fateful sitting in 1943. There are differing tales of the particulars of this meeting but the essence of the story is that the spirit of a young sailor appeared and told the spectators that he had gone down with his ship, the *HMS Barham*. Now the *Barham had* been sunk shortly before, but the Admiralty had hushed it up so that morale would not suffer. What seems to have happened is that when word got out that this medium was divulging military secrets, the government stepped in. D-Day was in the planning and the military was taking no chances that damaging information might come through to jeopardize the operation.

A Lieutenant of the Royal Navy named Worth attended two of Duncan's séances in Portsmouth, the home port of Britain's Royal Naval fleet, on the 14th and 19th of January 1944. Discrepancies abound, but what seems to be clear is that during the second séance a War Reserve Constable (policeman) named Cross came with Worth. When the third materialized form of the evening appeared, Cross lunged from his seat, overturning the chair of the man, a Mr. Homer, sitting in front of him, and clawed at the curtains. Worth switched on a flashlight, either before, during, or after the lunge, according to the varying accounts, and illuminated either the "spirit friend" or the medium, depending upon whom you believe. Worth claimed that Duncan was standing between the curtains trying to push a piece of white material, which was in front of her, down to the floor. (Didn't he think this was a strange way for her to try to hide it?) Cross claimed that he bent down and grasped the white material, which he said felt flimsy, like butter-muslin, but said it was pulled out of his hand from the front row of the audience. Mrs. Duncan wound up sitting on an upturned chair outside, or just inside, the cabinet wearing either one or no shoes, again depending on the testimony.

Cross supposedly cried to Worth, "Did you get the cloth?" to which the Lieutenant answered, "No, it has gone into the audience." Duncan is supposed to have commented, "Of course it has gone, it had to go somewhere."

The "cloth" had disappeared. The people in the circle asked the officers to search them but the officers refused. (Why? Did they suspect something that they didn't want to know about?)

A Mr. Gill, who had been sitting next to Mr. Homer, testified that Cross lunged forward, grabbed at the curtains, and fell into the cabinet on top of Duncan who could be seen sitting in her chair. The spirit form, he said, disappeared through the floor. Cross got up and pulled the medium out of her chair and into the room, and, he added, seemed scared.

Mrs. Gill, also sitting in front, maintained that a boy materialized and came out of the cabinet. He then vanished except for a small piece of ectoplasm on the floor about the size of a handkerchief. When the Constable jumped forward, she thought he was ill and trying to get out so she took hold of his arm. He plunged straight ahead, however, clutching at the curtains and falling onto Duncan. She said he could be seen with his legs stretched out, one on either side of the medium who was still sitting in the cabinet. She claims she cried out, "Oh, don't do it." (It is said that mediums can suffer great injury and shock if touched while entranced and producing ectoplasm.) She rushed into the cabinet after Cross, throwing her arms around his waist. She got turned around and found herself holding the medium who was now on an upturned chair outside the cabinet.

Another witness, a nurse named Russ, testified that Cross jumped onto a spirit form that promptly vanished through the floor. With nothing to grasp he clutched at the curtains but fell through into the cabinet. Duncan's chair was dragged away from the corner and she was found sitting just *inside* the cabinet wearing only one shoe.

What seems to have occurred, by my reckoning, is that Cross, seeing the apparition and thinking it was the medium with cloth draped over her, attempted to grab and expose her. As he jumped on it, the apparition dissolved and he clutched at the curtains to keep from sprawling. He evidently had grasped a portion of the dematerializing ectoplasm and, believing it to be "white cloth," perceived that it was being dragged away by someone in the audience. His scared look probably betrayed his shock. The impression that the medium was "pushing the material down" in order to hide it, is obviously the skeptical mind's interpretation of ectoplasm disappearing down to, or through, the floor. No white material was found in the room. And I think the officers didn't search because they finally realized that something went on here that did not fit in with their worldview.

Whatever happened, Duncan was tried in Portsmouth in one of the worst travesties of justice—and there have been many—of this century. The officials were hard pressed to find a charge against Duncan strong enough to put her out of circulation. The initial arrest was for vagrancy, which ordinarily would have ended with her release after the payment of a small fine. Instead, Duncan was sent to Holloway, London's notorious women's prison, for four days. The charge was changed to Conspiracy, which during a war can result in capital punishment. They finally resurrected the Witchcraft Act, an obsolete law put on the books in 1735, and the Larceny Act. She was tried at the Old Bailey, England's main criminal court, for "falsely pretending she was in a position to bring about the appearances of spirits of deceased persons."

The trial drew great attention, especially from Spiritualists who saw it as not only a gross injustice, but also a threat to their religious freedom. Many rallied around her with financial and moral support. Many well and not so well known people testified at the trial in her behalf. Even Prime Minister Winston Churchill got into the act.

Churchill, who had psychic abilities himself, wisely I think, picked a bone of contention that was more real to the public officials than spirits: money. He dashed off an angry letter to the Home Secretary demanding, "Give me a report of the 1735 Witchcraft Act. What was the cost of a trial to the State in which the Recorder was kept busy with all this obsolete tomfoolery to the detriment of the necessary work in the courts?"

But even the powerful Churchill couldn't prevent the wartime intelligence honchos from making sure this Spiritualist medium didn't reveal any military information that might hurt their cause. Duncan was convicted and sentenced to nine months in prison.

It is said that the prison officials, believing her conviction to be unjust, never locked her cell door and that she was constantly visited by jailers and other inmates for spiritual guidance. Churchill himself was said to have visited her. Churchill supposedly promised to make amends to Duncan for her mistreatment and many feel that he was largely responsible for the repeal of the Witchcraft Act in 1951.

When she was released, in September 1944, she vowed to give no more séances, but within a few months she resumed sittings. It must have taken a while for her to regain her old powers but regain them she did.

The letter I quoted earlier describing the ectoplasm emanating from Duncan as resembling egg white spilling from a broken egg in a pot of boiling water was from Mrs. Denise Iredell, daughter of Muriel Hankey. Mrs. Hankey was a very well known and respected member of the psychical research community. They both attended that séance in Edinburgh, in October 1949, five years after the medium was released from prison. Mrs. Iredell attended unexpectedly because someone else could not be there. Even her mother didn't know that she would attend.

Iredell reported that Mrs. Duncan was brought into the small sparsely furnished room in her black séance outfit after having been physically examined in an adjoining room. She was visible to all those present as she went into trance before the curtains were drawn and then partially opened. She reported that the red light was sufficiently bright to allow her to see the winking and smiles of a person seated opposite to her, and for him to see her expressions. The only times they could *not* see each other—she noted significantly—was "when materialized figures intervened; their luminosity made the surrounding area seem dark."

Albert asked for "Mrs. Hankey and her daughter" to step to the center, even though, as far as they knew, only two or three people knew that she was present. As they stood there ectoplasm "snaked" to the center near them at floor level and rose to about a foot and a half from their faces. Mrs. Iredell noted that the "characteristic smell of ectoplasm" was "markedly present."

(When I emailed the aforementioned Arthur Oram, a psychical researcher and long time Council member and former Vice President of the Society for Psychical Research in the UK, to question Mrs. Iredell as to what this odor was like, her response was "semen." I then mentioned it to another old friend, Arthur Ellison, a scientist and former president of the SPR and experienced researcher who had attended another [male] medium's ectoplasmic-producing séances, and he confirmed that the odor was indeed similar to that of semen.)

Mrs. Hankey and Denise instantly recognized the face that built up from Duncan's ectoplasm as that of an old family friend who had been dead for about five years. When an uncharacteristic mustache appeared on his upper lip instead of the small white trace of one that she remembered, she exclaimed, "Oooh, Mustache." The comment provoked a remark from the apparition that she felt was characteristic of him and she claims she would have recognized him from his tone even if she had not seen his face.

Afterwards, when she commented that the only two features that seemed wrong were the mustache and his blue eyes, her mother reminded her that the gentleman's eyes had been "remarkably" blue and that his moustache had been of the style the spirit form sported when he was younger. She saw a color portrait of him at a later date that proved her mother's memory to be accurate.

Albert requested that her mother sit down but asked her to stay in the center of the group because the next person was for her only: a young girl who passed with a condition in the lower part of her body. She said she knew of no such person but "Instantly the whirling mass of ectoplasm" around her legs "sprang like an Indian-rope trick rope to my face level", and resolved in the space of a few seconds into the "strong, clearly-defined features" of a schoolmate of hers who had died of cancer of the uterus a year previously. The young woman was unknown to her mother. She exchanged a few remarks with the friend and promised to carry messages to two people for her. The materialization then "collapsed to the floor and the amorphous ectoplasm was withdrawn."

She also reported in the letter that at a much later sitting in London both she and her mother found that Duncan's powers had diminished; the ectoplasm was so scanty that it merely produced "malformed features over her own face." Although they felt it to be poor, they never considered it to be deception.

The Witchcraft Act that had been on the books since 1735 was finally repealed in 1951 and replaced by the Fraudulent Mediums Act. It was probably under this law that the police raided a Duncan séance that she was giving in Nottingham in November 1956. Although Spiritualism was officially recognized as a legitimate religion two years before, evidently mediums were still subject to police harassment. They barged in and grabbed Duncan, strip searched her, and took flash pictures of her, declaring that they were looking for masks and other articles that she was using to deceive the public. Of course they found nothing, but the shock of being roughly handled took its toll.

It is a canon of Spiritualism that you never touch or shine a bright light on a materializing medium while they are entranced. It's believed that the rapid return of ectoplasm to the body can cause shock and even fatal injury. According to reports, the physician summoned after the raid found burn marks on Duncan's body. She went home to Scotland and later was taken to a hospital.

Whether her death was caused by the policemen's actions, by natural causes—she was after all obese, diabetic and not in good health—or by a combination of the two, she died on December 6, 1956, five weeks after the raid.

A century after Duncan's birth, Spiritualists and others mounted a campaign in the UK to clear her name or at least to have her pardoned. One of the problems her supporters have encountered is that relevant papers having to do with her arrest and trial are still classified and will not be released to the public for another decade or two. So it doesn't look like there will be any official pardon by the British government in the near future.

I hope, as more and more people learn about Helen Duncan, that the more important court of international human conscience will understand and exonerate her.

CHAPTER 22

THE RUSSIANS ARE COMING

All of the mediums cited thus far believed that they were conduits of spirits or of some divine power. Many contemporary "mediums" consider their abilities to be generated solely by their physical bodies in conjunction with their mental powers. This was especially true of some of the officially atheistic citizens of the former USSR. In the late 1960s word began to filter out from behind the "Iron Curtain" that a Russian woman known as "Nelya Mikhailova" amazed scientists with her psychokinetic powers. Conflicting reports from the then USSR either extolled her powers or denounced her as a fraud. (Same old story, *à la Russe*.)

The lady in question was an unassuming housewife from Leningrad named Nina Kulagina (Mikhailova or Mikhailovna was her maiden name), who discovered her psychokinetic powers one fateful day when she was extremely upset and angry. She walked toward a cupboard in her kitchen and saw a glass pitcher move to the edge of a shelf, fall off, and break to pieces on the floor. That incident set off a series of poltergeist-like events: objects moving, lights going on and off, doors opening and closing—in other words, the usual poltergeist stuff—except that she was in her forties, a little older than the usual adolescent subject, and she was aware that *she* was the cause of the disturbances.

Kulagina found she could control the "force" with her will. Reportedly she made use of it by causing a toy to move closer to her while she held her grandson in her arms, or by moving a bottle of nail polish without touching it and smearing her still-wet manicure. According to a Soviet writer, she gave new meaning to the Italian dish *Salt'im boca* by first causing a piece of bread lying some distance away from her on a dinner table to approach her in jerky movements, then proceed more smoothly and rapidly as it neared the edge of the table, and finally, as she bent down close to it, to literally jump into her mouth.

Kulagina was a brave woman. She was only about 14 when Hitler's army invaded Leningrad. She, like many Russian youngsters, joined the

Red Army and endured terrible hardships, bitter cold, starvation, lack of fuel or electric power, and constant bombardment and artillery fire for three years. She served as a radio operator in a tank and became senior sergeant of the 226th tank regiment. She and her family later served in an armored train that brought provisions to the besieged city, but her fighting days were ended when she was seriously wounded by artillery fire. She would later demonstrate this courage and self-sacrifice again in her work with scientists, allowing them to place demands on her that taxed and weakened her and probably contributed to her too-early death in 1990.

Russian investigators x-rayed her before a demonstration to determine whether or not she was concealing any devices such as magnets, or if her body retained any shrapnel that might somehow be responsible for her powers. It's always amazing to me what silly things scientists will do in the face of the unknown: How they thought magnets and fragments of metal could influence the movement of objects made of plastic, cardboard, or wood boggles my mind.

Many people, Soviet and others, filmed her demonstrations, conducted in full light. In a typical session she would warm up with something easy to move such as a compass. She would gaze intently at the object, her body leaning slightly forward, hands extended over and to the sides of it, her face showing the strain of her effort. After a few passes the needle would twitch or deflect and then often do a complete revolution or whirl around. At times the entire compass, case and all, would spin as well.

She would then move other objects, pen tops standing on end, match boxes, cigarettes. She could be selective, moving only one item among several. Some targets were placed under Lucite cubes or in sealed plastic boxes. Still they would move.

The strain on her, however, was tremendous. Kulagina would perspire and her pulse would race sometimes at more than 200 beats per minute. She lost several pounds of weight at each session, her blood pressure and blood sugar level would increase, and afterwards she would experience debilitating symptoms such as pain, dizziness, confusion, and temporary inability to speak and to see—much as Kluski had experienced.

Beginning in 1968, physicists and other scientists from Moscow University and the USSR Academy of Sciences studied her repeatedly. Under strictly controlled conditions she moved objects up to about 13 ounces, or more than 3/4 of a pound, from distances of up to two meters (about 6 feet) away. By concentrating on lab scales, she could make one side move downward while loads of up to an ounce were placed on the opposite side. She could also levitate and "suspend in air" objects such as a Ping-Pong ball. One such suspension was captured on film of rather inferior quality, but reliable witnesses have confirmed that she was able to do this on many occasions. Shields of plastic, paper, lead, steel, copper, and other materials proved ineffective in blocking the force.

She was able to dramatically change the color of liquid crystal film when it was placed near the objects she was moving. A dark green spot near the corner of the film would spread, changing to dark blue, then violet, dark red, and orange. The cycle would repeat itself over and over again for sometimes more than an hour. The researcher Larissa Vilenskaya reported that when a Ping-Pong ball that Kulagina had levitated was placed in a glass containing the liquid crystal, but not touching it, the crystal would go through the cycles of color changes.

Fluorescent crystals, which usually must be exposed to a light source to glow in the dark, would luminesce after Kulagina concentrated on them. She was also successful in getting substances, which normally only begin to react at temperatures of about 158 degrees Fahrenheit, to react at room temperature.

Like the Bindelof group and Ted Serios, whose talent is described in a later chapter, she was able to affect photographic film. In Kulagina's case she would mentally "draw" figures, such as stars, circles, squares, etc. on photographic paper that had been enclosed in black envelopes. She was able to expose film shielded by 1.5 mm lead sheets and other materials used for electrical insulation.

In biological experiments she was able to create invisible barriers in plastic insect-containing cases and in glass aquariums so that the insects or fish turned and changed direction when they encountered the "psychic boundary" she imposed. When asked to suppress the vital functions of mice, she moved her hands over them and they became still, as though unconscious. When she removed her hands, they immediately returned to normal.

The public became somewhat alarmed by reports that she was able to stop a frog's heart. The cruelty of such an act was appalling but even worse, if this were true, this power could be misused to perhaps harm or kill people. What actually transpired was that Kulagina was asked to influence an isolated (surgically excised) frog's heart that had been placed in a saline solution to keep it beating, and had electrodes attached to it in order to record its activity. Generally such a heart will continue to beat for 30 to 60 minutes or more after excision. When it stops it can be reactivated by electrical stimulation.

Kulagina was asked to try to make the heart beat faster, which she did. She was then requested to stop it using her PK. About 40 seconds later the heart stopped and would not start again when they tried to activate it electrically.

From the late 1970s to 1984 physicists and electronics experts in Leningrad and Moscow studied Kulagina. According to Vilenskaya, their published report noted that her hands emitted strong electromagnetic and acoustic impulses. The latter were picked up by piezoelectric sensors and were found to be in the ultrasound range. The magnetic impulses far exceeded the intensity of the Earth's magnetic field.

She was able to psychokinetically affect a laser beam, reducing its intensity by almost 80 percent and perhaps changing the properties of gas in the vessel through which the laser beam was passing.

Vicious and defamatory accusations of fraud by papers or magazines in the U.S.S.R. could not possibly stand up to the scientific validation of Kulagina's abilities. She sued one publication for defamation and won, forcing them to print a retraction of their statements in 1988—probably a first in Soviet Russia.

Kulagina died in 1990 after many years of courageous, selfless contributions to science. Unfortunately she met not only the usual fanatical skepticism that greets anyone with powers that don't fit in with the current level of scientific knowledge, but with the suspicion and restrictions of the pre-Gorbachev Soviet regime.

Nina Kulagina, who is the best known of Russia's contemporary psychics, had a direct influence on an American woman, the subject of the next chapter.

CHAPTER 23

A MINI-KULAGINA

One of the reasons I wrote this book is to encourage individuals to test their own powers. I don't believe that ectoplasm has disappeared from the face of the earth or that materializations are no longer possible. These phenomena have just gone out of fashion—or have gone underground, traveling incognito.

The negative attitude toward physical phenomena created by the many frauds who hopped on the séance bandwagon, and by the arch skeptics who panic at the thought that their mechanistic world-view might be undermined by "things that go bump in the night," has dissuaded people from believing in the reality of these occurrences and therefore from attempting to discover if they have a talent for producing them.

Witness the case of Felicia Parise. Parise was employed as a medical technician in the Hematology Department of Maimonides Hospital in the late 1960s, at the same time that Montague Ullman (of the Bindelof group again) established the Dream Laboratory there to study telepathic dreams. She had experienced many instances of ESP in her personal life, was interested in finding out more about them, and so volunteered to be a subject in some of his dream experiments.

Wired up with electrodes to monitor her eye movements and brain waves, she slept in a soundproof, electrically shielded room. A telepathic "sender" stationed in another room attempted to influence her dreams by concentrating on a randomly selected target picture.

At her first sessions Parise didn't have much success at picking up the target picture but reported on other events that transpired while she was dreaming. She dreamed of being involved in a car accident on the Verrazano-Narrows Bridge at about the same time that a close friend had a motorcycle accident while crossing it. The following night she dreamed that her grandmother was sitting unconscious in a pool of blood. That same night the old woman fell and cut her head. She was found sitting on the floor, dazed and bleeding, but not seriously hurt.

In the early 1970s Ullman and other researchers traveled to Moscow to observe Kulagina, and Ullman brought back a film of the Russian woman moving various objects and deflecting a compass needle. He also showed slides of her work with the frog's heart. The staff, including Parise, attended the gathering at which the material was shown. Also present was a well-known professional magician, Milbourne Christopher, who had authored works on debunking fraudulent mediums. The late Charles ("Chuck") Honorton, one of the principal researchers at the lab, reported that Christopher was extremely skeptical and expressed doubt in the genuineness of Kulagina's performance.

But Felicia was totally convinced by the film and by the first-hand reports from Ullman and Dr. Stanley Krippner that Kulagina was authentic. Christopher's pronouncements and Honorton's skepticism also annoyed her. Honorton had noted that on the film all the objects moved *toward* Kulagina as though a thread or strand of hair may have drawn them.

Without telling anyone, Felicia began to practice with small, light objects. Her grandmother was gravely ill, and one evening after returning from visiting her, Felicia attempted to move a small plastic pill bottle in which she kept a small quantity of alcohol for the overnight storage of her false eyelashes, which were very much in vogue in the early 1970s. In the midst of her intense concentration, the phone rang. It was the hospital telling her to come quickly; her grandmother was dying. She reached for the bottle to put it away and, to her astonishment, it moved away from her.

For the next month or so she worked with the plastic bottle increasing the movement and her control of it. It took a great deal of effort and exertion. In the summer of 1971 she wrote to Chuck Honorton who was conducting some research at the Psychical Research Foundation in Durham, saying that she had succeeded in moving a small alcohol bottle.

On his return he visited her in her apartment, jokingly asking how much of the alcohol she had drunk before she saw the bottle move. She was not amused. She placed the bottle on the Formica countertop in her kitchen, and with her fingertips placed lightly on the edge of the counter, gazed intently at it for several minutes. Finally Honorton observed it move about two inches to the right and *away* from Parise. The direction is interesting in light of Honorton's critical observation of the Kulagina film.

Honorton picked up the bottle, examined it, and said he wanted to try it. He placed the bottle on the counter and waited for it to "slide." It didn't

—until Felicia took over and concentrated on it once more.

Honorton described how he "became very familiar" with her kitchen that evening. He tried everything he could think of to get the bottle to move, pressing on the counter from the top, from underneath, jarring it, wetting the counter surface and bottom of the bottle with some of the alcohol. Nothing.

He told me once that he used a level to see if perhaps the counter was slightly tilted. It was—the bottle had moved *up* the slant.

Honorton, by the way, underwent a profound change. Even though he had been involved in PK research for years, conducting successful tests producing small, statistically significant effects on delicate instruments, this was the first time he had actually witnessed large scale, undeniable psychokinesis. He could no longer make excuses to himself about malobservation or possible fraud, and he found as many others had before that no amount of statistical evidence has the impact of a first-hand observation. He also realized that just as he doubted others' accounts, people would doubt his, and so he set about encouraging Felicia to develop her ability and to document it on film.

She learned to deflect a compass, occasionally to a full 360 degrees. Ever the investigator, he would unexpectedly grab her hands at times, passing them over the compass to insure that she was not concealing metallic shavings underneath her fingernails. He would also watch to make sure that her head was not near the instrument when it was affected, in case she should be accused of secreting magnets in her hair or mouth.

Felicia cooperated heroically for, as in Kulagina's experience, the work was debilitating. She would tremble, perspire profusely, develop a runny nose and eyes, and have great difficulty responding coherently for several minutes following a session.

She described trying to develop a rapport with the object (a characteristic found in other successful subjects in similar psychokinetic experiments), and focusing on the object until everything else seemed to disappear. She would then "pitch," or work herself into a state of excitement to the extent that she wanted it to move "more than anything else."

In March of 1972 a film was made in Parise's apartment confirming her abilities to move objects and deflect compasses. The photographer, an amateur magician, wrote an account of the filming, verifying its accuracy and noting that the ten-minute film took about four hours to shoot because Felicia needed frequent rests. He commented on her debilitating symptoms and also on an interesting effect the experiments had on her miniature pet poodle. It seems that when Felicia concentrated on the objects, the dog would begin to whine and wouldn't stop until the experiment was over. When she succeeded in moving an object (they were on the counter, out of the dog's sight), the dog would become very agitated and make furious digging movements on the kitchen floor.

Felicia kept honing her skill and eventually managed to deflect the compass by just staring at it. In Durham, the following summer, the compass needle stayed at 15 degrees from north even when she stopped concentrating on it. When the compass was moved to another part of the room, it would again point north, but when it was returned to the area where she had concentrated on it, it resumed the deflection of 15 degrees off north and remained that way for about a half hour. A film pack that had been placed underneath the compass was found to be almost totally exposed, and others placed at various distances from the "area of concentration" were partially exposed.

The excessive strain took its toll on Felicia. She became moody and resentful of the constant testing. She was also physically exhausted from it. No one can blame her for wanting to give up the experiments. She was doing important work in leukemia research and wanted to give that her full attention rather than being a guinea pig for the parapsychologists, and so she retired her compass and plastic pill bottle.

Parise's feats were not as spectacular as Home's or Palladino's, but perhaps she was not as innately endowed as they were or had their expectations. She modeled herself after a contemporary Russian woman, doing what she knew this woman had done. Was the strain a part of the PK, or did she expect to experience it because Kulagina had done so? Was the strain on both women more intense because they worked in bright light rather than in dim light or darkness? Or perhaps because they used only their own "force" and didn't "borrow energy" from others as well? There are so many as yet unanswered questions.

CHAPTER 24

THE MAN WHO COULD PUT HIS THOUGHTS ON FILM

In Gil's story you saw how the Bindelof boys were able to affect film. Their first attempts were "shadowgraphs" or images formed as though some radiation were penetrating the photographic plate from above and leaving an imprint of what was placed over it. They segued quickly to "thought" photographs in which images similar to what they were mentally projecting showed up on the film, such as the Native American charm that appeared when Gil was thinking of American Indians. Later they were able to obtain that astounding portrait of their "mentor" by uncapping the lens for a short time and pointing the camera at the center of the table in a dark room.

There is an alcoholic, poorly educated man living somewhere in the Midwestern U.S. who for a number of years could also impress his mental images onto photographic film. His name is Ted Serios.

Serios was "discovered" in Chicago where he was working as a bellhop or elevator operator in one of the large hotels. His career began when a fellow employee, George Johannes, an amateur hypnotist, discovered that Serios was an excellent subject. Johannes knew of work that had been done years ago called "traveling clairvoyance." This technique involves inducing hypnotized subjects into mentally traveling to various places and reporting on what they observed. The procedure is akin to what is known as "remote viewing" today, but under hypnosis the entranced subjects would get startlingly accurate visions of details. The traveling clairvoyants felt and behaved as though they were actually present at the place.

In some of these experiments "guides" were suggested to accompany the subject and help him or her find whatever information was desired. Johannes knew this. He was hot to find hidden treasure so he gave the suggestion to Serios that he was in the company of Jean Lafitte, the pirate who helped the Americans against the British in the Battle of New Orleans in 1815. (Lafitte was pardoned by President James Madison, but returned to piracy and disappeared somewhere in the Caribbean.)

Lafitte "accompanied" Serios for some time "showing" him places where booty was hidden, but none of these sites turned up anything of value. The pirate gradually faded away and Johannes urged Serios to go it alone. According to Serios they were successful in finding "treasure" in the Chicago area, which turned out to be very small amounts of money, sometimes only loose change. Once he detected a buried cache of several hundred dollars, but by the time they got to the vaguely perceived spot, a group of workmen who had been digging in the area had stumbled upon the money.

The idea occurred to Johannes that if Serios could somehow project the images he was getting onto film, the details might help them find the exact spot more quickly. He gave Serios a sealed camera and told him to go home and work on it. When the film was sent out for developing, it was returned with a couple of pictures on it. Serios suspected that Johannes had played a trick on him, so he went out and bought his own camera. He began by pointing it at a blank wall from a few feet away. When Serios began to get "impossible" pictures, he began to think that perhaps he was unknowingly walking and taking pictures in his sleep. He had himself locked in his room at night, but the pictures appeared anyway.

These initial experiments were done with an ordinary camera and film. He finally bought himself a Polaroid camera and started working day and night, occasionally getting "hits." He continued these exhausting experiments for many months but came up empty in the treasure department. Instead he became a nervous wreck and so run down that he was forced to leave his job. When he attempted to explain to others what he was doing, he was ridiculed and told to see a psychiatrist. So he did.

The analyst hypnotized Serios and told him it was all a dream and to forget all about these cockeyed pictures. The therapy worked. Serios destroyed about 300 pictures and apologized to friends and family for his wild and weird actions. He was convinced that he had been under some strange delusion. But after a year or so, he began to wonder again about the pictures.

He visited another hypnotherapist. The man had to take a phone call and Serios had to leave the office and wait in the reception room. Upon returning he showed the hypnotist six photos of India that he had shot while waiting. The receptionist verified that he had done nothing but point the Polaroid camera at the wall and shoot.

The hypnotist began a series of sessions with Serios (at his usual fee) in which Serios produced numerous pictures. The hypnotist took charge of them so that Serios would not destroy them if he had another episode of thinking he was a fake. This therapist suggested that Serios point the camera at himself, which became his standard procedure from that point on. More importantly, hypnosis lost its effect on Serios during this time and he could only produce pictures in his waking state.

Serios tried to find scientists who would verify his work but didn't meet with success until he was brought to the attention of Jule Eisenbud, M.D., a Denver psychiatrist originally from New York who was interested in and knowledgeable about "paranormal" phenomena. Great credit must to given to Eisenbud not only for the intelligence with which he pursued the study of Serios's ability but also for his patience and perseverance. Serios was not at all easy to work with. He was more often than not drunk, or on his way to being drunk. He would disappear without warning especially when he felt pressured. He'd sometimes participate in sessions only once or twice a week, claiming that the effort was so great that it caused him to cough up blood or bleed from the rectum—though Eisenbud never saw any blood. Eisenbud also found very soon that some colleagues began to shun him because of his experiments.

Serios came to Jule Eisenbud's attention through the efforts of Curtis Fuller, then owner and editor of *Fate* magazine. Fuller had published an article by Pauline Oehler, at that time vice-president of the Illinois Society for Psychic Research, detailing their tests with this unemployed bellhop in his forties who seemed to be able to project mental images of buildings on to Polaroid film by staring intently into the lens. Several examples of these photos were enclosed showing blurry but identifiable images of famous buildings including the portico of the Chicago Museum of Natural History, which had appeared in a session attended by one of the museum's paleontologists. Mrs. Oehler reported that a number of scientists, photographers and other observers who participated in these tests over a period of months found the conditions adequate to rule out fraud. The tests were carried out in full light with cameras and film supplied by the examiners who were able to inspect the equipment and Serios's person at any time.

Eisenbud initially rejected the invitation thinking that there was probably something fishy going on and reasoning that if the guy was genuine he would have heard of him from fellow parapsychologists. After a few more pleas by Fuller and others to investigate the case, Eisenbud finally promised he would stop in Chicago on his way back to Denver from a lecture trip to a Midwestern university. He invited his young cousin Jonathan, a college student who had done some experiments in telepathy and clairvoyance, to meet him in Chicago and assist him in examining Serios.

Just before leaving Denver, Eisenbud was warned about Ted's alcohol problem and that he might "fail to keep appointments." But Serios met them and Mrs. Freda Morris, a Ph.D. candidate who had been investigating Serios's phenomena, in a Chicago hotel.

After a few double scotches and some nervous preliminary shots, with camera and film—and booze--supplied by Eisenbud, Serios produced some "blackies," or photos looking like they had not been exposed at all. He would become agitated, his pulse rate would increase, his body wracked by tension as he sat cross-legged and pointed the camera at his face. After the first two failed attempts he asked if he might use his "gismo," a hollow plastic tube, which he would hold over the camera lens. Eisenbud, of course, examined the device carefully. Later this gismo became the object of accusations of fraud by professional skeptics, even though it wasn't always used. Gismos made of rolled photo paper were made on the spot by investigators who took all sorts of precautions to insure that no trickery was possible including stringing the gismo on a cord to make a 2-foot long loop that one scientist wore around his neck. He had to stay very close to Serios who needed to reach over to grab the gismo when he wanted to use it.

But finally, after about 2 hours of sporadic attempts, at Eisenbud's suggestion they put aside the hidden targets (photos in opaque envelopes) that he had brought. Serios then produced a blurry, skewed image of a structure that Mrs. Morris identified as the Chicago water tower. After another lull of a half-hour or so Serios said he had a hunch that he would produce something meaningful to both Jon and Jule. When he thought his heart was pounding at a significant rate, one of the signs that he was ready, he triggered the camera. At first the result looked like another blackie but Jon noticed something in the right hand corner that might have been part of a structure with a couple of windows. Serios declared that he was "hot" and wanted to shoot again. This time he produced a murky photograph of a building on whose marquee was an illuminated sign reading, "STEVENS." The building was a hotel that would become the Chicago Hilton. Jon and Mrs. Morris excitedly urged Serios to shoot some more but Eisenbud called a halt to the proceedings when he discovered that Ted's pulse rate was 132 and "pounding like an angry surf."

The name "STEVENS," Eisenbud revealed later, did have some meaning for him. On his way to Chicago earlier that day he was extremely upset by the negative response he received to his lecture at the university and especially by the criticisms of a "Dr. Stephens."

Eisenbud arranged to have Serios come to Denver where he could enlist the aid of his many professional friends and colleagues—at least those who didn't turn their backs on this embarrassingly crazy man—to study and document his unusual powers. They found that Serios worked best when demonstrating in their homes, one-to-one so to speak, rather than in front of a formidable group of scientists whose credentials probably intimidated him. And as in many cases of poltergeists or psychokinetic (PK) phenomena, he sometimes needed to get angry and/or frustrated to perform.

For instance, in the session mentioned above in which the investigator, Dean Conger of the Medical School at the University of Colorado wore the gismo around his neck, Serios was unable to produce anything for hours. Finally, "drunk as a skunk" and acting obnoxiously, Serios became furious because Jule wouldn't give him any more to drink and pushed him into his chair when Serios lunged for the bottle. Eisenbud suggested that they quit, at which point Serios exploded, "Goddammit, gimme the camera! I'll show you I can get one." He ordered Dr. Conger to put his hand over his own and hold the gismo. Serios held the tube with two fingers and Conger put his palm flat over it. Serios shot and exclaimed, "There, put that in your pipe and smoke it!"

What emerged was a photo of a double-decker bus. The rather fuzzy, but clearly recognizable vehicle is bathed in a grainy striated or striped pool of light against a black background. It is at about a 45-degree angle "exiting" the upper right-hand corner of the photo. The dumbfounded witnesses signed the print on the reverse side. Jule insisted that witnesses do this before the photo was out of their sight to prove that this was the actual print they removed from the camera and that no substitutions had been made.

Eisenbud always "assumed" that Serios was cheating and took precautions. For example, when it occurred to him that Serios might conceivably be flipping the time exposure knob as he handled the camera,

Eisenbud experimented and found he could approximate a "whitey" or photo that looked as though it was totally exposed, by doing so. Thereafter he taped down this knob. Serios had no trouble producing the whities with this new control. Some of them were produced with Serios holding the gismo over the camera lens and witnesses' palms placed over it, blocking any light from being admitted into the camera. Under normal circumstances a whitey would be the last thing you would expect from such a situation.

I find fascinating the psychological implications of Serios's development. He was limited by what he believed he could not do, even if the limitations made no sense. Later you will read about another subject with whom I worked who had many of these same psychological blocks and how we worked through most of them over a period of 18 months. As I reread Jule Eisenbud's account of his work with Serios, I was struck by the similarities of how these two men's beliefs affected what they could or couldn't accomplish. I believe the Bindelof boys, typical of teenagers, just accepted that if they worked at whatever it was they wanted to accomplish it would happen. It helped that some of them believed that "The Dr." was accomplishing these feats, not them. The belief that otherworldly spirits are responsible for these mind-boggling phenomena takes the burden off the gifted living persons who are most likely producing them. Perhaps that is why some of the séances of the nineteenth century produced such strong effects. Spirits, after all, weren't bound by earthly constraints and could do anything.

The very earthy Serios hated confinement of any sort. He needed to be free in every way, from not wearing belts or ties or even shoelaces at times, to taking off and getting dead drunk when the spirit (not spirits) moved him. For a while he had difficulty producing anything other than blackies or whities, which Eisenbud realized was probably due to his being confined, for control purposes, in a "monkey suit," which was tightly buttoned at the neck and wrists. A breakthrough came, as I mentioned earlier, when he complained about having to perform in the auditorium with the examining committee and was allowed to "take them on one by one" in their individual homes. Once they did this and removed the restrictions of randomly numbered lists and created a more casual, though of course still vigilant, ambience, Serios started to produce again.

He also had to feel free to come and go as he pleased, escaping back to his old haunts in Chicago, or prowling around bars and other rather disreputable places and getting into drunken brawls. He wanted to be boss,

Thought photograph of a double-decker bus by Ted Serios.
Source: The World of Ted Serios.

master of himself, and Eisenbud was intelligent enough to let him believe that he was in control.

We're told that he loved working with kids around. The children of one of the investigators provided the ideal audience. They would beg to hold the camera and/or the gismo, would shriek uninhibitedly in excitement when he got an image, and moan in disappointment when the pictures were blurred or began to fade. They mirrored his feelings and were totally accepting of him, uncritical of his person and his ability.

Because of the relaxed conditions, the invariably drunk Serios was able to become an "impresario," ordering everyone about and improvising experiments with cameras at a distance or at strange angles. He'd become frenzied and order cameras to be handed to him in rapid succession. The less they tried to control him the better the results; being dominant was a position his ego craved. Not that the observers were less watchful; Eisenbud would "graciously accord" control of certain conditions to Serios, which led him to comment: "Just so long as we know who's boss around here."

In these tests, by the way, witnesses often provided their own cameras and film and when they used cameras supplied by Eisenbud, they were allowed to inspect them before the sessions and to impound them afterwards for further inspection. Participants also made open paper gismos on the spot. These were always subject to inspection and often signed by the witnesses to avoid changes or duplication.

Each camera also produced control shots. The Polaroid prints were pulled and developed only by Eisenbud or observers in the presence of witnesses who were then requested to sign or initial any print that looked interesting before it left their sight. Chicago magician and slight-of-hand expert Lee Wayne Phillips stated in writing that he was completely satisfied that no trickery of any kind was used in the May 1963 session he observed.

For about a year, from March 1965 to May 1966, during a "hot" streak of sessions, Serios began moving away from the camera. He first asked others to trigger it while he held it, then asked them to hold the gismo and trigger it while he held it, and finally gave up the camera entirely. From a distance of only a few inches he gradually moved farther away so that finally the camera was 10 to 15 feet and more away from him. Some 30-40 pictures were made at various distances from Serios with other people holding the cameras and gismos. The greatest distance was attained in a hospital corridor with Serios some 66 feet away from the camera; the image was a strange one but certainly not the expected blackie that should have resulted, given the way the camera was positioned.

The most impressive session, I feel, was not only at a distance but also through a physical barrier. It occurred in a laboratory where physicist James A. Hurry had provided a Faraday cage, a small, electrically shielded room wrapped in fine mesh wire that screens out radio and radar waves. Hurry also provided the film and camera and arranged and supervised the test conditions. Serios was in the cage with one gismo, which Hurry examined and found unsuspicious. Hurry, Eisenbud, and two other observers were outside the cage with cameras and another gismo. The cameras were at least one foot from the cage. With Eisenbud holding the camera and Hurry holding the second gismo outside of the closed door of the cage, an extraordinary print was produced.

This picture clearly demonstrates that Serios's unconscious affected the images he produced. The test took place in February on Washington's Birthday. The hidden target, which Hurry had chosen, was of isochromatic stress lines, two circles or swirls of lines that resemble some abstract modern art. The image that Serios produced looked nothing like the target. It contains what looks like men in military uniform standing in a row facing in one direction. Afterwards, when he saw the target, Serios said it looked like two big "eyes looking at a line of people." You can easily see how his unconscious, knowing that it was a national holiday, could make the association and translate those "eyes" into military men watching a parade.

The experiments continued with Serios gradually expanding his repertoire of effects. At the home of Dr. L.B. Hall, Dr. Hall's son was asked to take the camera and gismo and first try a shot with the winklight (flash) disconnected. A blackie resulted, which was not wholly unusual. But with the next shot Serios, who was seated in a corner of the living room, asked him to take the camera into an adjoining study behind a vestibule wall. He also asked Hall's wife to put her hand over the lens. Serios held an empty camera in his lap and when he triggered the dummy, he yelled "now," and the son triggered the loaded camera. The print that emerged startled them all. It was a blurred image of Dr. Hall standing in the corner of the living room near where Eisenbud had been positioned at the moment of the shot. No one remembered Dr. Hall even being in that particular part of the room that evening. Eisenbud and Dr. Hall attempted to duplicate the photo by various means but could not succeed in creating the texture, distortion, geometry, or lighting of the mental image.

Later, with Serios still in the living room chair, and again using a dummy camera, Dr. Hall stood in his unlit study again behind the vestibule wall and aimed his loaded camera at a typewriter a few inches away from him. The resulting image is of a shelf of books, like many of Serios's images at an angle, in the darkened upper part of the photo. The bottom quarter or so of the shot is white.

There are about 13 or so of these kinds of "dislocations" where the camera would be pointed at Serios or at some particular area. A totally different area of the room would appear, sometimes with various members of the group in shadowy or blurry images in positions they had not occupied before.

Some photos resemble a few the Bindelof boys managed to obtain in which non-visible objects or figures appear in the room. Eisenbud and the others attempted to duplicate these pictures with multiple exposures but were unsuccessful. Even looking at the images reproduced in the book, which Eisenbud once told me were never as clear as the originals, you can easily see the differences in quality between Serios's productions and the attempted reconstructions.

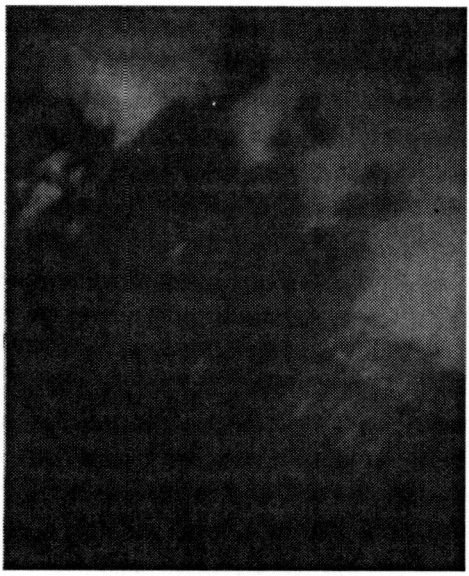

Thought photograph of men watching a parade by Ted Serios.
Source: The World of Ted Serios

Target picture. Source: The World of Ted Serios

On another occasion a few days later Serios, again improvising, suggested that they use three loaded cameras simultaneously. Serios sat on a couch pointing one camera at himself. Dr. Aaron Paley, whose home they were in, and Dr. Henry Frey stood about three feet in front of Serios pointing their cameras at him. Between them was Dr. Johann Marx, who put the palms of his hands over the two gismos held by the other two men in front of the lenses of their cameras. Serios then signaled everyone to shoot. (This whole procedure was recorded, by the way, on movie film by the medical school's Chief of Audio-Visual Education.) Serios's image looks somewhat like the top of a house roof with part of the walls and perhaps a couple of windows. Dr. Paley got what was expected—a blackie. But out of Dr. Frey's camera came a strange montage of blurry-edged images. There is Dr. Paleys' son in a place where he hadn't been just prior to the shot and at his left what looks like a man's arm or arms encircling the air. The lower half of someone's face is seen under the top arm. Below this, where a bookshelf should have been, is a blurred image of an abstract painting that was hanging on a wall at the opposite end of the room. Again they tried to reconstruct the picture through multiple exposures but when you compare the two there is a world of difference in the images, quality, and texture of the photos. The fake *looks* like a double exposure, with clean lines, proportions etc. It is very unlike the Serios thought photograph, which has a distinctly surreal quality.

Serios also began drawing sketches of hidden target pictures before attempting to reproduce them on film. Some of these telepathically perceived drawings are interesting not only for their sometimes striking resemblance to the target, but also for their psychological importance. A New York psychologist once chose a picture of the Hall of Mirrors at Versailles as a target. After choosing the picture, while alone in a room about 30 feet away from where Serios and Eisenbud were, she joined them. Serios said he was confused because he was getting *two* kinds of images. He then rapidly sketched a domed, pillared building but said he also "saw" sails. He then drew the sails of a sailboat. They set to work with the camera and after warming up with a "normal" shot and several blackies, Serios began producing images with the two themes: a domed, pillared building resembling Grant's Tomb and what seemed to be a skiff with sails down on a river.

When you look at the target picture what you see is the long, arcade-like interior of the domed room. Its long, vertical, arched mirrors are separated by panels, which do look somewhat like columns. Serios, obviously expecting a building as a target, thought he was perceiving the *outside* of the building with a dome and pillars and produced this in both his drawings and thought photos. Interestingly his unconscious mind was a little more accurate than his conscious perception, because the photo image contains rounded arches between the columns that are almost identical to the mirrors in the target picture. The "sails," Eisenbud realized, were a distortion of the name "Versailles," which to a poorly educated man like Serios would seem to be pronounced "ver-sails."

Eisenbud adds in a footnote that someone identified the building in Serios's thought photograph as the Four Courts Building in Dublin and the river scenes as resembling portions of the Liffey River, which runs past it. Why Serios's unconscious selected these scenes is a mystery. Did his unconscious mind scan his memory and/or the collective unconscious world-database as Edgar Cayce did, to come up with this combination of images resembling his telepathic or clairvoyant "reading" of the target? And for that matter, where did Gil Roller and the boys get the face of Dr. Bindelof? The reach of the unconscious mind seems limitless and the images it selects seem to involve many different psychological factors.

In many cases the experimenters choose targets that may not be interesting or may just not appeal to the psychic subject. In 1966 an experiment was conducted to see if Serios could get images while inside a shielded X-ray room. They also had him shooting through a lead-impregnated glass window onto film and cameras held outside the "tank."

One of the investigators had brought a target picture depicting what looked like a medieval tower overlooking a bridge. In a river in the foreground, about to pass under the bridge, was a man in a canoe. The bottom half of the picture, containing the bridge and canoe, was the actual target. Serios was shown only the top half, the tower. Before the session, however, Serios had opened a box of chocolates that his mother had sent him. Atop the candy was a card with daisy-like flowers on it. Serios stated confidently that the target he would later see would look something like the card.

Along with the target picture, the investigator had brought a painting for Eisenbud to see. The painting had nothing to do with the experiment. He wanted Eisenbud's opinion, as an analyst, on its content. Part of this picture had daisy-like flowers on it, which was rather similar to Serios's card.

Versailles photos and drawings. Source: The World of Ted Serios

Some of the images produced by Serios that evening are large daisy-like shapes. While Eisenbud makes the observation that a few of the petals have a canoe-like shape and could easily be, therefore, a combining of the two images—the daisies and the target—it was obviously the flowers that were foremost in Serios's mind. This kind of "displacement" is fairly common in psi experiments.

Psychic photography has been around almost as long as photography itself. There have been many cases of "spirits" showing up next to or behind the portraits of living people. These spawned the inevitable frauds, of which there were plenty and which gave psychic photography a bad odor, in much the same way as charlatans contributed to the decline of séances.

The most famous of these "spirit" photos is of course that of Abraham Lincoln. My guess is that Lincoln and his wife were quite talented psychically. We know that they held séances in the White House and there is the famous incidence of Lincoln's precognitive dream about his own death. Less well known is the story of the Lincoln photo.

Mrs. Lincoln, garbed in "widow's weeds" and heavily veiled, appeared at a photographer's studio unannounced, requesting that her portrait be taken. She would not remove the veil until the photographer, a Mr. Mumler, was ready. She gave her name as "Mrs. Lindall," but when Mumler developed the picture he realized who she really was because standing behind her, his hands on her shoulders, looking down on her with a pleasant smile was the late president. There is some controversy regarding Mumler so I can't say for sure that this was not fraud. However, Eisenbud says that in the "spirit photo," Mr. Lincoln appears in his "Long Johns"—and I hardly think he would have posed in such a manner while he was alive.

Even lesser known was a Japanese counterpart of Jule Eisenbud's named Tomokichi Fukurai, a professor at the Imperial University of Tokyo at the beginning of the 20th century. While Fukurai was investigating two women subjects who seemed to be telepathic or clairvoyant, he accidentally discovered that a photographic plate had somehow been imprinted with the image of a (Japanese) calligraphic character. He assumed it was a result of the subject's psychic concentration and began a series of experiments, including one in which the sensitive was directed to mentally imprint a Japanese symbol on a photographic plate sandwiched in between two others. After many successful experiments with a variety of subjects, he published his work in 1913. It was also published in English as *Clairvoyance and Thoughtography* in 1931. This was the first time this term was used and underscores Fukurai's contention that these were not spirit photographs but resulted from the minds of the subjects.

Predictably, Fukurai was severely attacked. Despite his integrity and the innocence of his subjects, he resigned from the University. One of the subjects with whom he worked died from "influenza"; the other committed suicide.

Felicia Scatcherd, a British spiritualist, mentally imprinted written messages and symbolic drawings on unopened packs of photo plates. She called them "skotographs," Greek for "dark writing." And in 1911 Ochorowicz, whom you may remember from the "Katie King" investigation, working with another potent medium, Stanislawa Tomczyk (who later married psychical researcher Everard Fielding), obtained "psychographs" of "etheric hands" on sensitive film. The images were larger than either his or the medium's hands and one was wearing "the shadow" of Stanislawa's ring. Ochorowicz picked up a silver thimble of hers and put it on his own finger. The medium mused, "Perhaps the thimble will pass to my hand." They repeated the experiment with her (unadorned) hand at least a foot away from the plate. The developed image shows four fingers; on one is a thimble.

Other experiments in thoughtography were carried out in America and France in the first two decades of the century but then because of the fakes that entered the business, psychic photography fell into disrepute and disappeared from references for the next thirty or so years.

I should mention one similarity in the photos that Fukurai and Ted Serios produced—their graininess or striation. These grainy lines that appear in the background of the Japanese pictures and in some of the eerie pools of light in the Serios pictures also showed up in another source. Eisenbud found a picture in *Modern Psychical Phenomena* published in 1919 and written by the psychical researcher, Hereward Carrington, which looks like a burst of light against a dark background. Radiating from this light burst are the same types of grainy striations found in Serios's and Fukurai's pictures. Unfortunately there is no information given as to the picture's origin. Its caption reads: "Vital radiations' issuing from the human body and impressing (directly) a photographic plate."

Recently I managed to get a clear print of Dr. Bindelof's picture—I had seen only poor copies previously—and it was a revelation. Not only does the picture have the same sort of fuzzy outlines as the Serios photos, but to the left of Bindelof's face is a patch of graininess very similar to these other psychic photos. (See pages 184 and 185.)

Serios was also able to project his thought images onto videotape. In 1967 an experiment was conducted at the TV studio of the University of Denver Mass Communications Center to see if he could do this. The number and caliber of the witnesses and assistants in attendance was impressive. There were not only photographers and technicians but also professors of Electrical Engineering and Senior Research Engineers from the Denver Research Institute, and a Special Consultant to the Institute. They participated as well as observed, making gismos out of paper on the spot, holding them, holding cameras, and observing and filming Ted's movements.

Serios, supplied with quarts of beer, got many blackies and some unidentified structures on the still Polaroid cameras. He would occasionally rise from his chair and approach the video camera, hold a gismo up to the lens, and go through his procedure of working up energy and then, with an explosive gesture and sound, forcefully project his will at the camera. He kept looking at the monitor, which was a few feet away from the camera. Three fleeting images were imprinted on the video film, but these were only discovered afterwards when the film was replayed and scrutinized.

A second session, about two weeks later, this time at the studios of NBC affiliate KOA-TV, produced even better results. This session was also attended by the station manager, professional cameramen, and reporters from the station and from the *Denver Post*. They worked from 2:40 p.m. until 5:30 p.m., when they took a dinner break and got some coffee and fresh air into Ted who by this time had imbibed several quarts of beer. They resumed at 7:00 p.m. At times, before and after the break, Serios would get up, approach the video camera and go into his routine, eventually exploding with a grunt or a Karate-like yell. Sometimes he'd demand, "Well, did ya see anything?" If not, he'd stomp back to his chair in disgust, muttering, and a couple of times flinging his gismo to the floor.

About 9:00 p.m., after the experiment had more or less ended, one of the attendees who had brought an envelope containing hidden target pictures opened them to reveal one of old-fashioned trains and another of a row of parked cars. The technicians were starting to gather up their equipment before leaving when Ted went over for one last try declaring, "I'll put something on this thing if it kills me." This time there were flashes of something on the monitor. When they replayed it, they found images similar to some that had appeared on the Polaroid film but rotated about 90 degrees. They are portions of a wheeled vehicle (auto or train?) with part of a trolley bus moving in from the left side and some other images that had appeared earlier on Polaroid.

In a little more than a minute of elapsed time there are 11 bursts of imagery lasting from 2 frames or 1/12 of a second, to a complete cycle of 61 frames, or about 2 ½ seconds. One image might change to another during a given burst, or at times a wisp of an image might appear fleetingly. In viewing the film strip you can see Serios's face through the gismo—it's not round because he's squeezing it—as he begins to grimace with effort, then only part of one eye is visible as the image moves into the frame. As the image recedes or fades you start to see, little by little, part of his face reemerge.

Eventually his abilities began to fade. There were long sessions in which nothing was produced but whities or blackies. Serios had always warned Eisenbud that one day the curtain would come down, "Ker-boom! That's

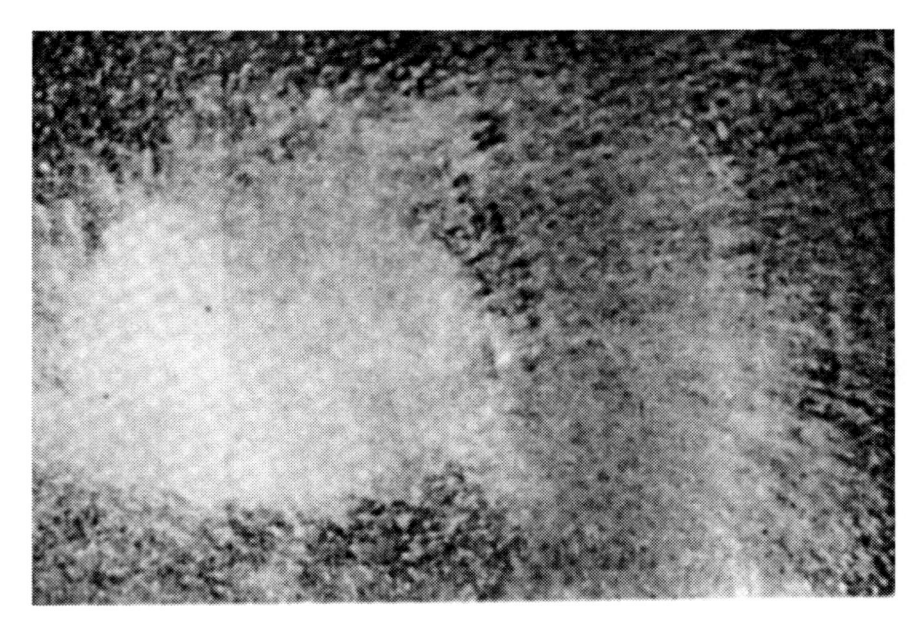

"Vital Radiations"

Fukurai's subject's grainy production. Source: The World of Ted Serios

Thought photograph of Trajan's Column by Ted Serios. Source: The World of Ted Serios

Bindelof "portrait."

all brother." In a session on June 15, 1967, Serios, frustrated because he kept getting blackies when he felt he should be producing pictures, exploded. He demanded that the Swedish journalist who was holding the camera turn it around so that the back was facing him. He smashed his fist down on it with all his might and exclaimed, "Develop *that*, now!" The picture that emerged is of drapes or curtains. Later Eisenbud realized that the image signified "The End," at least for a long while. He never managed to produce pictures under test conditions again.

Of course, after Eisenbud's book came out, there were "investigations" by the professional skeptics and a series of derogatory "debunking" articles, which I will not dignify by mentioning here. They did accomplish their objective; they threw doubt on the validity of the Serios-Eisenbud work, but no magician has been able to duplicate the pictures produced by Serios under the same, or any other, conditions.

I have only presented a small portion of the fascinating material reported on by Eisenbud here, but I heartily recommend that you read *The World of Ted Serios* to get a more complete picture—no pun intended—of the tremendous work done by both these remarkable men, Ted Serios and Dr. Jule Eisenbud.

Jule Eisenbud passed away on March 10, 1999, at the age of 90. My friend, Stephen Braude, a close friend of the Eisenbuds, wrote an obituary for *The New York Times* stating that the Serios work was sound and that no one had been able to reproduce the photos Serios got even under their own conditions. But the published obituary gave the impression that the work was spurious. They quoted a skeptic who reviewed the Serios book when it first appeared stating that Eisenbud had "little notion of what experiments" were. They also quoted the present director of the American Society for Psychical Research only as saying that his professional standing helped shield him from the sting of such criticism. As Stephen Braude said to me, Eisenbud met the same treatment in death that he had received in life.

Since this book is primarily about "table tilting," I am going to end this chapter with a quote from a biographical chapter Eisenbud wrote for my first book, *Men and Women of Parapsychology: Personal Reflections*, published in 1987, about his own experience with séance phenomena:

> About this time [early 1940s] I had my own first encounter with homegrown

psychokinesis. A friend of mine, a young British composer, and I managed to get invited to a weekly table-turning session held by three elderly dowagers. In the substreet dining level of an East Side brownstone we all sat around a heavy card table which within minutes took on a personality of its own and soon began wild gyrations and movements back and forth across the length and width of the room, often backing one or another of us into a corner before dashing off to harass someone else. There was no doubt in my mind that the good dowagers started things off with almost deliberate muscular movements on their own part but, as far as I could see, once the table got fired up and began madly careening about, sometimes in response to a request for it to answer a question with some specified movement, there was no possibility at all that muscular aid on the part of any of the participants, who were doing their best just to hold a finger or two lightly on the table as it skidded across the bare floor, and scrambling furiously to keep up with it, could have been responsible for what took place.

The weekly meetings ended for the season after one session at the close of which the table, seemingly possessed by a stamping, whirling, rushing will of its own, led us out the door and up the steps and into the street and the startled gaze of a couple of dumbly uncomprehending passersby. I recall that we all, seemingly with one mind, abandoned the table frenziedly at this point and rushed back into the house and hopeful anonymity. I don't recall whether the now completely inert table was later retrieved or not, but I presume that it was. Curiously, my composer friend, his girl friend, and I were able to get very much the same results in later sessions held in the large living room of my own apartment, with my wife simply looking on but, for some reason, taking no part. We discontinued these sessions after only two or three go-arounds because it was always pretty much the same thing. (How blasé can one get?)

CHAPTER 25

BREAKING MENTAL BARRIERS

Serios, with Eisenbud's help, was able to psychologically wean himself away from the loaded camera and, at times, the gismo. However, even though he got some clearly paranormal pictures with investigators' palms covering the gismo's opening, Ted wasn't able to get a successful image when masking tape covered the gismo. Triggering the camera at the precise moment, in fact, using a camera at all was probably also a psychological "crutch." It was how he *thought* he had to work. It was more a ritual that he came to rely on than a necessary part of producing the phenomena. He believed he needed these props to succeed. Eisenbud confessed that Serios was not able to spend time on developing new techniques; he had made a promising start with an unopened film pack for instance, but that approach was not pursued. Eisenbud regarded Serios's dependence on these crutches as no more significant than an athlete's dependence on a particular bat, club, or racquet.

When Serios's powers were waning, Eisenbud tells us, they did some sessions at distances of several feet and, at Ted's suggestion, at several miles, from the camera with experimenters getting the signal to shoot over the telephone. At the closer distances Serios would often require the person holding the camera and the gismo to give the tube a slight squeeze when he gave the signal to shoot. Sometimes, when the camera was only a few feet away from him, he would throw the gismo to a third person whom he would order to provide the needed squeeze.

Eisenbud also reported in *The Journal of the American Society for Psychical Research* that in one long-distance experiment, when Serios was five miles away from the camera, Ted got only blackies, but he seemed to have gotten them this time by PK-ing the camera's mechanism, that is by psychokinetically jamming the shutter. This incident especially reminded me of another subject that Gil Roller and I worked with over a period of almost two years who also affected cameras.

Nick, a person of average intelligence but quite gifted psychically, was nervous about people taking his picture. A few times he seemed to cause the shutter to jam or to prevent the flash from working when he didn't want to be photographed. As I mentioned in an earlier chapter, he once reluctantly allowed a woman to whom he was attracted to take his picture The camera functioned normally and his image was clear on the two shots she took of him, but a small "lightning flash" of static electricity appeared near the bottom of each of his pictures. All the other pictures on that roll of film were normal in appearance and a photographic expert at Kodak who examined the prints could find no explanation for the anomalous effects. (Years later I told Jule Eisenbud about these photos and he said that he had seen similar effects produced by other subjects.)

I met Nick in 1970. We were both teachers at the same school. He was a rather unusual character but not one that I liked very much at first. Two years later, when I was going through some difficult emotional times, we began to speak about personal things and I discovered that he seemed to have psychic abilities. I encouraged him to learn more about his gifts, recommending books and journals and urging him to educate himself and to develop his talent. We began to see each other out of school and because of our common interests grew closer. In the summer of 1973 Nick moved in with me and in September of that year we enrolled in two courses at the New School for Social Research in Manhattan. One was an Experimental Parapsychology course taught by Bob Brier, who is now a well-known Egyptologist. The other course, entitled "Paramechanics," was taught by Gilbert Roller. It was in Gil Roller's class that the radio experiment began.

The experiment was Gil's idea and it took place long after the Bindelof group had broken up. He was working with a "table tilting" group in New York's Hudson Valley near his weekend house, getting raps and minor phenomena. As part of these sittings he had experimented with a small AM transistor radio. The radio would be placed in the center of a table around which they were sitting. It was tuned between stations or at the end of the band so that it emitted only a soft hiss with, at times, occasional static.

The group discovered that if they "counted down" aloud from ten to four, to establish a rhythm, then mentally continued on to zero, and on "zero" together directed their mental energies toward the radio, it would often emit a loud "click" or "pop."

Gil told us about the experiment in class and decided to have his students try it. Since the class was rather large, we broke into two groups.

We discovered that when Nick was in the group, the radio would give a loud, sharp "pop," quite distinct from ordinary static. When he wasn't in the circle, the sound wouldn't occur.

At the next class meeting the following week, Nick, who was very excited with the results, felt that he could generate the sound by himself. He placed his hand over the radio, at a distance of a few inches, and it began to make the popping or clicking sounds. When he removed his hand, the sound would stop. I should emphasize that these weren't random sounds, but were of an extremely sharp, precise nature, quite distinct and different from background noise. It sounded something like popcorn exploding in random bursts.

We continued the experiment on a weekly basis, trying to figure out if the phenomenon was electromagnetic in nature or if he was affecting some physical mechanism in the radio. We never found out, although there was no great effort made to consult electronics experts who might have been able to give useful information on the technical aspects.

At first the radio would only respond if Nick held his hand directly over it. If another person's hand, or even a thin sheet of paper were placed between his hand and the radio, the sounds would cease. However, sometimes he'd stand behind someone and put his hand behind this person's head or neck and ask them to place their hand over the radio. Then the thing would "perform" as though Nick's hand was directly over it. This, of course, made no sense to me, but this is what he *thought* he was doing—sending "energy" through the other person. It was the first mental crutch I noticed.

Nick also felt that he was "taking energy" from the group members. He would sometimes walk behind people, holding his palm near them while extending the other hand toward the radio. When he was near members he liked or felt had a great deal of "energy," the signals (pops) would become louder and/or faster.

As is the case with most psychic phenomena, we found that the experiment didn't always work. In early February 1974, for instance, Nick visited Gil's new class to demonstrate his talent but was unable to do so. He attributed his failure to his feelings of nervousness and lack of confidence with a new, and perhaps skeptical, group. His second attempt with this same group was successful; he was able to get the radio going at once. This time he was more relaxed and comfortable with the group members. He felt he had developed a rapport with them at the last meeting by giving some of them psychic readings and discussing the experiment.

Two nights later we met at the Manhattan apartment of a woman named Joan who had been a student in Gil's first class and had become interested in the experiment. She was also anxious to be healed of a physical condition she had before we met and hoped that Nick could do some psychic healing on her as he thought he could. He was not very effective with the radio at first and soon asked Joan's mother, whom he felt "had very little energy," and Joan's male friend, Eric, to leave the circle temporarily. He said he felt a "negative force" from Eric that he attributed later, in private, to jealousy. He claimed that the feeling that he had to "perform" was inhibiting him as well.

As everyone became more relaxed, the sounds from the two transistor radios we were using that night became louder. We found that he could start and stop the sounds at will. With his hand placed over the radio(s) he would say "start" and the clicks would begin, "stop" and they would cease. He seemed to be completely in control of the sounds.

Still, if someone covered the radio with their hand or a thin sheet of paper, the sounds would stop. Again this made no sense to me and I suspected that it was a psychological rather than a physical barrier that was stopping the sounds.

At the end of March we met at the Rollers' Manhattan apartment, a small penthouse atop the Des Artistes building on 67th Street and Central Park West. This session was important not because of its success but for its failure to produce results. A guest observer that evening was Montague Ullman of the Bindelof group. Now a well-known psychiatrist and parapsychologist it's possible that even though Ullman was receptive to the experiment, he intimidated Nick. It's possible that Nick was picking up some negativity from him or that this distinguished older man may have represented a father or authority figure to Nick. Nick had trouble with authority figures so it's more than likely that Ullman's presence put the kibosh on the first performance. At a second meeting with Ullman, the radio worked like the proverbial charm and even seemed to monitor Ullman's heartbeats.

It might be interesting to note that in the 18 or so months that we conducted the experiment, Nick was never able to get the radio to click in the presence of his family. We tried it several times in his parents' home, and although he seemed to be eager to perform for them, the radio remained resolutely silent.

Nick's initial outward confidence probably hid his deeply seated feelings of inferiority or insecurity. I think perhaps he had these traits in common with Ted Serios. Like Ted, Nick was a "charmer," too. He delighted in amusing groups of people with his stories, which were often gross exaggerations of fact or complete fabrications. He was especially charming with women.

Perhaps they both had a need to feel above the laws of society—and of physics, as we know it.

But back to my tale: At subsequent successful sessions with Gil's classes we gradually weaned Nick away from the radio so that now he could get it to click while he was standing outside the circle and didn't need to hold his hand over it. He moved around the room, standing behind the group members who usually sat in a circle around the table on which the radio was placed.

In June 1974, we held a session at the Rollers' Hudson Valley home. Nick spent the day relaxing next to the small waterfalls and stream behind the house and walking through their densely wooded property. That evening we met at the home of a local attorney, Mrs. B. The group participating in the experiment was very receptive to psychic phenomena, having participated many times in sitter groups or séances with Gil. There was a high level of receptivity, excitement, and energy in the room. Under these ideal conditions Nick was not only able to make the radio respond well but he would also pick up a good deal of information psychically from those in attendance.

As in most of the successful sessions with Ted Serios, there would usually be a warm-up period for Nick in which the sounds were weak, then the "clicks" would generally grow stronger and he would be able to control them more effectively. He might get them to go faster or slower, "count to ten" with him, and so on. But at this session the radio responded immediately, strongly, and loudly.

His feeling of being "energetically charged" may also have had to do with the fact that he was well rested; that afternoon he had fallen asleep on the lawn next to the waterfall and stream. Nick always claimed to get energy from moving water. Other psychics, Ena Twigg for example, also claimed to be "energized" by trees, grass, and especially moving water. In addition, his confidence was high; the group was composed predominantly of women—of the nine of us, only Gil and Nick were male—who were extremely enthusiastic about the experiment. He seemed excited about displaying his "powers" to the group and of being the center of attention.

That evening, when his eyes were closed and he was standing about three feet away from the table with his head averted, I took the opportunity to put my hands over the radio shielding it from view. The radio continued to respond to his commands. When I told him to open his eyes, he saw that my blocking the radio had not diminished his effectiveness. From then on that particular barrier was eliminated. Later that evening he went a distance of about 20 feet from the group and issued his orders to the radio. The response was immediate and strong, beginning when he said "start" and ceasing immediately when he would say "stop."

At each step in the development of this phenomenon Nick was limited by what he believed he could not do. For instance, he thought he could produce the signal only on the AM band. When we switched to FM or the Marine band he couldn't get it to work, until one night, while he was preoccupied, Gil quietly switched to FM without Nick's noticing. The popping was uninterrupted and as strong as ever. When we informed Nick and he saw that he could do it, that barrier was also broken.

By slowly breaking down psychological barriers during good sessions, we were able to get Nick to increase his distance from the radio to about 35 feet from behind a closed door and to combine the radio response with telepathy or clairvoyance experiments.

Our sessions were interrupted by our marriage in August of 1974. When we returned from our honeymoon trip we had another meeting at Mrs. B's in Hudson. While Nick was in an adjoining country kitchen with the connecting door closed, a member of the group, seated as usual around the dining room table on which the radio was placed, suggested that some of us quietly leave the room through an arch into the living room. Nick, by using a combination of ESP and PK, was to affect the radio so that it would "click" out the number of remaining persons. The radio clicked eight times, which was correct. We repeated it. This time six people remained and again the number of clicks was correct. On the possible chance that somehow Nick could detect by extraordinary hearing ability or some other means how many people were moving around, we decided to look instead at a playing card chosen randomly from a deck, concentrate on whatever number card turned up and see if he could "click out" the number. Again he was successful. The radio clicked six times. The card was the six of clubs. We continued with other cards and each time the radio responded with the correct number.

This number guessing became part of many of our subsequent sessions. That this response was on an unconscious level of awareness became most evident in the sessions we conducted that winter at the New School with yet another of Gil's classes. Nick got his best results when he would wander down the hall, sit in a phone booth, peruse the bulletin boards, take a drink from the water fountain, or be otherwise occupied while the experiment was going on. We would have a class member check on him occasionally to make sure he was not in the vicinity of the room, even though our numbers were chosen quietly and the heavy door was windowless.

If they chose large numbers, over 15 or so, the radio would give a flurry of clicks and it would be difficult to tell if it had given the correct number. But if the numbers were small, the clicking would be precisely correct *each time*, so long as Nick was not consciously aware of what was transpiring. He would not know if the radio had responded correctly or at all, until we called him back into the room and told him. He would be quite amused later when we would play back the audiotapes of the session.

One evening about a year later a student in another class suggested that we decide upon a series of numbers, such as 2-3-2. Nick was out of the room and out of earshot so he did not even hear the suggestion. We quietly agreed on the sequence: 4-3-4. After a few seconds of silence the radio "tapped" out the sequence slowly, precisely, and correctly, with appropriate short pauses between numbers.

Interestingly, when he came back into the room and we attempted to have him "guess" the numbers that we wrote down, or choose the numbers on a small calculator, he was not successful, never guessing more than chance. The radio would click out numbers but the answers would *usually* be wrong. When he was not consciously trying to do anything, he was invariably correct—or at least the radio was.

Another indication that he was acquiring the information on an unconscious level, or that it was acquired through some form of ESP, may be illustrated in a session that took place in lower Manhattan in January 1975. The group members that night included a physicist, Dr. G., and a clinical psychologist, Dr. L., who wanted to try to get a "message" from the radio by having it click as we recited the alphabet, much as the Bindelof boys had done at first. One of us would begin reciting the alphabet, and at certain letters the radio would emit a flurry of loud and rapid sounds. The "answers" given to the group's questions seemed to me to be productions of Nick's unconscious. For example, he was at that time immersed in Andre

Puharich's rather far-out book, *Uri: A Journal of the Mystery of Uri Geller*, published the year before (1974). The "source" of our radio's message identified itself as SPECTRA, the supposed alien organization that contacted Geller in the book, and the message had to do with setting up a meeting between Nick and Puharich. The message in part came out, "Puharich . . . meet . . . chek circumstances to introduction." (As in the Bindelof written communications, there is the hallmark misspelling of these kinds of unconsciously processed communications.) I knew too that Nick wanted to meet Puharich and compared himself privately to Geller. (Someone had told him once that physiologically he resembled the Israeli metal-bender.) I knew the "message" was coming from Nick's unconscious fantasy material.

To a question about the source of the radio phenomenon, the answer was "G wave." Since neither Nick nor anyone else in the room except for Dr. G., had any knowledge of what G (gravity) waves were at the time, we conjectured that Nick probably picked up this information telepathically from Dr. G's subconscious and, again unconsciously, had the radio "click out" the term. Dr. G. said that he was not consciously aware of associating the phenomenon with G-waves but was intrigued—and impressed—by the "answer."

Many of the sessions included healing. Nick knew of my long interest and involvement with psychic healers, had read about healing, and felt that he could diagnose and help heal people psychically. He seemed to have some success with Mrs. B who had a hearing problem and whose physician testified that the hearing in her affected ear had unexpectedly improved after a few sessions with Nick. There is no conclusive proof that the improvement was a result of Nick's healing efforts, however. It might simply have had to do with Mrs. B's *belief* that she was being healed and that she in effect healed herself, or perhaps to a combination of the two factors.

Nick would use the radio to "monitor" his healing energy. As he made passes with his hands around the head and body of the person on whom he worked, the radio would make its popping sounds. When he stopped, it would fall silent.

The healing aspect of the experiment played an important part in March 1975, while Nick was demonstrating at another class of Gil's. A woman volunteered to be a healing subject and was dramatically relieved of a problem she was suffering with that day—a pain and immobility of her left arm and shoulder, which she believed to be a severe attack of bursitis. I didn't attend that class but learned from Nick, Gil, and later the woman, Mrs. F., that she began to feel some relief and Nick reported that he felt "her system balancing out." By the next morning the woman, who the day before had not been able to move her arm, was able to extend it up over her head without pain.

Mrs. F., as it turned out, was a successful publisher and a friend of a well-known parapsychologist, Dr. Russell Targ, who was based in California and who was visiting New York. Targ was invited to attend our next session at the Rollers' penthouse apartment on 67th Street. There was a good deal of static or interference that night but Nick was able to get his "popcorn sounds" going pretty quickly although rather weakly. We tried distancing Nick from the radio because we knew from experience that he sometimes got better results away from it, but the apartment and terrace were just too small. I took a chance and suggested that Nick go down to the lobby—we were on the 11th floor of a building with high ceilings—and try to affect the radio from there. By this time I felt he had the confidence to do so. Right after he left the room, the radio's "popcorn" effect started up, more loudly and clearly than when he had been there. It stopped for a short time twice. Later Nick reported that he had tried to keep it going but was distracted on the elevator, first by a man who entered with two dogs, and next by a woman who took a phone call on the elevator intercom.

Marion Roller called the lobby and we continued the experiment with Nick on the phone. He was able to hear the radio responding to his mental and verbal signals. The "popping" continued to be louder and more precise than it had been when Nick was in the apartment. Dr. Targ, who was returning to the west coast, suggested that he try the experiment over the phone from his lab in California and we set up the time and dates for the experiment.

As had been arranged, Targ called our apartment on Staten Island at 8:15 p.m. New York time, on March 24, 1975, from his laboratory. Listening in with my ear close to the receiver, I could hear that Nick was able to get Targ's radio in California to emit the signals. Actually, he had attempted to do this just prior to the phone call as well and Targ reported that his radio *had* begun to "pop" just before he made the phone call.

There were several interesting things about this experiment. For the first time there was only one person (Targ) rather than a group, near the radio. Secondly, on our side, I was the only other person with Nick—

another first. Thirdly, the 3,000 mile distance seemed to have little effect, if any, on the phenomenon, and fourth, at one point when Targ held the radio in his hand, unknown to Nick, it stopped "popping." This was consistent with previous experiments but we weren't sure of the reason for this happening. From this experiment it seemed that the signal might be affected physically by someone holding the radio but I am more inclined to believe that Nick clairvoyantly perceived that Targ was holding the radio thus setting up a psychological barrier. It might be argued that Nick didn't perceive it when I held my hands over the radio in that earlier session, but he was preoccupied with the other participants and then, too, he might have been "psychically on guard" more with a stranger than with me.

The clairvoyant hypothesis was borne out the next evening when, by prearrangement, another phone hookup was made from Targ in California to Mrs. F.'s townhouse in New York. That night Gil and members of his class met us at the townhouse. Nick was able to describe Targ's surroundings and felt that another man was in the room with him and described him. Targ confirmed that his colleague at the time, Dr. Hal Putoff, was there and fit Nick's description. They were taping the phone call.

Nick had difficulty getting any response from the radio and this time felt he could do better *away* from the group. (There were some strained group dynamics at work that are too complex to go into here.) I stayed on the phone and Nick went upstairs to use an extension. I was able to hear his commands and the response of the radio in California. Targ said it was not as strong as it had been the previous night but was adequate. This was the first time that Nick had attempted, successfully, to activate the radio on two successive nights.

Nick had come a long way in the eighteen months or so since he believed he could get the radio to click only if his hand was right over it.

Unfortunately, although Targ felt at the time that the experiment should be continued, especially since it was repeatable, because of his other commitments it was never carried out. Nick got involved in becoming a "psychic analyst" or therapist and, I believe, lost interest in the project.

The Serios and radio experiments showed that repeatable, reliable PK experiments are possible with talented subjects, and that PK as well as ESP is not necessarily diminished by distance. The implications may be far-reaching. For instance, if (transpersonal) healing is a function of PK, then the claims of "distant healing" must be taken more seriously. The well-known healer Olga Worral caused rye seedlings in a laboratory

200 miles away from her home to grow at an extraordinarily fast rate by concentrating her healing "prayers" on them. And more recently, the effect of prayer or conscious healing thoughts has been tested by having a "healing circle" of people pray for a number of heart patients, for example. At the end of the experimental period these patients had a significantly lower death rates or complications than a matched control group. Other laboratory evidence has also shown the positive effects of distant healing. Perhaps, as with Nick's radio performance, being away from the subjects might enhance the concentration and effectiveness of the treatment. This is of course speculation; many more studies are needed.

It might be helpful in understanding these psychokinetically talented people to take a closer look at their personalities. Certainly Eisenbud did an excellent job of analyzing Serios in his book and journal articles. Nick had a good deal of innate psychic and psychokinetic ability: he demonstrated spontaneous telepathy, clairvoyance, and precognition many times in our everyday life. He also had a volatile personality, tending toward physical acting out. One day, when he was extremely angry with his mother and could not vent his rage, he (unconsciously) caused a glass bowl that I had placed next to me on our kitchen table to explode. He was in the living room, out of sight of the kitchen at the moment, and came running in when he heard the noise, not knowing consciously what had happened. The bowl, which shattered into thousands of pieces, was identical to one I had given his mother for Mothers' Day and therefore became an unconscious focus for his anger. (He couldn't "smash" her so he pulverized the bowl.)

He seemed also to have a more than usual desire to not only gain attention but also to be considered unusual, a "super-person," and indeed he seemed to hold this conviction himself. He resented any type of authority or authority figure or any restrictions placed upon him, feeling that he was above the rules that other people are subject to. Once a policeman who stopped him after he ignored a red traffic light complained to me that Nick made him feel as though *he* had done something wrong. He was very persuasive and charismatic, perhaps owing to this feeling of being beyond normal conventions, and was able to convince others many times that indeed these things were his due. (That policeman never gave him a ticket.) As is common with feelings of superiority, however, there was a deep sense of insecurity and a continual need to prove himself.

He often admitted his tendency to be a "ham" and to try to be the center of attention, in any way he could. He told many tales of his accomplishments, his incidents of deviant or defiant behavior as a child and youth to combat authority (especially the police, the defenders of law and order).

He claimed to have friends and relatives who were Mafia "biggies" (members of the glamorous underworld who lived by their own laws and defied acceptable societal rules) and of knowing and being friends with famous celebrities. I later discovered that these claims were strictly products of his imagination or gross exaggerations of the truth. I believe a part of him actually came to believe many of his fabrications.

He had, in short, what psychologists would call a fantasy-prone personality. As Eisenbud noted of the psychic Wolf Messing, there are a small number of people, including psychics and sensitives, who fully experience what they fantasize and have great difficulty in distinguishing their fantasies from reality. He notes that the feature that separates them from those completely out of touch with reality is that they are demonstrably sane and lack the well-known characteristics of paranoid personalities.

Eisenbud also observes that they often come to believe their stories and that these distortions of memory may serve to bolster their sadly sagging sense of inner worth. They may be prone to the special fantasy that has come to be known as the "family romance," in which the person fantasizes that he is really of noble or aristocratic birth. A form of the "family romance" that Nick and Messing seemed to share was in name dropping, accounts of "giants" (of science and politics in Messing's case, of celebrities in Nick's) who took special notice of them. Eisenbud speculates that many magicians and show persons may be given to this kind of grandiosity. As he says, "What could be more self-enhancing than putting on a show in which one does things that are plainly impossible, or gaining the applause of a packed auditorium."

In summary, Nick believed that he was someone special who could do things that defied the laws most people live by. Combined with an innate psychic ability, his belief enabled him to do whatever he believed was possible. He was not able to do what he considered "impossible" at each step of our experiment until he was shown otherwise, was inspired, or developed enough confidence to transcend each barrier.

Perhaps the altered states induced by hypnotism and alcohol helped Serios to feel that he too could transcend physical laws, as we know them.

D. D. Home, Palladino, Duncan, and the other spiritualists believed that otherworldly forces were responsible for their phenomena, but Serios and Nick had only their own very earthy resources on which to rely.

I know of only one other case of someone affecting a radio in this same way. In the 1990s Stanley Krippner investigated a Brazilian medium who, among other feats, seemed to cause stones to fall from above, as Gil had done twice, both indoors and outdoors. This gentleman, Amyr Amiden, used a small radio occasionally to monitor his energy in the same way that Nick did. The radio, tuned in-between stations, would emit the same kind of popping or clicking sounds that have been described here, but Amiden didn't seem to attempt to control them or use them for any other purpose.

CHAPTER 26

THE IMPACT OF KENNETH BATCHELDOR

In September 1966, a report appeared in the *British Journal of the Society for Psychical Research* entitled "Report on a Case of Table Levitation and Associated Phenomena." The article was written by a little-known English psychologist named Kenneth J. Batcheldor, who with two friends decided to try "table tilting." None of them had ever had any experience with moving tables, or felt that they possessed any sort of "mediumistic" ability. They were not Spiritualists and didn't expect to get anything more than the kinds of movements that were easily explained by unconscious muscle action. They were all, therefore, quite surprised when in their eleventh session the 15-pound table suddenly rose up off the floor. Batcheldor remarked that although he had heard of the supposed phenomenon of levitation he never really believed it. When it happened, he said, it came as quite a shock. Having stumbled upon a genuine force, they became determined to continue the meetings and find out all they could.

With his friends, Miss P. M. Coghlan and Mr. William G. Chick, he sat for 200 sessions from April 1964, to December 1965. They were occasionally joined by Mrs. Chick and/or one or two other relatives or friends. However, Mr. Chick was absent from 120 of the sittings and at those sessions nothing happened that could not be attributed to unconscious muscle action. Of the 80 sittings Chick attended, 70 resulted in major (paranormal) effects.

Their sittings typically lasted about two hours with a half-hour break. They would turn on a tape recorder, the type with seven-inch spools, sit at a table in the center of an ordinary living room with the main lights off, and place their hands palms down on the table. Batcheldor reported that they didn't pray nor have music, except once when the table spelled out "musick" and they obliged with a song. He maintains that no one went into trance and that they conversed, sometimes animatedly. (Interestingly, Montague Ullman maintained that Gil didn't go into trance, but Gil told me several times that as soon as the lights went out he had an overwhelming desire to sleep and his chin would go down onto his chest.)

Before anything occurred, there was always the initial waiting period, which lasted anywhere from one minute to as long as half an hour. A quick start usually was followed by a good session, but a slow start didn't necessarily mean a bad one. Sometimes, after starting slowly, very little happened, but at other times things would pick up in the second half of the session.

Like the Bindelof boys they first got creaks or cracking noises in the wooden table. Most of these "crepitations" seemed normally produced, but interspersed were sharp taps, scrapings, and soft thuds. These other sounds sometimes came from the chairs, the floor, or the walls. After a few minutes of these noises the table would usually slide along the floor for a few inches then, after a pause, it might tilt up on two legs before dropping again. The sliding and tilting varied in character: sometimes the table would glide slowly and silently, other times it would scurry rapidly and noisily for six feet or more, causing the sitters to get up and scramble after it.

Their first total levitations occurred in darkness and were only sensed by touch and the sound of the table falling back to the floor. These levitations also varied and the table could float down in complete silence or crash to the floor with such force that they feared it might go through the floorboards. It would sometimes rotate slowly and at other times spin around.

They decided that, because they were working in darkness, they needed a more objective means of checking on the reality of the levitations, so Batcheldor made an electrical apparatus to detect when they occurred. It consisted of four switches, one on each table foot, joined to a battery and small red bulb. The bulb was mounted in the center of the table and would light only if all four legs came off the floor. (The switches would close only when the pressure of the floor was taken off them.) The little light not only confirmed their sense that the table had risen but also added visible evidence of its altitude (shoulder or chest height) and that all their hands, fingers and thumbs, were indeed on *top* of the table. Thinking they might be accused of mass hallucination, Batcheldor replaced the light with a buzzer that would sound, so that it was heard on the audiotapes they made of the sessions. Because it would continue to sound until the table came down again, the buzzer also enabled them later to measure the length of time the table was in the air. (It sometimes stayed up for about

20 seconds.) There were some bugs in the system, which they corrected, and while it didn't preclude clever fraud, the three friends had satisfied themselves that no one was fooling the others.

Batcheldor's series of experiments with "sitter groups" were similar to the Victorian séances but without "spiritistic assumptions." They were purely trying to understand the manifestation of large-scale psychokinesis or macro-PK from a scientific viewpoint.

Batcheldor was a psychologist and in these experiments he concluded that tight controls tended to interfere with the "psychological conditions necessary for the strong manifestation of psi." In other words, tight controls would do away with cheating but would also inhibit true phenomena from happening.

The Victorians believed that spirits were lifting tables, sending messages, and so on—spooky but okay, that's what spirits did. If you dropped the spirit idea, however, it meant that you, the living sitters, or at least *one* of you—horror of horrors—had this awesome power. Most people are scared to death, or at least into inhibition, by the thought. However, if you thought that somebody in the group *might* be cheating, then maybe these things were not so scary after all.

With this concept in mind, Batcheldor deliberately conducted his groups under loosely controlled conditions, even sometimes starting things going by giving the table a nudge. He found that when the group *thought* something paranormal was happening, *real* phenomena began to occur.

Early on he noticed that some ostensible paranormal occurrences "grew" out of normal events. Creaks that at first seemed to come from thermal expansion or to stresses in the wood of the table gradually became far too loud and frequent to be attributed to those causes. Small movements probably owing to involuntary muscle action turned into larger movements and levitations. These "artifacts," the creakings and small movements, would cause an intense expectancy of further psi events, and that expectancy or belief might in turn release PK and cause the genuine raps and levitations to occur.

The "instant belief" that some phenomenon was about to happen, he maintained, was one of the most important factors in successful sittings. "Long-term" belief didn't matter as much. A long-term attitude of doubt can be changed in an instant, as we saw in Chuck Honorton's case when he saw Felicia Parise move the little plastic bottle. For the ordinary person, he realized, something evidently has to happen to *create* belief. "Such belief," he said at a 1982 conference in Cambridge, England, "is then involuntary, and possibly only this form is likely to be 'pure,' or free from intellectual reservations."

This statement echoes what Jerome Frank of Johns Hopkins University in Baltimore found when he investigated people who had been cured at Lourdes. He said they "didn't interpose their critical faculties," that is, they were able to inhibit the critical, analytic parts of their brain/mind. They believed *absolutely* that they were to be healed–and they were. This absolute belief was what Batcheldor felt was needed to voluntarily induce Macro-PK (as opposed to the involuntary PK that occurs in poltergeist cases).

Batcheldor also felt that a belief easily arises that a particular sitter is the "medium" or the primary source of the phenomena. Once that belief is established, the group won't get any results in his/her absence. He felt, therefore, that apparent dependence on one person was not a conclusive argument against the "group force," the energy coming from the entire group rather than from one person. His theory was that certain special or talented sitters didn't directly produce the phenomena but triggered the group by their effect on the expectancy and belief of its members. He felt that they were focal points for the phenomena, which was powered by the group as a whole.

In the Bindelof group there was no doubt a great deal of energy generated by this highly libidinal pack of teenagers, and their combined force certainly contributed to the production of the PK, but Gil was the only one who had exhibited Recurrent Spontaneous PK (RSPK, or poltergeist-like phenomena). He was also the only one able to get results with other groups. And Batcheldor's idea certainly doesn't seem to hold up in the cases of super-stars such as Kluski, Palladino, or especially Home, who could just walk into a strange house and cause furniture to move and whose ability Crookes measured in the laboratory. But I think Batcheldor is correct in saying that the sitter-group is a "creative situation in which firm beliefs—whatever form they may take—will largely shape and determine the results."

Batcheldor found that a big problem in his sittings was in retaining belief while avoiding emotional resistance. Large-scale effects tend to have a disturbing effect on sitters and to cause many to react in various defensive ways. Batcheldor identified two types of resistance, which he called "ownership resistance" and "witness inhibition." Ownership resistance refers to the reluctance to possess paranormal powers. (Gil never felt comfortable accepting that he was the "medium" of the Bindelof group.) Witness inhibition refers to the disturbed feelings or reactions to witnessing paranormal displays, as in Gil's first séance when the armchair moving towards them startled the owners of the boarding house. Ownership resistance and witness inhibition both spring from fear of the unknown and the uncontrolled.

Resistance can lead to all kinds of interference, such as explaining everything away in "normal" terms, making counter-suggestions ("This won't work!"), or distracting by talking about irrelevant things. It can also lead, as we've seen, to complete refusal to continue with the experiment.

One way Batcheldor sought to overcome resistance was to encourage lots of noise, laughter, singing, and light chatter. He felt that this could maintain belief by preventing cognitive analysis while at the same time keeping a light-hearted tone. The sitters could laugh at their own fears.

He also saw the advantage of proceeding slowly to allow gradual desensitization to the phenomena to take place. He felt that development usually takes weeks or months because of the need to gradually build up belief and also gradually dispel fear. For the would-be sitter group, he felt there was no short cut to developing psi abilities.

Batcheldor also reasoned that because the sometimes amazing and coordinated macro-PK feats of poltergeist agents were spontaneous, we don't have to *learn* how to do PK. That is, some level of the mind already knows how to do it. (Nobody taught my ex-husband, Nick, how to shatter that bowl.) The rub is doing it *intentionally*. To learn how, the sitters had to get into a proper state of mind. He found that the results in his sitter-group were mostly "intermittent and freakish" probably because average persons could only, or mainly, achieve the necessary moments of "instant belief" through involuntary response to artifacts. To him, this meant that the sitters had no real control over their PK.

He managed to get consistent control in his first group, however, by "training" the table movements to respond to a spokesman's command. Instead of the table "jumping about" unpredictably, they got it to stay still until given an order—to move, "walk," or levitate. The table would immediately obey their oral commands.

The Bindelof group discovered that by themselves.

To produce the phenomena, it is of primary importance to prevent the conscious mind from interfering. Batcheldor did it by occupying it with "noise and nonsense," thereby distracting it, or by attempting to quiet it down into a "psi state" of heightening suggestibility.

The state he described as the "blended state"—a blend of conscious and unconscious—even though he maintained that none of his sitters was entranced, sounds very much like what earlier sitters called a trance state. This state, he said, implies perfect belief and freedom from resistance. (I'm reminded here of Home when he carried the hot coals to his hostess speaking in a slow trance-like way but able to function on a conscious level at the same time.)

Distraction, then, is helpful in the conscious state because it diverts the mind, but not during the "blended" state because it will break the state and immediately cause, for example, a levitated object to drop. That might be what happened when Lennie, Gil, and Larry levitated the bridge table so high that Larry couldn't reach the top. When he complained and pulled on the leg, it caused the distraction that sent the table crashing to the floor.

Batcheldor also discussed the *suggestion* model, that is, making suggestions or "appeals" to the sub- or unconscious mind. Suggestions may be verbal or non-verbal, as from hearing or feeling artifacts or experiencing previous PK occurrences. The non-verbal suggestions may be far more effective because they may rivet the attention and displace analytical thought. Batcheldor says that success "usually comes after a certain delay, or during a distraction," as in the case of Felicia Parise reaching for her plastic false eyelash container to put it away when she was distracted by her grandmother's imminent death.

The early researchers like T.J. Hudson, whose book Gil and his friends had read, wrote at length about suggestion. They too saw PK as a goal-oriented process in which an idea of the desired goal is "planted" in the subconscious, which later "realizes" the idea. *How it does this*, of course, we don't know, but we don't need to know the answer to that mystery to do it.

The people who led the many "spoon-bending" parties held in the 1970s and 80s made good use of suggestion to obtain their results. I took part in one such party in Cambridge in 1982 where Batcheldor spoke. After a banquet dinner with wine, a group of us, perhaps 30 or so people, met in a large comfortable sitting room with the goal of bending cutlery. Some of the locals had brought their own flatware but some of us had swiped tableware from dinner. I filched my small silver coffee spoon. As we sat around relaxed and in high spirits, the leader told us what we could expect. We were supposed to chant, "Bend, bend, bend!" while lightly massaging our forks and spoons. After a while, this experienced and authoritative man told us, we would feel an "urge" or "knowledge" that the metal would bend. We were to act upon the urge and try to bend our object. It would probably appear to "melt," he said, for a second and then "harden" again so that it might take a few tries to bend it completely. He also asked that the first person to get some bending tell the group.

With his words firmly implanted in our minds, we laughed and joked and chanted and rubbed. . . and suddenly I got the feeling that I could bend my spoon. I tried it and, lo and behold, it "gave" as though it was a licorice stick then immediately hardened again. I looked at it. Sure enough, there was a slight bend in the handle. I held it up and shouted excitedly, "Look, it bent! I bent it!" The floodgates broke. Everybody's flatware started to bend. After two more "urges" and tries, I got the spoon to bend completely in half. Some people had forks that twisted like corkscrews, the tines becoming a tangle of unkempt Medusa's hair. A journalist friend was wearing a copper bracelet, which at one point in the frenzy he started to wind, ribbon-like, around his index finger. "Don't stop me," he said, "It's like an orgasm; if you distract me it'll stop it." I think that's the state of mind Batcheldor was talking about.

The effects of suggestion and belief were dramatically illustrated by Uri Geller's televised feats of metal bending in the 1970s. Immediately people from all over the world who saw him began bending cutlery and restarting broken watches.

Julian Isaacs, a British researcher, used some of Batcheldor's theories in his work screening subjects for laboratory metal bending (PKMB) experiments. He employed the same techniques that I mentioned earlier for spoon-bending parties. He would lecture the group to convince it of the reality of PK and suggest that the metal-bending would spread further in the audience—which it did. He persuaded them to loosen up and enjoy themselves in a "silly" way to try to bend cutlery. Isaacs pointed out that the roles of humor and amusement to diffuse the tension of an encounter with PK, to relax, to prevent over striving in the PKMB task, and to block analytical thinking are identical in the sitter-group and metal bending situations.

Dennis Stillings of the Archaeus Project tells of a metal-bending party that he was asked to conduct for a group of medical professionals. Everything was wrong, he said. It was a small group of primarily skeptical people who were into deep relaxation techniques, which is not usually conducive to metal bending. He had brought with him a quantity of forks and spoons, which he had tested for toughness and the bent ones were either thrown out or were bent back into their original shape. He had also brought, in case he should find a metal-bending prodigy, a small tray of "really tough and unusual materials." Among these was a three-pronged cast-steel fondue fork with its haft imbedded in an ebonite handle.

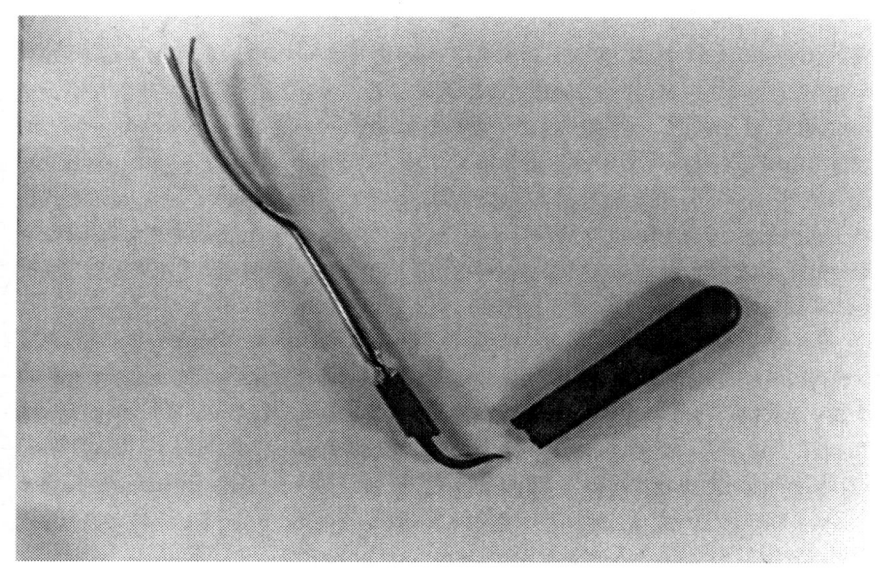

Bent/broken fondue fork. Courtesy Dennis Stillings

Stillings began with Jack Houck's routine, which encourages a true party atmosphere. He told them to "imagine a point of intense white light in the middle of your brain. Bring it down through your arms and put it into the metal. At the count of three we will all command the metal to bend." After they shouted, "Bend!" three times they went into a concentrated meditative state. After ten minutes passed with nothing happening, Stillings, in his own state of embarrassment, decided to do a little "artifact introduction" in order to "break state." He saw that the fork being held by the person in front of him looked as though it was a little bent. (Perhaps he had not straightened it out very well before the party.) He exclaimed, "Look! We're getting some bending!" That broke the unproductive meditative state and people started talking to each other. Soon forks and spoons were bending away. One physician stroked the side of a knife blade and became excited as he saw it begin to droop. Another turned a strong fork into a series of waves, and the psychiatrist who held the fork that Stillings "saw" bending tied it in knots.

This last individual then went over to the tray of "tough items" and took the heavy fondue fork with the ebonite handle. He began stroking it lightly and Stillings watched in apprehension from about eight feet away, worrying that the man might hurt himself if he forced it. He was about to warn the man when he noticed the tines beginning to fan out. As he continued to watch, a bend of about 15 degrees formed in the last centimeter of one tine, a bend that would be impossible to make without the use of a tool. Then suddenly the fork exploded. Fragments of ebonite struck against the windows and walls. The psychiatrist sat stunned, shaking his hand in pain. What had happened was that the part of the metal haft imbedded in the ebonite had bent, even though it hadn't been touched directly, shattering the brittle ebonite. The now exposed haft was bent about 20 degrees.

Some time later Stillings took it out to show someone and noticed that the bend was at a much greater angle than it had been on the night of the party. The metal had continued to bend in storage. Whenever he showed the fork to someone, he would insert the tip of the haft back into the fragmented handle as it had originally fit. The fit was tight at first but some months later, when he tried to do it again, it would no longer slide into place. The extreme tip of the haft had begun to curl back on itself.

That psychokinetically bent metal continues to bend is a phenomenon that has been noted in demonstrations by Uri Geller and others. Stillings noted that he is particularly susceptible to "retrocognitive dissonance" and admitted having a tough time with this phenomenon. But, he maintains, "This fork was truly bent by forces which have not been taken into consideration by normal science."

One Canadian sitter group also did metal bending. These people, who came to be known as the "Philip" group, were greatly influenced by Batcheldor's work, as well as that of his friends Colin Brookes-Smith and D. W. Hunt.

Iris Owen, wife of researcher and poltergeist expert, Dr. A. R. G. (George) Owen, had read reports of the work Smith, Hunt, and Batcheldor had done in the 1960s. Iris shared her husband's interest in PK phenomena. They observed that some people who were naturally endowed with PK ability could often bring it under voluntary mental control. But, they wondered, could ordinary people have PK in a form too weak to manifest itself in large visible or audible ways? Does the average person have PK latently or potentially? And if so, can they be trained to use it?

No ordinary person, they reasoned, could lift a heavy object of several hundred pounds in weight, but a group of six or eight people could. Why couldn't six or eight people then, pooling their efforts, raise a table through PK?

In 1973 Iris and seven other members of the Society for Psychical Research of Toronto decided to explore these questions. They wanted to find out (1) whether or not a "spirit medium" was necessary, (2) if the PK was produced by a discarnate entity or by the living group members, and (3) if they could produce these effects in full light. The group consisted of an accountant, an engineer, an industrial designer, a scientific research assistant, and four housewives, none of whom claimed mediumistic abilities.

Long before, as members of the Toronto SPR, they had discussed hauntings and attempted to investigate sightings of ghosts. They wondered if these apparitions were the products of collective hallucinations and if so, might not a group of people who had mutual rapport see a ghost together as a group? They discussed how they might create an apparition that could be proven to exist—their own "manufactured" ghost.

They decided that they'd have to invent their own ghost, someone who had never really lived. And that's how Philip came to be.

Sue Sparrow, one of the eight members, made up Philip's life story: He was an Englishman who lived in the mid 1600s at the time of Oliver Cromwell. He was a Catholic supporter of the king and was unhappily married to Dorothea, a frigid noblewoman. He met and fell in love with a gypsy named Margo and secreted her in the gatehouse of his home, Diddington Manor. Dorothea discovered the affair and accused Margo of witchcraft and husband stealing. At her trial, Philip, afraid of losing his reputation and possessions, failed to protect Margo and she was burned at the stake. Stricken with remorse, he committed suicide by throwing himself off the battlements of the Manor.

The group familiarized themselves with the story and in their first meetings discussed the story, making suggestions and filling in details so that they all had the same clear picture of this tragic tale. They discussed aspects of his character and personality and agreed on what he looked like, things he liked or disliked, and so on, and especially his feelings for Dorothea and Margo so that they had a clear mental picture of him. An artistic group member drew a picture of him. They also decided that once every century or so, Philip's ghost would be seen on Diddington's battlements and that year, 1972, was such a year for the ghost to reappear.

They started by sitting in a circle, sometimes around a table, meditating. They put Philip's picture on the table or, if no table was used, on a piece of aluminized cardboard on the floor hoping and expecting that he might materialize there.

They never sat in complete darkness, although they did sometimes illuminate the room only with candles or colored lights. They held two meditative sessions per evening broken by a relaxed exchange of experiences and views. They met regularly once a week for a year. Except for a perceived mistiness around the circle at times, nothing of real value occurred.

Then Iris read the Brookes-Smith and Batcheldor reports. The group, which by now was a close-knit unit, decided to copy the methods used by the English researchers with a couple of variations. They still were intent on producing a materialization and opted against sitting in darkness, fearing they might miss their "ghost" if he showed up. Instead they used colored lights behind a sheet of frosted glass.

They found it hard at first to relax and converse normally after their year of meditation, and even though they were intimate friends, they felt self-conscious about singing. But the sessions became less forced in a few weeks and they found it easier to tell jokes, recite poetry, or just chat while intending to produce "Philip."

The change paid off. During the third or fourth new session they felt a vibration in the top of the table around which they were sitting. Because of the noise they were making at the moment, they weren't sure they "heard" anything but were positive they "felt" a rap. As the session proceeded more raps occurred, first lightly then more strongly and louder until there was no doubt in their minds. Then, to their surprise, the table started to slide about the floor, quickly and randomly with no apparent purpose. It slid away so quickly that they had difficulty keeping up with it.

They were rather nonplussed. They were expecting, at least consciously, an apparition, and not this sort of manifestation. While they were speculating out loud about the cause, one woman said, "I wonder if by chance Philip is doing this?" There immediately came a loud rap from the tabletop.

They adapted to the new situation using one rap for yes, two for no.

Philip had not materialized but they had successfully obtained phenomena in full light with a "non-mediumistic" group. Even though "he" wasn't a real spirit, they were interested in what he had to say.

Sitting around an ordinary folding card table, they'd start the session by each saying, "Hello, Philip." A rap would occur under the speaker's hand, the raps moving around the table to answer the person addressing Philip.

If the questions became too intense, the raps would grow feeble or might stop altogether. They found that the best procedure therefore was to break for songs, jokes, and chatting before resuming the questions.

The table took on a personality. It would sometimes rush across the room to "greet" a latecomer. If they got into a conversation that seemed as though they forgot him temporarily, Philip would demand their attention with a series of raps, or the table might suddenly slide across the floor.

As in other groups, the raps were varied. If they made a remark concerning Philip's wife, Dorothea, they got "extraordinary scratching sounds" from underneath the tabletop. A good joke might elicit a loud series of raps giving a "rolling" effect as though the table was laughing. And as they sang some of their favorite tunes, they'd get loud raps keeping time to the music.

They inquired into aspects of Philip's life, asking only questions that could be answered with "yes" or "no." His answers were what the questioner would have expected. If there was doubt in the mind of the person questioning, the raps were usually hesitant. When the questions became too personal, they would hear loud scratching rather than knocks. His answers to questions regarding history were correct *when the group knew the facts*. For instance, when one member asked concerning Charles I's execution, "He was beheaded when Cromwell came to power, wasn't he, Philip?" the answer was "yes." In actuality the king lost his head (literally) some years after Cromwell's ascendancy but nobody in the group was sure of the particulars.

Another time he was asked if he enjoyed going to chocolate houses in London and seeing the ladies, to which he replied a hearty affirmative. Chocolate, however, wasn't known at that time and chocolate houses weren't introduced until more than a hundred years after Philip's "death." To another question about the king's love of pets, Philip indicated that Charles I loved cats. This was not historical fact but the person who made the query had an ardent love of cats. It seems that the questioner was able to elicit answers that he or she expected.

Like Dr. Bindelof, Philip responded quite literally. Once when asked to give a rap under each person's hand at the table, each person felt a rap under his or her hand at exactly the same moment.

Another parallel with the Bindelof boys occurred in the summer of 1974 when the Philip group took a rest. Individual group members experienced poltergeist-like happenings in their homes. Remember Larry's cracked watch crystals and the switched clothing labels? Once the energy is started, it may be difficult to contain it to the sittings; it may break out from the subconscious in various ways.

Also like Bindelof, Philip could refuse to show up. When someone said jokingly one time, "Philip, if you won't talk to us, we can send you away and get somebody else," the raps ceased altogether. The group felt that the threat had disturbed their rapport. They knew from Brookes-Smith that they had to have complete faith in their ability to produce the phenomena in order to do so. They resolved not to threaten Philip again. It took them most of that evening to coax his raps back again.

The group obtained other phenomena as well. They sometimes used heavier wooden tables that produced louder raps than the bridge table. (An offspring of their octet, the "Lileth" group, used a Plexiglas and metal table, which also gave raps.) They recorded many sessions by taping a microphone under the tabletop and were able to capture them on a video of a Canadian TV talk show on which they appeared. In the tape I saw the boom mike lowered to the table, which I believe at that point was turned over on its back, and dull thuds could be heard in response to their prompting. This all took place in front of a large studio audience and under glaring TV lights.

Raps also resounded from adjoining plaster walls and the floor of the room above them when requested. (Philip was told to say hello to George who was meeting with a few other people in the room above them. The raps were produced in the floor of Owen's meeting room.)

There was also flickering of certain lights in the room in which they met that was not due to any known cause. They would ask Philip to "flick the lights" and there would be immediate compliance. One time one of the red bulbs in the light panel switched off, leaving an illumination more pleasing to the eyes. They found nothing wrong with the bulb and no one had gone near it to turn the control knob.

This incident reminds me of the time Nick, Gil Roller, myself, and a few others were sitting around a table in a lower Manhattan apartment doing the radio experiment. Suddenly the hanging light over the table went out, leaving us in darkness. I volunteered to turn it back on—we assumed that the knob of the dimmer switch had somehow slipped around—and both Gil and Nick protested simultaneously. They preferred the light to be off. At the end of the session the woman who lived in the apartment went to turn it on and found that the knob had been turned past the "clicking" point to "off." Some force would have to be applied for it to have been in that position and no one was near it. With those two PK-gifted men in the room, both evidently more comfortable without the overhead light, we were not surprised.

But, returning to the Toronto bunch, the table would also slide about the heavily carpeted room on one or two legs, often escaping from their hands and landing in a corner or wedged into a doorway in an attempt to follow people out of the room. Once, when they were tired of chasing it around, someone suggested that it turn over on its back with its legs in the air while they had a rest. It did exactly that. It turned over gently and then flipped upside down. Much to their amusement it would chase after people on two legs then thump the airborne two down on the floor and raise the other two like a bucking bronco. The time it chased one member out the door and wedged itself in the doorway, only two of the group members were near the table and it "had escaped all hands."

On a smaller scale, Philip was able to cause objects to stick to the table top in much the same way that D. D. Home had done when he caused a table laden with china and glass to tip and nothing fell off. The Toronto group always "shared" candy with Philip by putting one piece on the table for him. Someone teasingly made a move to take "Philip's" candy, telling him to hang on to it. The table was tipped to a 45-degree angle but the candy didn't move. They tested this effect with other candies and all of them stayed put. Subsequently they manually tipped the table and at much less than the 45-degrees, the candies slipped right off.

There was an occurrence that reminded me of engineer Crawford's theories of ectoplasmic rods emanating from medium Kathy Goligher's body and pushing up from underneath the center of the table to levitate it. In trying for levitation in a fully lighted room, the Canadian group felt distortions in the tabletop, lumps the size of oranges appearing to rise from the middle of the table. They were not able to duplicate these effects.

Because of a cold and flu epidemic that caused members to miss some sessions, the Philip group discovered that they could get the phenomena with as few as four people attending. Any four would do. If the quartet was feeling tired or perhaps coming down with an illness, the raps and movements would be weak but they still occurred.

Remarkably, Philip and his group were able to get movement of the table and raps for TV under bright lights and with a large audience. They claimed to have had the table levitate completely an inch or so off the floor and for a short period, but there is no record of it on tape. They did not get the materialization they had sought as their original goal, nor did they get the more spectacular manifestations that Home, Palladino, Kluski, or for that matter, the Bindelof boys did. The question is why? Were the more powerful manifestations a result of spirit intervention or the *belief* that all-powerful spirits could do what poor mortals could not? Did "ordinary" people like Batcheldor, Smith, and the Philip group unwittingly limit their powers by what they *thought* they could not do (as Nick did at each psychological barrier in the radio experiment)? Or perhaps are we merely dealing with the fact that some people are more psychokinetically talented, that is, that they have more of this PK energy than others?

It may be that PK, like other psychic abilities, functions in the way that musical talent does. Some people are born with absolute or perfect pitch. For example, I was born with considerable inherited musical talent, but not absolute pitch. When I was a music student at Hunter College I carried a tuning fork around with me and after much practice could, if asked to sing an "a," reproduce it to within a half tone. I have friends, however, who have "tin ears," can't carry a tune in the proverbial bucket, or hear when an instrument or musician is out of tune. Only very rarely does a Mozart or a Mendelssohn come along—a musical genius with technical know-how.

I suspect that Home, Kluski, Palladino, and few others were "PK geniuses." Gil Roller was probably a very talented individual who, with the addition of other less "talented" people, learned how to do PK with their beliefs, imaginations, and creativity directing them. We don't know how many talented people there are out there who have never explored, or who are afraid to explore, their abilities. But it does seem that sitters who believe that spirits are responsible for the phenomena get larger and more awesome effects. Belief in one's own capacities often has its limitations.

The Philip group was widely read in psi history and research. Perhaps they accepted that they could cause tables to move and levitate, produce raps, have objects "stick" to the table, or flicker lights, but materialization, which may involve ectoplasm, is perhaps a little too close to belief in spirits for comfort. Not only that, but ectoplasm is messy stuff that comes out of bodily orifices, and while that group was like a family, such displays could be considered too intimate for a mixed group of friends. Or it could be that they just didn't have enough "genius" to produce such mega-feats.

More recently, an Australian group of researchers in Sydney, who were inspired by the Philip group and the works of Batcheldor, claims to have been able to replicate some of their successes.

But the Australian researchers, eight people led by Michael Williams, obtained no results in trying to emulate the Philip group. After 5 months of trying they scrapped that approach and switched to Batcheldor's suggestions. Sitting in semi-darkness and concentrating on the table itself, rather than on their fictional entity—they had named him "Skippy Cartman"—they finally got results. They experienced faint raps, then groans and finally some movement, with their flimsy folding card table eventually spinning on one leg.

According to an article by Ruby Lang that appeared in *Phenomena Magazine* online, the group has been filming its sessions. In the video footage the table-legs are purportedly shown "lifting off of the ground and the sitters virtually being dragged along behind the table as it starts to build up momentum and spin around on one leg." She also notes other effects, including the video camera light fitting faltering and going out as the movement begins and the appearance on the infrared video footage of balls of light, which "appear to roll across the floor in random directions near the sitters."

The *Australian Journal of Parapsychology* rejected the film as being "too ambiguous to be definitive evidence of PK," so the jury is not yet in on this case.

CHAPTER 27

THERE'S SOMETHING TO BE SAID FOR SPIRITS

In 1982 another group ostensibly getting macro-PK effects came to my attention. It was called the Society for Research on Rapport and Telekinesis or SORRAT for short. (Telekinesis is an older term for psychokinesis.) Experimental parapsychologists, many of whom are the worst of skeptics when it comes to macro phenomena, had told me that SORRAT was not to be taken seriously. They implied that there were a lot of shenanigans going on out in Missouri where this group was based.

On the other hand, I knew that the main investigator, Dr. William Edward "Ed" Cox, a colleague of J. B. Rhine's, had actually moved to Rolla, Missouri to study them and now believed in their genuineness. Cox was a large man with a shaggy mane of white hair who towered over the crowds at conferences. He was a striking figure I had seen at other meetings and knew to be a respected researcher as well as a member of a magician's organization. I had also heard that he had debunked some clever fakes.

For the SORRAT group Cox had devised, at Rhine's suggestion, a "mini-lab"; one was a 5.5-gallon fish tank, the other was about twice that size but both were secured to a wooden platform, locked and sealed, and further secured by heavy-duty steel bands. He had placed objects in these tanks in the basement of the house where SORRAT's meetings took place, and set up a movie camera that operated only when there was movement. He claimed that he had captured on film the movement of the objects, as well as written messages, the interlocking of seamless leather rings, and so on. I had not seen his film, but another one, which unfortunately put me off. This was a visually funny but cruel parody made by sardonic psi researchers using stop-film techniques to simulate the movement and interaction of objects. It gave me, and most of the others present, the idea that this was all hogwash and that Cox was the deluded dupe of some charlatans. I no longer hold that opinion.

Let me back up and tell you a little about SORRAT. John G. Neihardt,

Poet Laureate of Nebraska and Plains States Poet Laureate and an author and authority of the Omaha and Sioux peoples, founded SORRAT in 1961. Neihardt's philosophy of "pragmatic mysticism" combined "physical and non-physical reality." He considered scientific observations only one form of knowledge. Another form was the mystical experience, which he felt could not be explained. However, Neihardt was familiar with the history of psychic phenomena and the scientific work done up to that time. Not unlike Batcheldor, his idea was that *"rapportment"* among the group members would promote psychological conditions most favorable for the development of PK. He believed that the "element of mental unity" would be the key to achieving phenomena.

In a lecture he gave on ESP in 1966 he observed that "All power in nature tends toward the form of a circle," using as examples whirlwinds and centrifugal and centripetal forces that remain in a cyclical balance throughout the solar system. He drew on his deep understanding of American Native cultures noting that "Everything that the Sioux did in their ceremonies was related to the prayer circle, and when the Hoop of the People was broken, the . . . tribal system began to fall apart." He continued, " Perhaps a circle of experimenters around a target object . . . helps the unknown power with which we are dealing to be condensed, although doubtless the psychological effect of linking with one another as an entity, a group, has much to do with helping telekinesis to happen."

Joining Neihardt in the SORRAT group were college age men and women who were interested in psychic phenomena and/or who felt they possessed some psychic ability. A young student named John Thomas Richards helped Neihardt recruit the others. Richards's book, *SORRAT: A History of the Neihardt Psychokinesis Experiments, 1961-1982*, published in 1982, is the source of much of my information on SORRAT.

At the beginning, in September 1961, Neihardt and the young people sat in wooden chairs around a 40-pound wooden table in Neihardt's living room at Skyrim Farm. They kept their hands on the table with little fingers and thumbs touching those of the person next to them, trying to replicate the conditions of the Victorian séances that Neihardt had read about. They would take turns, some sitting, some observing, cameras and flashlights ready to capture the phenomena or cheating. At this point they sat in darkness. Later they used indirect lighting. Neihardt cautioned the group to be open but vigilant and "not take any wooden nickels," that is, to be open-mindedly skeptical of any phenomena they produced. And it was he who eventually consulted J.B. Rhine about verifying their phenomena and welcomed the investigations of W. E. Cox.

They met every Friday night for two months before they obtained some light raps from the floor of the room. Some of them ran down to the basement to see if they could find anything causing the noises, but the raps seemed to be coming from between the floors or from the wood itself. Over the next months the raps grew louder and came from various pieces of furniture as well as the floor. They constantly examined the objects, at one point taking a chair completely apart, to see if they could find some other explanation for the sounds. Remembering the Fox sisters' "confessions," they even took off their shoes and put cushions under their feet but this precaution did not diminish the sounds emanating from the floor.

The table would vibrate too quickly to be caused by shaking. They described it as like electrical vibrations but more rapid and subtle than holding an electric razor. The top of the table would develop cold spots, as though ice had been left on it for a few minutes.

The group eventually disbanded because of personal problems and conflicts. Richards left to continue his education and returned in 1965. The sittings then resumed with different members, including Neihardt's daughter and two granddaughters. Another young man, Joe, occasionally went into trance states and claimed to have out-of-body experiences. Elaine, Richards's wife, also seemed to have some psychic talent. But they kept the meetings secret because of some unfavorable publicity engendered when Neihardt, in December 1966, gave a lecture after Batcheldor had published his report in the *Journal of the Society of Psychical Research*.

In this second round of sessions, Richards reported that the pleasurable, soothing vibrations in the tabletop put them into a pleasant mental state of "rapportment" with one another, "and with whatever entity, agency, or psychological manifestation of our group's united subconscious minds . . . was involved in producing" the PK.

Taking Batcheldor's lead, Neihardt suggested they sing to improve rapport. So they sang, talked, and joked to achieve that "happy good feeling of unity" that the séance groups of Home and others "seemed to experience over and over again."

These sittings produced much larger effects than their previous table tiltings, "walkings," and levitations. They felt cold breezes flowing upward from the center of the tabletop just before tiltings took place. On Neihardt's 85th birthday, January 8, 1966, they got complete levitation after celebrating with cake and goodies. There were only five of them present: Neihardt, his daughter Alice, Joe, Richards and his wife, Elaine. The table vibrated and then rose two or three inches from the floor. They began having raps answer "yes" or "no" questions.

Richards says that he and Elaine experimented at home with a light metal tray table. When they asked if deceased entities were present, the raps informed them that two (known) deceased persons were there. They asked if it was Dr. Neihardt's late wife, Mona, and received one affirmative loud rap. Other questions followed until they asked, "Can you move the table?" Instead of replying with raps, the table began to move, swing on one leg, then levitate, sticking to Richards when he reached for his camera, then floating up to the ceiling where it clattered against the overhead light fixture. He was able to photograph it and the photo may be seen in his book and on the paperback covers of Volumes 1 and 2 of *The Year of the SORRATs*, another of his publications.

Once they reported the incident to Neihardt and "spirits" became involved in their circle, the phenomena became stronger. The table at Skyrim "walked" up and down staircases and levitated to the ceiling over Mona's sculpture stand. Other poltergeist-like phenomena occurred as well. A table walked into the garage and jumped onto Neihardt's car. The car door opened about 6 inches with no one touching it. It then walked toward the "Prayer Garden" on the grounds before stopping. (The participants speculated that they were cold and wanted to return indoors so the table halted.)

The phenomena continued and grew stronger with the introduction of spiritualism. They evidently duplicated the "earthquake" effect and Neihardt's chair supposedly levitated with him in it. They got apports of different kinds and automatic writing and messages in later years, including some claiming to be from Neihardt, who died in 1973.

The sittings continued for many years at the Rolla home of Dr. and Mrs. Richards who, it would seem, were the catalysts (mediums, if you wish) of the group. There were accusations of fraud by some parapsychologists, but never against Cox whose integrity was not questioned. In reading over Cox's reports on the mini-lab preparations, you are struck by their genuineness.

In the Proceedings of the Parapsychological Association (*Research in Parapsychology, 1983*), Cox outlined the series of filmed experiments with the mini-lab he had begun in 1979 at the suggestion of J. B. Rhine who became interested in SORRAT before Cox did. Cox was a certified magician and no fool when it came to sophisticated trickery. The construction of the mini-labs was carefully thought out. He inverted both glass aquarium tanks described above and secured them to wooden platforms, which extended about 10 cm. beyond the front and sides of the tanks. Except when he periodically rearranged the target objects inside them, they were kept locked and sealed. He used heavy-duty steel straps to secure them plus a lock and special seals. For instance, he went through the trouble of buying special varicolored string in Europe, so that it could not easily be matched here. He would tie it to the lock and with a match melt the ends together. He would take any remnant of the string away with him along with the key so that the Richards's never had access to it. In addition he often attached onto the string a white tape bearing his private Notary Seal imprint.

Cox got a local locksmith, a Mr. Henson, to agree to lock "*securely*" the larger of the tanks for a special test. Henson also agreed to provide a notarized and detailed statement concerning anything he might find to have occurred inside the tank. So Henson jammed a key into the lock, breaking it, and applied special glue to both the broken-off portion and the shackle itself. In the mini-lab were a pile of seven different coins, a heavy serving spoon, a small piece of plywood containing a wood screw, and several other target objects. He was specifically asked to note the absence of any writing instrument.

The mini-lab was carefully placed in a special room in the Richards' basement. Cox placed a pen on the outer platform of the tank and left. Two days later "all seven coins had been moved onto assigned spots in two straight rows, the spoon was bent, the screw released, and other target objects disturbed." The pen was inside the tank and produced writing on prepared paper placed inside. A penny and an X-ray packet also were found inside.

When the mini-lab was returned to the locksmith, Henson and his assistant could find no way anyone could have gained entry to the tank. They took nearly half an hour to remove the Master Lock because of the quantity of glue they had injected along with the broken-off key.

So intrigued was Henson, that he asked if he could have another shot at it—for no cost. By the way, he had no idea of the PK or spiritual nature of the tests. He had asked Cox if he was a magician, to which Cox replied, truthfully, in the affirmative.

Cox delivered the smaller (5.5 gallon) tank to him, which contained assigned places for two rows of four quarters each. When Cox went back he found the glass had been cracked—I guess in Henson's zeal to make an absolutely foolproof box. They both felt the crack was insignificant so Cox inserted a pile of eight quarters and several other target objects in the tank. Henson secured the lock and the tank was placed again in the basement room. A week later Cox returned with the mini-lab to Henson's shop. Inside the tank were a balloon and a now orderly array of six of the quarters. The other two coins were now outside the tank on the front platform. Henson, nonplussed decided that he should have purchased a new tank and "preferred to discount the effects."

Henson tried once more. He even installed a second steel band crosswise to the base and "booby trapped" the tank. This time Cox, who the locksmith still assumed was performing magic tricks, promised "to enter" eight quarters and a heavy lock, supplied by Henson. Four days later, both the lock and coins were found inside the mini-lab.

In his notarized statement the locksmith commented that he found it "difficult" to believe that Cox had forcibly inserted various large objects into the sealed tank, particularly the heavy lock. "It was simply far too well secured and tight . . . The pen-writing, spoon-bending, screw-unscrewing, and entry of the pen, and [other objects are] totally inconceivable." He maintains that the effects occurred exactly as described.

So the SORRAT produced direct writing, just as the Bindelof group had, but succeeded where the Bindelof boys didn't by getting coins to enter a box and have two seamless rings interlock. Unfortunately very little of these phenomena from the locksmith's series were captured on Cox's films, a single levitating coin, which seemed to have been caught exiting through the glass front, and the erratic movement of two quarters that had been "expelled" from the tank.

Although Cox never professed to believe in the "spirit as agency" theory, Richards and the rest of the SORRATs are confirmed spiritualists, believing that the phenomena are caused by discarnate entities. Even though the Philip researchers addressed their "ghost" and exhorted him to perform, they did not actually believe that they were dealing with a surviving personality. Batcheldor's groups excluded the spirit hypothesis altogether. Neither the Batcheldor nor the Philip group obtained the magnitude of phenomena that SORRAT, the Bindelofs, or the other spiritually oriented sitters achieved. Did the latter groups have stronger "mediums" or more energy? Or is it that the belief that the force is coming from mysterious realms, not from mere mortals, allows these "larger" effects to occur? There may be an advantage to believing in spirits.

In the 1990s there was widespread interest in a small spiritualist group called Scole in the UK that had been meeting for several years and who had been under investigation by three well-known researchers. The "mediums" of the group were a husband and wife living on a farm in a rural part of England. Unfortunately for researchers, the couple was not particularly interested in scientific verification of their phenomena. The first reports I heard were of frustrated investigators who complained that the sittings were held in a basement in total darkness. A gentleman I met at a conference said he had observed little points of light, similar to those produced by Kluski, that bounced around the room and sometimes came to various participants. One landed on his palm, he said, and as it did so he closed his hand only to feel it withdrawn as though by a filament or thread.

That detail made me skeptical, although I knew that ectoplasmic threads have been produced by legitimate mediums, so it didn't necessarily signify cheating. What really got my attention was an email communication I received from my old friend Prof. Arthur Ellison, past president of the British Society for Psychical Research, who was one of the three investigators and who has since passed away. (The other two were Prof. David Fontana, president of the SPR, and Montague Keen, a Council member, who has also now passed away.) Arthur also experienced the lights, but when one landed on him he felt it *penetrate* his chest. Now that effort is a little hard to fake. It is also reminiscent of Bindelof's "finger" penetrating Ellie's cheek or pressing under a tooth.

Also convincing was an incident reported by another investigator, Ivor Grattan-Guinness. When one of the lights came into his hand he put his other hand over the first, cupping the light within it. He reported that the light "ricocheted" about between his palms until he opened his hands and released it.

More convincing was that the lights would respond to the sitter's spoken or silent requests. The small points of light would settle on sitters' hands to allow closer inspection. Larger areas of light would brush against them, producing tactile as well as visual effects. At times the lights would make an audible "ping" as they hit the table with speed. They would then appear almost instantaneously under the table, apparently passing through it. Montague Keen told me that one light entered a glass of water he held close to his lips and made "appropriate swishing noises as it agitated the water." He claimed that it was too close to his lips to allow control by any "rods, threads and similar nefarious appendages."

I attended Keen's informal presentation of some of the findings at a meeting here in the U.S. He showed photographs, ostensibly produced a la Serios, that is, thoughtographs. However, besides the Serios-like pictures they purportedly also affected Polaroid and 35 mm Kodachrome films on which were written passages of poetry or prose, esoteric symbols, and other materials. One of the more impressive examples was a poem, handwritten, with some words crossed out. They had said the spirits were sending something for Keen. Upon investigation it turned out to be a poem by Wordsworth, which was very meaningful to Keen. What was particularly interesting was that it was a version of that poem that had only been printed in one edition of Wordsworth's works. Keen tracked the manuscript down in the Yale University archives and found a copy in Wordsworth's sister's handwriting that looked very similar to what appeared in the film. But that particular page had also been printed in the 1960s, I believe, by a well-known auction house catalogue so it is possible that the mediums had laid eyes on it at one time in their lives. Like the "paranormally" produced one, it also had certain words crossed out. This production is very reminiscent of some of Ted Serios' photographic "reproductions" of objects he'd seen in books.

There were other impressive samples of their phenomena, but a few scientists I knew were muttering "fraud" as they emerged from the mind-boggling display. I can't blame them. If they have had little education in séance phenomena and the constant bad press such things elicit, these phenomena would certainly exceed their "boggle threshold." But more experienced researchers are also skeptical because the Scole séances were usually held under the group's rather than the investigator's conditions, the written poem had been accessible to the public, and in addition had "the appearance of being copied."

So the jury is still out on the Scole group, too. Although they asked the spirits' permission to allow infrared photography of their sittings, I don't believe they ever received it and the group has now disbanded. If the photos and writing on film are genuine, they are remarkable examples of séance phenomena.

Sir William Crookes became a believer in spirits because of his contact with Home and Cook. Perhaps he was influenced because he was convinced that the phenomena were real and had no other explanation for them. Many researchers propose the "super-psi" theory, which essentially holds that the extent of the capabilities of the human mind is unknown, limitless perhaps. Others have, like Crookes, become convinced of the continuation of personalities after death and see the information given by mediums as too complex to be the result of psi.

My own bias, as you have already surmised by now, is that these phenomena are the products of living beings, although belief in outside or discarnate forces greatly helps in their production. But I may be wrong. Because the Bindelof boys also "contacted" a man on the moon doesn't mean that the features and information of Helen Duncan's phantoms came exclusively from her telepathic abilities. I don't think either opinion can be proved conclusively with what we know at present.

I do firmly believe that the powers displayed by these special people, whether mediated by spirits or not, have profound implications for science. How, for instance, could Home and the others change the gravitational field of an area? What exactly is ectoplasm? How can it be exuded, molded into thought forms, and then either be dissipated or be reabsorbed into the body? By what physical or mental means can people imprint their mental images on photographic paper, or on video and audio tape for that matter?

If the phenomena are genuine, and by now I think you may be convinced that they are, our current knowledge of the mind and body, our whole concept of physical laws, is woefully limited.

EPILOGUE

The Bindelof experience altered the lives and changed the perceptions of all those involved; some in only subtle ways, others profoundly. It especially affected Montague Ullman's choice of career. He became a psychiatrist and parapsychologist and is best known as the founder of the Dream Laboratory at Maimonides Hospital in Brooklyn, New York, where some of the most important work in paranormal dreams was done in the 1960s and 1970s. He has authored and co-authored several books on dreams and is a highly respected member of the scientific community. He also wrote of his experience with the Bindelof boys for Rhea White's journal *Exceptional Human Experiences* (and later reprinted in the *Journal of the American Society for Psychical Research*).

Ullman took charge of all the materials, messages, photo plates, and minutes of the meetings etc., and over the years got the group together to discuss their experiences. (These materials were subsequently donated to the Parapsychology Foundation in New York, where they are available for study by serious scholars.) According to Larry's notes, a few of them got together in New York in November, 1946, and attempted to sit several times without Gil who was reluctant to join them. They only managed "slight but inconclusive" results or none at all. However, after lunching with the president of the American Society for Psychical Research, who impressed Gil with the importance of what they were attempting, Gil consented to sit with the group. On November 26, Gil, Howard, Tom, Monty, and Larry got "table movement and levitation." The same group, with the addition of George Kaiser, met once more on December 9, and again got some results including movement, levitation, and a message spelled out by the table tipping as they called out the alphabet. The message was "Larry bad 66th St.," which Larry said, "meant nothing to anybody including me."

Ullman tried to get a group started when he was in the service during World War II, but it was unsuccessful. Larry also attempted a sitting once in California when he got together with Maryann Meader and an aged Hereword Carrington (the man who had investigated Gil when he was a child). The only member who had any success in producing physical phenomena in adult life was Gil; he sat with various groups and got table movements and other large-scale phenomena but nothing approaching what the disciples of Bindelof had achieved as teenagers. Gil also had many odd things happen around him. For example, one day when I was visiting him and Marion in their penthouse in Manhattan, Gil told me that a strange incident had taken place a short time before our get together. He was to attend a meeting downtown and made sure he put a certain letter that he thought was important in his briefcase. As the meeting progressed he realized that the letter would actually be detrimental to him. When he opened his briefcase, the letter was missing. Upon returning to his apartment, he found the letter on his desk.

I questioned him, saying that perhaps he had absent-mindedly taken it out and laid it down before closing his briefcase, but he insisted that was not the case, that he had put it purposefully in his briefcase before he left. He could have been mistaken, of course, but there are many people with psychic or psychokinetic abilities who report such disappearances and reappearances of objects. Larry's missing dentures might be another such case.

The other original sitter, Lenny (Leonard Lauer) who started the experiments with Gil and who brought in most of the subsequent participants, became vice-president of a metallurgical company, married twice and raised a family. He continued to have an active intellectual life and was especially interested in psychology.

Unfortunately Lenny died of a heart attack in 1988, the day that I was to call him to set up an interview. However, he had made a tape recording recounting his experiences with Gil, Larry, and the rest of the Bindelof group, which I used to fill in some details of the first experiments.

Larry Levin, who changed his name legally to Gilbert Laurence in 1940, lives in California, north of San Diego. He has two children from his first marriage to Flo. Larry and Flo started a successful business and moved to Los Angeles in 1947, but "Gil-Larry" never lost his love of theater. In addition to his business he participated in several theatre, writing, and radio projects including assisting Rod Amateau, the producer-director of the Burns and Allen show and other sitcoms, in a 1960 New York show, "Venus at Large." After Flo's death, he sold the business and became more immersed in theatre activities, taught theatre classes at UCLA and UCI, and hosted radio shows on which he interviewed many well-known entertainers. During the 1990s he was a theatre critic for several publications, including *Stages*, and was an active member of the American

Theatre Critics Association.

Larry is currently in an assisted living residence with his second wife, Pat, who suffers from Alzheimer's disease. He still reads voraciously, and enjoys plays and good films on TV. Larry attributes his longevity to his continuing involvement with Dr. Bindelof. You might remember that he was the one member of the group who believed, and still believes, that Dr. Bindelof was what the messages said he was—a spirit. Larry has carried Bindelof's picture with him all these many years and feels that Bindelof has helped him throughout his life.

In about 1970 Larry contacted the rather eccentric Tom Loeb in California. Larry and Monte visited Tom just before he succumbed to cancer. Tom had attempted a literary career and had at least one story published in the *New Yorker* magazine, but eventually wound up, he claimed, smuggling marijuana from Mexico and running guns. Gil, remembering Tom's stories as a young man, didn't put much credence in this story, although he said he wouldn't have put it past him.

Howard Frisch, ever retiring, went into the rare book business and lives quietly with his partner in New York. Reticent as always, he claimed to be uninfluenced by his experiences with the sitter group. I believe he just enjoyed being a part of a special group of talented, brilliant young people. He and Gil remained friends until Gil's death.

Gilbert Roller became an artist, filmmaker, writer, and TV producer. He taught TV production and direction at the Fashion Institute of Technology, and a course in "Paramechanics" or physical phenomena at The New School for Social Research, where I first met him. It was he who first introduced me to the work of Sir William Crookes and the phantom Katie King. Gil seemed to excel at whatever he attempted. He was an accomplished musician, a fine photographer, and a skilled painter. As many psychic people are, he was enormously creative.

Gil accepted the "paranormal" as a normal part of life. Despite occasional feigned indifference, he did care about imparting what he had experienced and knew to be true. In his book, *A Voice From Beyond*, and the classes he gave, he tried to enlighten the public that such phenomena do occur. He did not include his own youthful experiences in his book, however, nor did he mention them in his courses. However, with Montague Ullman he made two presentations on the Bindelof experience, one at Maimonides Medical Center and the second, more recently, at the Parapsychology Foundation in New York. (A video of that lecture is available at www.parapsychology.

org.)

I should mention here a postscript on Olga Roller. In May 2003, The Lincoln Center Library exhibited a display on the history of musical theater entitled Broadway Show Original Cast Recordings, which Gil and Marion Roller visited. To their surprise they encountered a lovely enlarged photo of Olga on stage in Victor Herbert's *Eileen*. As Sara Velez, assistant chief of the Rodgers and Hammerstein Archives of Recorded Sound reported on NPR's *Weekend Edition* on December 28 of that year, she had been trying unsuccessfully to find any recording of Olga's voice. She was therefore very pleased when Gil called her and said he had an unpublished test-pressing of Olga singing a song from that show.

Olga Roller on stage at the Schubert Theatre.

Velez reported that Gil met with her and a sound engineer who played the old scratchy pressing for them. Tears came to his eyes as he heard his mother's voice once again. Velez was impressed with the beauty, musicianship, and sensibility of phrasing the recording demonstrated and told Gil that they would be thrilled to add the recording to their collection.

The recording was "cleaned up" and sounded lovely on the CD that *Weekend Edition* sent the Rollers of the program. It is the only extant recording of Olga Roller's voice.

Gil informed them that Olga, who had been born in Vienna in 1884, had died in New York in 1968. He was very moved to have heard his mother's voice one last time.

I said a sad goodbye to Gil a week or two before his death from cancer on October 20, 2004, at the age of 89. We knew it was the last time we'd see each other and, with a soft smile, he assured me he would still be around. Gil was ready to go, perhaps to solve the mystery of Dr. Bindelof.

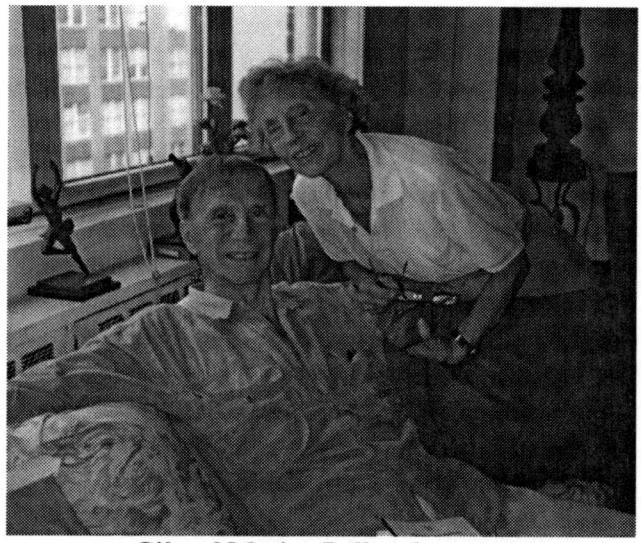

Gil and Marion Roller, Aug. 1993

APPENDIX:
SO YOU WANT TO DO IT TOO?

After reading all that's come before, I hope that some of you would like to explore your psychokinetic talent, alone or in groups. Going it alone might be problematic. You saw how Kulagina and Parise strained to achieve the movement of objects, but if you must, start with something easier than a plastic bottle. Try deflecting the needle of a small compass or moving a light hollow tube that rolls easily, in other words, something that's relatively easy to move.

From what we know of laboratory work you must strive to "become one" with the object and concentrate all your attention on it. However, remember that Parise's first success came, after a long period of trying, when she was distracted and emotionally charged by the imminent demise of her grandmother. Now I'm not suggesting that you do in Granny to achieve your ends, but perhaps a break or distraction while keeping the objective in mind might help.

You might try throwing a spoon-bending party with a group of like-minded individuals. Since it might only be a one-time event you don't need to have a faithful following willing to commit a substantial part of their leisure time. Make sure you have a lot of cheap cutlery around. (Hide the silver you inherited from Aunt Martha!) If you have inexpensive, thin, stainless forks and spoons that you've picked up in a close-out store, people will be more likely to believe they can bend them than a formidable, heavy butter knife. As we've seen, plastic can also be bent, but again, people are more likely to remember Geller's spoon-bending feats and want to try it with metal. (Look over the procedure that Julian Isaacs used and the details of my spoon bending in Chapter 25 to help you get started.)

But if you're interested in more spectacular macro- or large-scale-phenomena I suggest the sitter group approach. You need to find some kindred spirits (earthly and/or otherwise) who share your enthusiasm and goals. Remember both Batcheldor and the SORRATs considered rapport and common goals to be essential to successfully producing phenomena. It may also be helpful if the prospective sitters have had some psychic experiences and/or are very open to and comfortable with them. You don't want anyone in the group who is negative or antagonistic to the views of the others. I know of groups that have failed miserably because of underlying personal antagonisms that only came out after the group had been meeting for a while. So choose carefully.

Group members must be sufficiently motivated to commit one evening a week to the project for an indefinite period of time. The Bindelof boys started out with a core group of two or three and built on that. The SORRATs started with a larger group some of whose members dropped out, but they have maintained additions to the core group of more than 20 people. It seems rapport, patience, and perhaps some psychic or psychokinetic talents are more important than numbers.

It's a good idea to meet regularly and proceed slowly. Sporadic meetings will thwart any momentum the group is gathering. Remember the Bindelofs got their most consistent and strongest results when they began to meet every Saturday night. Slow progress, according to Batcheldor, is necessary so as not to encounter ownership resistance or especially "witness inhibition." You don't want to freak out anyone so that they get scared and throw cold water on the doings. So go slow, but at the same time allow your imagination to flow freely to see how much you can accomplish. Time is needed for rapport to develop and to overcome fears and psychological barriers, as we saw in Nick's development with the radio experiment.

I wouldn't encourage cheating, or as Batcheldor would say, "creating artifacts." There must be a feeling of unity and a certain level of trust in the group. You don't want to feel someone is pulling the wool over your eyes, one-upping, or making a fool of you. Besides, it's been my experience that you will get creakings and table movement just from involuntary muscle action. In a small group I was involved with some time ago we got a little round table to move rapidly around the room with us following. I was never convinced that it was anything more than our own unconscious pressure on the table causing it to scurry around. The group broke up before we ever got anything unequivocally "paranormal."

As we've seen throughout the book, total darkness is unnecessary, but dim lighting seems to facilitate things. Leaving a light on in another room or using a red bulb or covered lamp might be a good idea. I think candles tend to be distracting with their flickering and unless they are in a glass container that hides the flame they can be too bright for someone facing them. However, scented candles have become very popular, and if the group likes them, why not?

Find what works for your group. Batcheldor felt that the circle must have absolute belief to achieve phenomena. The SORRATs felt that belief would evolve and encouraged open-minded skepticism.

But try, as Batcheldor suggests, putting aside your critical faculties. Don't worry about controls, at least until something seemingly important happens, then trust judiciously. Remember what Gil Roller said: When phenomena occurred, the boys would make sure their little-fingertips were touching and their feet were firmly in contact with those of the guys on either side.

SORRAT says, "love wisely." Don't squabble, but make an effort to achieve "at-one-ment" in the group. Try not to get hung up on trivial nonsense and remember the Golden Rule, which is a good habit to acquire outside of the circle as well. It will be easier if each member of the circle is in agreement with the goals or the purpose of your meetings. Rapport, harmony, accord, concord, unity (and any other synonyms you can think of) are the watchwords you want to focus on.

Each person should be "educated" as to what to expect and to what some of the possibilities are. Reading and discussing the literature—especially this book, of course—will help in achieving a commonality in the circle. Knowing about sitter or séance groups will help them accept the PK as natural. After all, it is!

And don't forget to keep things light. Keep in mind what your goal is but also keep the atmosphere pleasant. Converse, joke, sing if you like (happy songs that most or all or you know) and expect that something will happen.

Avoid negativity. Keep a positive attitude; don't even *think* something won't work. Remember, you don't know what the limits of possibility are, or even if there are limits.

Whether you believe that spirits are responsible for the phenomena or that the energy producing them comes from the living sitters doesn't matter. You need to keep in mind that even agnostic, scientific proponents of "super-psi" admit that ESP transcends time, space, and physical barriers. You've seen, in this book, examples of self-levitation, ectoplasmic production, and formation into hands, limbs, and even walking, talking people. You've seen thoughtography, materialization and dematerialization, and all manner of feats that are considered "impossible" by a linearly oriented world. Is anything impossible? We don't know that. Assume that nothing is and you may go as far as your unconscious will take you.

If you are not spiritualists, you might encourage the naming of the "force" to focus your efforts and/or endow it with an identity, as the young Gil did naming the poltergeist force "Liz" or the group in Toronto creating "Philip." If your belief encompasses "discarnate entities," then by all means speak and request "signs" from whatever spirits you feel are attending.

One word of caution: Dabbling in "demonic" forces is not recommended. Knowing your sitters is important. Anyone who has a history of mental problems or violence should not be invited to participate. On a milder level, in the later Bindelof sittings, sub- or pre-conscious anger was acted out by breaking and throwing pencils and paper around. Violence attracts violence. If you believe, as I tend to, that these phenomena come from our unconscious selves, a psychopathic or violent personality might produce some unpleasant and unwelcome effects. It's very unlikely that anything like that would happen—I know of no cases--but I don't think it's beyond the realm of possibility.

Most often, as successful sitters have noted, you start to feel the oneness or unity with the others in a very pleasurable sensation. And the more phenomena occur, the more the group's belief in them will grow, and the stronger and more consistent they will become.

With today's low-light camcorders and other technological devices you could even record your successes for the world to see. I wouldn't attempt such recordings or inviting guests until the phenomena occurs pretty consistently. Expect, especially at first, to have evenings where nothing at all happens. You saw how a new member or a skeptical guest could put a damper on the proceedings. Recording equipment may also make the "spirits" camera shy, so don't attempt to introduce new elements until the group has gained confidence in their ability to perform.

Happy tilting!

SOURCES:
FOR EXPLORING ON YOUR OWN

Good and great mediums have emerged from all walks of life and from the four corners of the globe. Of necessity I've only touched upon some: I've had to leave many important ones out. For the interested reader who would like to learn more about these extraordinary people, I'll provide some suggestions and sources of information below.

I have also not included the work being done on EVP (Electronic Voice Phenomena) or ITC (Instrumental Transcommunication), electronic voices and images purported to be imprinted on tape or seen/heard on radios, telephones, computers and television sets. Whether these sounds and images are proof of survival after death or psychokinetic effects created by the living is still a topic of controversy. Anyone interested can find a range of information—and probably misinformation-- by Googling EVP and/or ITC.

Which reminds me, another word of caution is necessary: Searching the internet can be very productive, but you may find avid, uncritical proponents of spiritualism as well as many professional debunkers' sites. These latter groups, arch-skeptics, are as fanatical as some of the anti-psi religious fundamentalists who consider any psychic manifestation as the work of the devil. I will attempt to steer you to the more reliable Web sites of serious investigators and scientific organizations.

If you liked Home and Kluski you'll love Mirabelli and the Schneiders. The book by Anita Gregory, *The Strange Case of Rudi Schneider*, is out of print but might be obtained from online bookstores. You can find some information on Rudi and his brother Willi on the web at www.harryprice.co.uk/Seance/Schneider/schneider-fodor.htm.

Carmine (or Carlos) Mirabelli was considered by some researchers to be the most powerful and talented medium who ever lived. You can begin your reading with the Brazilian/English site: members.tripod.com/-Mirabelli/index.htm or on the ISS site at: www.survivalafterdeath.org/mediums/mirabelli.htm.

This last site, www.survivalafterdeath.org, is that of the International

Survivalist Society, which is based in Vancouver, Canada. It contains some excellent articles on physical and other mediums plus the complete book *Intention and Survival* by Dr. T. Glen Hamilton, a Vancouver physician who experimented with physical mediums in the early 20th century. The book contains many photographs of these mediums including ectoplasmic manifestations. The site also has the complete *Researches into the Phenomena of Spiritualism* by Sir William Crookes in its online library.

Another interesting site contains information on direct voice phenomena including the work of the late British medium Leslie Flint. On it you may hear samples of voices heard at his séances: www.xs4all. nl/%7Ewichm/dirvoic3.html

An extensive library of books on spiritualism and psychic phenomena may be found at: www.spiritwritings.com/library.html. There are many classics of psychical research in their collection as well as many links to other interesting sites.

Websites of other legitimate organizations include:
The Society for Psychical Research: www.spr.ac.uk/
Membership in the SPR will give you access to their extensive on-line library including many books and articles on physical mediumship. Highly recommended.
The Parapsychological Association: www.parapsych.org
The Parapsychology Foundation: www.parapsychology.org/
Survival Research Institute of Canada: www.islandnet.com/sric/
The American Society for Psychical Research:
www.aspr.com/ There's not much on physical mediumship in this entry but you can see a picture of Dr. Ullman and read an article on dreams by him in the Newsletter section.

There is more to research than the internet, of course. The complete story of Ted can be found in *The World of Ted Serios* by Dr. Jule Eisenbud (First Edition: William Morrow & Co., 1967; Second Edition: McFarland & Company, 1989) and in articles from *The Journal of the American Society for Psychical Research*.

For more information on the Toronto experiments see Iris M. Owen's *Conjuring Up Philip: An Adventure in Psychokinesis*, Harper & Row, 1976.

For readers who would like to read more on Scole, a full report on the researchers' findings was published in the *Proceedings of the Society for Psychical Research,* November 1999. There is also a popular book on Scole, *The Scole Experiment* by Grant and Jane Solomon, which was published by

Piatkus Books.

This should be enough to get you started on your quest for answers to the mysteries of physical phenomena.

ACKNOWLEDGMENTS

Many people have assisted me in putting this book together. First and foremost of course was Gilbert Roller, aided and abetted by Larry Levin, aka Gilbert Laurence. Although I never got to meet Leonard Lauer, the third member of the young triumvirate who originated the Bindelof sitter group, a lot of the early details were gleaned from a tape he made for his family about his experiences.

I am also indebted to Dr. Montague Ullman who preserved the minutes and materials from the séances and made them available to me.

To Martin Ebon, a posthumous note of gratitude: Martin took me under his wing imparting sage advice and encouragement throughout the years. He believed in the importance of this book and urged me on when I got discouraged.

Other supporting angels include Dr. Larry Dossey, who I can't thank enough for all his many acts of kindness, Professor Stanley Krippner, my mentor and friend, and Mary Rose Barrington, who is an inspiration.

I would like to thank Professor Stephen E. Braude, the real maven on physical phenomena, and Dr. Eric Eisenbud for permission to use the Serios photos. Thanks as well to Dennis Stillings for his additions to the metal-bending section, to Michael Colmer for his help with the Helen Duncan chapter, and to Professor Peter Mulacz of Vienna, Austria, for the translation of Princess Metternich-Sandor's *Geschehenes Gesehenes Erlebtes* (*Happened Viewed Experienced*) and D.D. Home candle illustration.

To Barbara Deal, Mary Bringle and Susan Stavola, thanks for your good advice. I am also grateful to Lisette Coly and Dr. Joanne McMahon who helped facilitate my research at the Eileen Garret Library of the Parapsychology Foundation and to Dr. Carlos Alvarado who is so generous in sharing his prodigious knowledge.

To all the others who have advised, encouraged, pushed, and goaded me, thanks for your confidence in me and for understanding that I can't thank all of you here.

INDEX

The names of spirit guides are presented in quotation marks.

"Albert," 149-158
Aksakoff, Alexander, 102-104, 114

Baggally, W.W., 121-122
Batcheldor, Kenneth J., 202-208
Beraud, Marthe, 125-130, 135, 153
Braude, Stephen, 114, 186

Carrington, Hereward, 8, 120-122, 127, 227
Churchill, Sir Winston, 156-157
Cook, Florence, 102-115
Cox, Edward (Ed), 218-224
Crawford, William Jackson, 130-135, 215
Crookes, Sir William, 75, 88-114, 205, 226

Doyle, Arthur Conan, 39, 61, 128
"Dr. Bindelof," 31-33, 39-40, 48-53, 60-66, 179, 182, 229, 231
"Dr. Rinchner," 34, 60-62
Duncan, Helen, 148-159, 200, 226

Eisenbud, Jule, 170-188, 189-190, 200
Ellie, 6, 23, 46-47, 56, 59, 224
Ellison, Arthur, 157, 224

Feilding, Everard, 119-122
Fink, Eddie, 6-9, 30 120
Fontana, David, 224
Fox Sisters, 72-75

Frisch, Howard, 1718, 23, 33, 47, 51, 56, 58, 61-62, 227, 229
Fukurai, Tomokichi, 181-182, 184

Geley, Gustav, 125-126, 137-140, 153
Geller, Uri, 196, 208, 210
Goligher, Kathleen, 130-134, 215
Gursararson, Loftur Reimer, 144

Hankey, Muriel 157, 158
Haraldsson, Erlendur, 144
Hodgson, Richard, 115, 118-119
Home, D. D., 77-87, 89-101, 136-137, 226
Honorton, Charles (Chuck), 165-166

Indridason, Indridi, 133, 142-146
Inglis, Brian, 119, 124-125, 128
Iredell Denise, 152, 157, 158
Isaacs, Julian, 208

Joseph, Horace, 18, 43, 51, 53

Kaiser, George, 17, 33, 45, 227
Kaiser, Leo, 15, 33, 42, 45, 53-54
"Katie King," 102-115, 130
Keen, Montague, 224-225
Kluski, Franek, 136-141, 142, 145, 161, 216, 224
 as Teofil Modrzejewski 136-137
Krippner, Stanley, 165, 201

Kulagina, Nina, 160-163, 165

Lauer, Leonard, 9-17, 21-28, 33, 35, 39, 44-45, 51, 56, 58, 60-64, 66-69, 228
Levin, Larry, 2, 13-15, 19, 22-23, 25, 29-49, 56-69, 207, 214, 227-229
  as Gilbert Laurence 228
Loeb, Tom, 17-18, 30, 39, 42, 54, 60, 62 229
  aka Tom Newman
Lodge, Oliver, 114-119, 132
Lombroso, Cesare, 113-114

Meader, Marianne, 56, 60-68, 227
Messing, Wolf, 200
Modrzejewski, Teofil, 136-137
  see Franek Kluski
Myers, F. W. H., 10, 114-119

Neihardt, John G., 218-221
Nick, 189-201, 214-216
Nielsson, Haraldur 142, 144-145

Olafsson, Bjorn, 143-144
Oram, Arthur, 154, 157
Osty, Eugene, 134-135
Owen, Iris, 210-214

Palladino, Eusapia, 102, 113-123, 124-134, 200, 216
Parise, Felicia, 164-167
"Phillip," 210-217

Richards, John Thomas, 219-223
Richet, Charles, 114-118, 125, 135, 139
Rhine, J. B., 218, 220, 221

Roller, Gilbert, 1-70, 90, 120, 132, 168, 179, 189-207, 214-216, 227, 231
Roller, Marion, 69, 197, 228, 230, 231
Roller, Olga, 6-9, 18, 46, 198, 230-231

Scole Group, 224-225
Schneider, Rudi, 134
Schrenck-Notzing, A. von, 10, 125-128, 135
Serios, Ted, 168-188, 189, 193, 200, 225
SORRAT, 218-224
Stillings, Dennis, 208-210

Targ, Russell, 197-198

Ullman, Montague, 1, 15-16, 22, 25, 33-34, 38, 42, 51, 54, 56, 58, 164-165, 192, 202, 227, 229

Vilenskaya, Larissa, 162-163

Williams, Michael, 217

Zorab, George, 82, 111

INDEX 241

Printed in the United Kingdom
by Lightning Source UK Ltd.
133288UK00001B/300/A